CHOICE OF CONSCIENCE

CHOICE OF CONSCIENCE

Vietnam Era
Military and
Draft Resisters
in Canada

DAVID S. SURREY

PRAEGER

PRAEGER SPECIAL STUDIES • PRAEGER SCIENTIFIC
A J.F. BERGIN PUBLISHERS BOOK

Library of Congress Cataloging in Publication Data

Surrey, David Sterling.
  Choice of conscience.

  "A J.F. Bergin Publishers book."
  1. Vietnamese Conflict, 1961–1975 — Draft
resisters. 2. Americans — Canada. I. Title.
DS559.8.D7S97   959.704'38   81-18170
ISBN 0-03-059663-7   AACR2

All rights reserved
J.F. Bergin Publishers, Inc.
670 Amherst Road
South Hadley, Massachusetts 01075

Published in 1982 by Praeger Publishers
CBS Educational and Professional Publishing
A Division of CBS, Inc.
521 Fifth Avenue, New York, New York 10175 U.S.A.

0123456789   056   987654321

Printed in the United States of America

To Jane Benedict and Esther Rand,
who have been inspirations to
myself and others
through their politically active
Choices of Conscience

CONTENTS

ACKNOWLEDGMENTS

I used to think that acknowledgments were a mere formality. They're not. Books, at least this book, could never have been written without the help of those listed below and doubtlessly others whom I have inadvertently and apologetically overlooked.

First of all, those at the Vietnam Era Research Project at the Center for Policy Research in New York City not only allowed me to use their original data but made it financially possible for me to do so. At the time that research for this book was conducted, the project was funded by the National Institute of Mental Health (R01 MH26832). The project's senior staff — Drs. Arthur Egendorf, Charles Kadushin, Robert Laufer, George Rothbart, and Lee Sloan — both encouraged me to be the first user of the material collected in Canada from this nationwide study of the Vietnam Era generation and made themselves readily available for my needs. It should be noted that any conclusions drawn in this work are my own and not necessarily the project's.

More specifically from the project I would like to thank the research assistants Laurie Michael Roth, Florence Neumann, and Herbert Phoenix for their initial time-saving computer assistance; Humanistic Sociologist and Computer Ace Mark Gallops for his last-minute computer rescues, and Administrators Miriam Kahn and Mindy Marks for simply being there.

Although the entire senior staff was more than generous, two made immense contributions. Charles Kadushin somewhat successfully exorcised my anthropologically engrained terror of "data" and then encouraged me to employ thematic analysis and to develop assimilation scales. As well, his critical readings of chapters seven and eight, despite book deadline pressures of his own, were essential in avoiding some major pitfalls.

Beyond all those associated with the project, however, I thank Robert Laufer. Over five years ago, before any data had been collected, even before I had been officially hired, Bob told me I could, would, and should write a book on those men who opted for Canada during the Vietnam War. His careful reading of virtually this entire manuscript, parts of which we could not always agree upon, led to a substantial alteration of the final outcome — for the better. In addition to all of the above was his willingness to generate ideas, from the initiation of the book to the actual title used.

Outside of the Vietnam Era Research Project, several other individuals contributed to various stages of the manuscript. Karl Kuivinen, stopping off between the South Pole and Greenland, offered a number of insights; Carol Gordon helped maintain perspective on the entire work and added key comments to the first two chapters; John Judge (formerly of C.C.C.O.) and Robert A. Seeley of the Central Committee for Conscientious Objectors provided comments on the first two chapters and, more importantly, worked for an organization so long so important to so many; Richard Blot religiously scoured the entire manuscript; Cover Design Artist Gene Suchma was imaginative but not weird; and, finally, my students at the Center for Labor Studies, Empire State College, had no choice but to read versions of this work and gave me no choice but to hear their comments.

I would also like to give special thanks to Rayna Rapp and Jack Colhoun, whose Ph.D.s have not interfered with their politics. Rayna's reading of the entire manuscript, sometimes with the author hovering over her shoulder, added immensely to the quality of this undertaking. From her encouragement to her rather strong views on punctuation, she helped mold the outcome.

Jack Colhoun, a military exile and a leader of AMEX-Canada also read almost the entire manuscript. Jack, who has returned to the United States for the same reason he left — to bring about political change — provided input which could not be obtained from any other quarter. His influence greatly improved the strength, accuracy, and political direction of this work.

Long before the possibility of this manuscript existed, I began to learn about these issues as a paid anti-war organizer in Michigan. I would not have learned so much without the support of the following people: R. Kenny Letherer; Patricia O'Mally Letherer; Marion Anderson; Tommy Costello; Tom and Dawn Lohr; Joseph E. Lopez, Jr.; Bob Loucks; Terry Miller; Roberto Rodriguez; John Rozboom; Lucy Ruonavaara; Lee Shinkle; Ed and Aileen Schultz, and Rosalie Riegle Troester.

For the mechanics, I thank the wonderfully patient typists Cassandra Blunt, Anne Lewis, and Mattie Wyatt. Especially I thank my major typist, V. DeNice Rivera, who typed the bulk of this work and put up with a lot of, shall we say, pedantic demands for deadlines. At J.F. Bergin I owe a great deal to Judy Garvey and Jeanne Ray Juster, but most of all to my editor, Betty Chandler Hunt, who did so much more than put the commas in the right spot.

Naturally this book could not have been written without the cooperation of the scores of war resisters interviewed in Canada as well as their friends, wives, and lovers. These people made me more than welcome on my several trips to Canada and put up with questions both good and bad. More importantly, they reached a political decision for which my admiration has grown immensely. Although their names cannot be cited due to anonymity mandated to all respondents by the NIMH grant, they know who they are.

Finally there are two people above all others who are responsible for the completion of this book. Jim Bergin, president of J.F. Bergin Publishers, pushed, flattered, negotiated, and demanded to get this project started — and finished. At the same time, he did not let this book interfere with our valuable friendship — a slick act.

Most of all I thank Michelle Fine, whose contributions from reading and editing every word and every version of this work seem minimal when compared to the stronger solace she has provided throughout and beyond the duration.

The above debts can never be repaid; I can only say thanks. *Thanks.*

Introduction

Our nation's self-image was severely damaged during the Vietnam Era; mythologies of national invulnerability and righteousness crumbled. By the end of the Vietnam Era, Americans of all generations had undergone an often traumatic re-evaluation of their beliefs. Personal values and the nation's values were questioned in an unprecedented fashion. Many came to the harsh realization that the United States was neither invincible in warfare nor infallible in its moral judgment. This work focuses on just one set of responses to Vietnam, with an in-depth examination of so-called "draft dodgers" and "military deserters" who resolved their conflicts by relocating to Canada. By studying this select group, we hope to gain insights into the broader implications of the Vietnam Era for the United States.

This book grows out of a personal involvement with antiwar activities during the Vietnam conflict, and with the development of a national data bank dealing with the impact of the Vietnam Era on age-eligible males. From the late 1960's on, I counseled hundreds of men on draft and military decisions. Later I worked on the Vietnam Era Research Project (Center for Policy Research, New York) — a national study funded by the National Institute of Mental Health and the Veterans' Administration. Data from this project provide the empirical foundation for much of this work. The project (VERP) involved structured interviews with 1440 men in the United States and Canada,[2] designed to assess the impact of the Vietnam Era on age-eligible males, providing an extensive data bank — from which much of this work is drawn. Unfortunately, funding was not available to examine the impact of the Vietnam Era on women who played major, and frequently neglected, roles during this period. They range from the 193,000 who served in the military, and the 7,456 in Vietnam (Dullea, 1981: A1, B12), to the women who constituted a significant portion of the exile community in Canada.

This book focuses on the Canadian component of the research.[3] A four- to five-hour structured interview was conducted with each respondent to explore three phases of his development: childhood; the "period of greatest concern about Vietnam" (for nonveterans/draft dodgers) or the time spent in the military (for veterans/deserters); and the present. To supplement the qualitative and quantitative survey information, participant observations in Canada with dodgers and deserters, their friends, wives, and lovers (including many Canadians) were conducted, and are constantly updated through communication with several people in the U.S. and Canada.

The book is divided into four parts, with a concluding chapter. Part One, "Who Shall Serve?", provides a historical overview of methods of military procurement and assignment, and the forms of resistance from Colonial Times to the Vietnam Era. (The Mexican and Spanish-American Wars — minor by U.S. standards albeit major to others — were excluded because they conform, in general, to the other military conflicts of U.S. history.) Across these conflicts, the systematic patterns of class discrimination are traced, with particular emphasis on the Civil and Vietnam Wars. The section ends by examining the extent of breakdown in authority in both the civilian and military sectors during the Vietnam War.

Part Two, "From the Cradle to Canada," shifts focus from the development of a military procurement system to the development of the men in this sample of war resisters. This section traces pathways followed by these men from the time of their childhoods through the point at which they decided to seek exile. Analyses of family values, social class, and relationships distinguish the families of these men from those of other draft dodgers and military deserters, and most clearly from other American families. Particular attention is paid to the period just prior to each respondent's exile: the time when his core values were systematically challenged.

Part Three, "Canada: Refuge or Home?" explores the ways in which Canada reacted to these men, and how they in turn responded to Canada. Draft and military resisters, as political refugees, are compared to other immigrant groups as they experience new host societies. Special attention is paid to the distinct experiences of the draft dodgers (generally from relatively higher social classes) compared to the experiences of military deserters. Canada's history, its role in Vietnam, and its complicated relationship to the United States are examined as factors which influenced resisters' abilities to settle into Canada.

Part Four, "Assimilation: An Uneasy Process" follows the lives of these men from the time they arrived in Canada through the decisions they made after President Carter's amnesty allowing most the possibility of returning to the U.S. Upon arrival, most resisters joined a tightly knit dodger/deserter community. These ties soon weakened, and most groups did not remain active. Eventually, schisms developed within the resister community, between dodgers and deserters, and between those who wished to return to the U.S. and those who wished to assimilate. The impact of the discriminatory amnesties granted by Presidents Ford and Carter receives attention.

The concluding chapter reviews the legacies of the Vietnam conflict, and their implications for the future. An examination of what has happened to the resisters in this sample serves as the point of departure. We return, then, to the war's lasting impact on Americans. What we as a nation have internalized, distorted, and denied about Vietnam, is of central significance.

COMING TO TERMS WITH TERMS

The concept of *social class* pervades this work. For our purposes the term social class incorporates more than sociology's standard socioeconomic status (SES), based on indicators of education, occupation, and income which are generally utilized to differentiate various groups within a society. While these indicators are applied in this work, social class is conceived more broadly. "Class" summarizes a set of lived relationships including values, attitudes, and perceptions, as well as opportunities and pathways available. Class is discussed, therefore, as a composite of life influences, opportunities, and experiences.[4]

From Colonial Times forward, social class has affected the question of who served in the military and in what capacity. Class distinctions are evident in who became a draft dodger or a deserter, as well as in who ended up in Vietnam. Canada's relative acceptance of the draft dodgers and reluctance to admit military deserters exemplify further the influence of social class. Dodgers were generally viewed as middle class at least, and were welcomed; deserters were considered lower class and less warmly received. Class distinctions among who was, and was not, granted amnesty mirror the class bias which has typified military history before, during, and since the Vietnam Era.

Another concept which requires elaboration is that of *"survivor."*[5] The nature of the sampling technique used affects the data in ways which should be clarified for readers. A snowball method was employed. We began with 6 dodgers and 6 deserters, selected randomly from the membership lists of various activist organizations. From these 12 starting points, nominated friends and then friends of friends were interviewed, until 60 interviews were complete. These respondents, therefore, represented men more interconnected than many others who exiled to Canada. These men can, in a meaningful sense, be considered survivors. They have remained in Canada since, at the earliest, 1962, and have maintained some contact with other resisters. They are neither so assimilated as to be isolated from these networks, nor have they returned to the United States.

A few items of format should be explained. Anonymity was guaranteed to all who were interviewed. Real names would not be used. Because of the extensive use of quotations in this work, rather than using fictitious names, the original three-digit coded identification numbers, such as "(402)", precede individual statements. When quotes have been edited, three dots (. . .) are used; when the respondent pauses in answering a question, a dash (—) is inserted.

The final issue as to terminology is the question of what labels to use to describe the men in this sample. As a group, they can be considered *resisters* or *war immigrants*. Beyond this, however, the labeling becomes more problematic. Consultation with a dozen activists, researchers, and policy analysts on the subject yielded at least two dozen uncompromisable terms. The central issue boils down to whether or not it is correct to classify these men as draft "dodgers" or "evaders" and military "deserters." Some argue that these terms represent negative stereotypes, and should be replaced with terms such as "draft resister" or even "self-retired veteran." While the validity of these arguments cannot be questioned, the men who comprise this sample, overwhelmingly refer to themselves as "dodgers" and "deserters." Williams (1971a: 90), himself a draft dodger, argues that the term "deserter" should *not* be replaced. Such a change only "defers to popular prejudice instead of trying to change it." The same argument applies to "dodgers." The "resisters" in this sample are therefore labelled "dodgers" and "deserters" throughout the text.

While the term "resister" refers here to those dodgers and deserters who remained in Canada, one must recognize that "resisters" can include all dodgers and deserters: the thousands who went to Holland, Sweden, and other countries; the tens of thousands who lived underground in the U.S.; those who refused to cooperate with military authorities, leading to hundreds of thousands of "bad paper discharges" during the Vietnam Era; the men and women of all ages who took passive-to-active stances against the war; the hundreds of thousands who held deferments to avoid the draft during this period; and the "reluctant volunteers" who joined the military in special programs specifically to avoid Vietnam. Despite the focus of this work, these other men and women need to be recognized as resisters of the Vietnam Era.

The 49 dodgers and 11 deserters in this Toronto sample represent only a fraction of all who chose exile in Canada. The actual number of dodgers and deserters who went to Canada will never be known. The Canadian government did not permit immigration officials to formally question potential immigrants about their military status, nor did that government keep formal records of this kind. The estimates vary widely, depending at least partially on the politics of the estimator. One of the many Canadian government reports places the figure at 15,000. Higher tallies include one amnesty group's report of 30,000; a sympathetic reporter-writer places the total at 40,000; others feel the number is between 60,000 and 100,000, and finally, there is one projection as high as 120,000.[6] The 60,000-to-100,000 estimate seems to me to be the reasonable range.

Responses to the Vietnam War are the focus of this work; however, not all protest activity during the "Vietnam Era" focuses on the war. In particular, the rise of the civil rights movement predates the antiwar movement and is at least its rival in terms of militancy and long-range consequences. At times the antiwar and civil rights movements merged; more frequently they remained distinct. A great deal of dissent surrounded other issues during the Vietnam Era — particularly loss of faith in our leaders and political institutions, and the emergence of the women's and environmental movements. However, while it would be interesting to pursue roots and connections of these movements, such a project is beyond the scope of this work. When these issues are explored, they will be examined in terms of draft dodgers and military deserters.

Thus the men in this sample represent just one aspect of what happened to Americans during the Vietnam Era; but reaching an in-depth understanding of these men can place the era itself in clearer perspective. Currently the Vietnam Era remains a phase of our history which has either been rewritten in myopic script, or has simply been ignored.

NOTES

1. The potential for disagreement over the definition of the term "Vietnam Era" is high. Here, Vietnam Era refers to the most narrow, perhaps most ethnocentric, definition: the period of large-scale U.S. ground troop involvement from the Gulf of Tonkin incident on August 4, 1964, to the ceasefire on January 27, 1973.

2. The 1440 men were sampled using a randomized stratified design, with six categories of respondents each sub-stratified by age and race: *Vietnam Veterans; Vietnam Era Veterans,* men who served in the military but not in Vietnam; *College Nonveterans,* using distinct operational criteria for blacks and whites — the former involves two or more years of college, the latter involves four or more years; *Non-college Nonveterans; Military Deserters;* and *Draft Dodgers.*

3. Original empirical findings are reported for (1) the dodger and deserter sample, derived from interviews with these 60 men; and (2) analyses comparing responses of the resisters and those of the veterans and nonveterans from the VERP Northeast sample ($N = 380$). Time did not permit comparative analysis of resisters with the entire national sample ($N = 1440$). Trends discussed for the Northeast, however, have been found, for the most part, to be generalizable to the national sample.

4. For a more detailed discussion of social class see: Harry Braverman, *Labor and Monopoly Capital: The Degradation of Work in the Twentieth Century* (New York: Monthly Review Press, 1974); Alfred Szymanski, "Trends in the American Class Structure," *Socialist Revolution,* 2(4) 10 (July-August), 1972; Edward Thompson, *The Making of the English Working Class* (New York: Pantheon Books, 1974). Dr. Rayna Rapp's critical insights were also extremely useful in steering me towards an understanding of this complex issue.

5. Conversations with Dr. Robert Laufer led to the terminology "survivor" and, more importantly, an understanding of why it is appropriate.

6. The lowest figure is cited in John Graham's "The American Amnesty Debate" in *New Statesman,* 87 (1974), p. 349; the "higher tallies" are cited respectively in Graham; Lucinda Franks' *Waiting out a War: The Exile of Private John Picciano* (New York: Coward, McCann and Geoghegan, Inc., 1974), p. 161; Saul Levine's "Draft Dodgers: Coping With Stress, Adapting to Exile" in *American Journal of Orthopsychiatry,* 42(3) (1972), p. 432; Robin Mathews' "On Draft Dodging and U.S. Imperialism in Canada" in *Canadian Dimension,* 7 (1970), p. 10; Alfonso J. Damico's "In Defense of Amnesty" in *Dissent,* 21 (1974), p. 90.

PART ONE

WHO SHALL SERVE?

Historically, the state's desire to procure and maintain military manpower has been answered by non-cooperation of varying degrees from those who were to fill this need. Since the Jamestown Colony, the government's methods of raising a military have progressed from heavy-handed bribery to selective conscription, returning to bribery of the poor with the all-volunteer military, and now to reconsideration of conscription. Those who were to become the troops have responded with reactions ranging from compliance to open resistance.

Underlying the variety of methods used to conscript and assign military manpower from Colonial Times to the present day, one constant pattern persists: protection of the higher social classes, resulting in a patent discrimination against the lower classes. Chapter One, "Selective Servitude: Colonial Times through Korea," provides a class analysis of these patterns, tracing their evolution from overt to covert discrimination. Chapter Two, "Vietnam: The Well Ran Dry," continues the analysis with an in-depth examination of how the conflicting forces of procurement and resistance came to a head during the Vietnam Era. By examining the nature and consequences of the class discrimination in the military and civilian spheres, with an analysis of who resisted, when, why, and how, these chapters combine to provide the genealogy of the draft and military resisters who chose exile in Canada.

From Colonial Times through the present, men from the highest social classes consistently enjoyed access to the greatest number and diversity of avenues out of or away from dangerous assignments within the military. Military needs determined which classes would be disproportionately targeted. Throughout the Civil War, the military consisted largely of combat troops, filled primarily by unskilled men procured from the lowest social classes. By the time of Vietnam, the modern military demanded a shift to men with greater training and skills, linked to higher, but not the highest, social classes. Historically military needs were modified: the higher classes were consistently protected from danger inside and outside the military.

CHAPTER 1

Selective Servitude: Colonial Times Through Korea

Benjamin Franklin:
The question then will amount to this: whether it be just in a community, that the richer part should compel the poor to fight for them and their properties for such wages as they think fit to allow, and punish them if they refuse?

(Cited in Gates, 1970: 24)

September 1, 1863, Newspaper Advertisement:
The New York Draft Assurance Association will this week, for $10, guarantee any undrafted party exemption from the draft. For $25 we will furnish an acceptable substitute.

(Cited in Milton, 1942: 138)

Selective Service "Channeling Memo" (1965):
The process of channeling by not taking men from certain activities who are otherwise liable for service, or by giving deferment to qualified men in certain occupations, is actual procurement by inducement of manpower for civilian activities which are manifestly in the national interest. While the best known purpose of Selective Service is to procure manpower for the armed forces, a variety of related processes take place outside delivery of manpower to the active armed forces.

(Cited in Reeves and Hess, 1970: 194)

COLONIAL TIMES THROUGH THE REVOLUTION: THE TRADITION BEGINS

Conscription in the colonies began with the first settlement at Jamestown where legal incentives were needed to fill the ranks of the defense militia. Plymouth Colony in 1663 saw the first "universal" manpower law: all able-bodied men had to undergo military training. From this time forward, conscription grew, but only at local levels. By the American Revolution, over 650 different statutes for raising and maintaining armies existed. The thirteen colonies never centralized conscription and centralization was usually avoided even within colonies (Gates, 1970: 156; Useem, 1973: 72–73).

Despite the large number and diversity of local ordinances, twin themes emerge. First, the rich could get out: by paying cash (commutation), buying munitions, and/or providing a paid substitute (substitution). Second, the poor had little choice; they could not afford the options available to the rich, and their financial conditions often forced them to accept cash bounties for service (Gates, 1970: 156–157; Murdock, 1967: 16–17; O'Sullivan and Meckler, 1974: 5–10).

By the time of the Revolution, the question of how to create a large army rose to levels of intense debate. The Continental Congress rebuked General George Washington several times when he requested centralized compulsory service. Eventually, each colony adopted some form of conscription (based on the pre-Revolutionary models). The colonies were to deliver a quota to the Continental Army; however, meeting these quotas usually received secondary priority to local defense (O'Sullivan and Meckler, 1974: 7–8).

Both the individual colonies and the Continental Congress resorted heavily to cash bounties to induce voluntary enlistment. This led to more problems, as the colonies often outbid the Continental Army's fee of $200 for the duration. New Jersey, in 1779, offered $250, and Virginia $750; each also issued land and clothing. By 1780 New Jersey has raised its offer to $1000 (O'Sullivan and Meckler, 1974: 7, 15–16; Murdock 1967: 17). General Washington became so frustrated by being outbid that he threatened the governor of Rhode Island: if this problem continued, the Continental Army would not "bestow any extraordinary attention to the defense" of Rhode Island (O'Sullivan and Meckler, 1974: 7).

The conscription which existed in each colony throughout the war perpetuated the pre-Revolutionary theme: if you had money you would not have to serve; substitution and commutation were built into the laws. As an extreme example, one town — Epping, New Hampshire — hired enough substitutes from other towns to keep all of its own citizens home (O'Sullivan and Meckler, 1974: 8–9).

Parallel to the efforts made to raise any army, varied methods of resistance sprouted. Beyond the general opposition to a centralized draft, local resistance to any conscription began to foment. In Virginia, draft records were destroyed in two counties and potential draftees staged a protest sit-in in a third. There were also anti-draft demonstrations throughout that state, resulting in several deaths (O'Sullivan and Meckler, 1974: 5–15).

Inside the military, resistance also was in evidence. Desertion rates during the Revolution were very high, with perhaps 50 percent of the militia deserting. The problem grew so severe that in Virginia the fee for turning in a deserter was raised from two pounds to 60. Informers were tempted by promise of a draft exemption (Higginbotham, 1971: 400; O'Sullivan and Meckler, 1974: 9).

Canada played a most significant role for the dissenters at this time. *Per capita*, more chose exile to Canada during and immediately after the Revolution than during the Vietnam Era. At least 60,000, out of a population of 2,780,000, fled to Canada either to avoid the war or to remain loyal to the crown (this number includes entire families rather than individuals, which would be the case 200 years later) (B. Mitchell, 1974: 33–34; Siebert, 1966: 256).

In addition to desertion, overt draft opposition, and flight to Canada, legal forms of avoidance were established prior to and during the Revolution. Married men, teachers, deacons, or fathers could receive draft exemptions in many localities. Avoidance on principle also existed in Massachusetts from 1661, Rhode Island from 1673, and Pennsylvania from 1757, when Conscientious Objectors (CO's) were recognized as an exemption. At this time CO's were exclusively from the traditional Peace Churches — Quakers and Mennonites. CO's usually hired substitutes to take their places. These legal forms of avoidance were firmly embedded in our manpower procurement system from its beginning (O'Sullivan and Meckler, 1974: 4–5; Schlissel (ed), 1968: 28).

Raising an army throughout the Revolution thus involved limited local drafts which the well-to-do could escape, cash bounties to induce men to join, and substitution fees for the same purpose. Anti-draft activities, desertions, the option of Canada, and exemptions further filtered those who served, and those who didn't. To the extent that the higher classes served, they chose to do so.

Immediately after the Revolution the standing army dropped to 80 men; leaving a beleaguered federal government's defense to local militia in conflicts against Indians and Daniel Shays' rebels. Because of a provision in the 1787 Constitution, these militia could be placed under federal control to "execute the laws of the Union, suppress insurrection and repel invasions." A much stronger 1790 proposal by Secretary of War Knox for a federal draft and universal militia was soundly defeated by Congress (Gates, 1970: 157).

WAR OF 1812: ALMOST A NATIONAL DRAFT

With the War of 1812, the question of how to raise an army re-emerged. The bounty system was reintroduced, with a bonus of $16 for five years of enlistment. When this failed to draw the desired troops, the sum was raised several times until it reached $124 for five years in 1814. The federal government issued $2,012,439 in bonuses during the first ten months of 1814 (Murdock, 1967:17).

In 1812 Congress approved President Madison's request for an army of 166,000 men. Each state had to provide a proportionate number of men by whatever means were deemed appropriate. In most cases, the states employed the "traditional" methods of raising militias — limited local drafts with substitution and commutation for the rich, and bounties for the poor. Three New England states which were opposed to this war simply refused to cooperate. Fearing those states might secede, Madison did not persist (Gates, 1970: 157).

After the capital was burned in 1814, Madison called for a federal draft to raise 40,000 men. Both the House and Senate approved his request; however, the war ended before the implementation of the draft. (Gates, 1970: 158; Useem, 1973:72).

The 1814 draft law, although not enacted, signifies two historical shifts in manpower procurement. First, the law amounted to the first federal military procurement law. Second, it established quotas: the population of each state was divided by socioeconomic class. Each group had to provide recruits or means for recruitment. Each could send "volunteers" (often given cash bonuses) or simply provide monies (commutation). Had this "representative" method of raising an army gone into effect, the military would have remained a poor man's army, consisting of men without financial options other than accepting cash bonuses for enlistment (Gates, 1970: 158).

CIVIL WAR: NEAR BREAKDOWN

Initially during the Civil War the federal government relied on the traditional means of raising an army — an offer of money. Federal bounties for joining the Union Army in May 1861 were $100 for three years' service for whites and $10 for blacks. As the war intensified, manpower needs soared, and bounties went higher — $300 for whites for three years, or for re-enlistment. Local bounties, too, provided for militia service, and after the draft riots of 1863, these bounties soared. By 1863 the bounty system, which had worked reasonably well in the past, was failing (Murdock, 1971: 218ff.).

One problem with the bounty system was "shopping around". Bounty jumpers would enlist in one area, collect their bonuses, and then desert to another region where they would again collect bounties for enlistment. Many Canadians obtained large sums on bounty-jumping tours, returning home with substantial profits. Confederate agents in Canada would use the bounty system as a profitable method of returning home: they would enter the United States, enlist, and once in the South, desert with their bounty to the Confederate Army, where they received a second bonus as Union deserters.

The bounty system proved to be an expensive method of recruitment. During the war, in addition to the $300,000,000 paid in federal bounties, local and state governments paid another $400,-000,000 for militia bounties. The state and local bounties, unlike the federal ones, were paid in advance, encouraging further bounty jumping. Furthermore, the quality of enlistees who stayed was poor. General Grant complained that eight bounties paid for only one good soldier (Lonn, 1928: 49; Murdock, 1971: 218ff.).

Federal Enrollment Act: A Limited Draft

To call the draft controversial was to be rather too mealymouthed.
(McCague, 1968: 4)

When one considers the controversy and bloodshed surrounding the 1863 Enrollment Act, this statement on the Civil War draft belies reality. This Act departed from, and at the same time reinforced, historical traditions of procurement. As a departure, for the first time a national draft was established. As reinforcement, with national conscription to determine who should serve, the historical class discrimination was strengthened.

By 1863 it was clear that the bounty system had failed to rally enough able-bodied men around the flag. As a result, draft debates were again heard in Congress. In February 1863, the Federal Enrollment Act was passed. On March 3, it was signed into law by President Lincoln.*

The Act worked as follows: each local district was assigned a quota of men to fill per draft call (there were four calls in all). This quota was to be met by volunteers, paid substitutes (often induced to service by local or state-raised bounties), or draftees. The bounty-induced volunteers served as the major means of recruitment. Available manpower was divided into two categories: the first consisted of all single men from 20 to 45 years of age, and all married men aged 20 to 35; the second was all married men from 35 to 45.

As in the earlier conscription ordinances, a series of exemptions

*The description of the Act which follows is derived from the following sources: A. Cook, 1974: 50ff.; Gates, 1970: 159–160; Milton, 1942: 129ff.; Murdock, 1969: 6ff. and 1971: 62ff.; Schlissel (ed), 1968: 89; Useem, 1973: 73).

allowed certain men to be excluded. Exclusions were granted for the following: the mentally disabled; sole supporters of aged or widowed parents; 51 different physical disabilities, including having no teeth; and after February 24, 1864, Conscientious Objectors, i.e., Peace Church members. The CO's were permitted to perform alternative service or, as in the Revolution, to hire a substitute. These exemptions excluded many persons from the draft pool. Local districts also freely exercised discretion in permitting exemptions for men already drafted: in effect, cancelling the draft. Avoidance through exemptions was extensive, with over 70 percent of the men in the first draft call escaping through this means.

Combined with these exemptions, the retention of commutation and substitution reinforced the "selective" nature of the draft. Under commutation, any man drafted could simply pay a fee of $300 to the Collector of Internal Revenue to fulfill his military obligation. However, in the summer of 1864, commutation was terminated for two reasons. First, the draft was supposed to supply men, not money. Of the initial 133,000 men drafted, almost 87,000 took advantage of commutation. Second, as governmental responses to the draft riots will illustrate, it was feared that if the system remained so blatantly unjust, the poor would explode again.

Substitution was conceived of as a more productive method of buying one's way out of the service. During the war, 116,000 men served as paid substitutes. Until commutation ceased, the going fee for substitution was also $300, since few chose to pay a substitute more than they would have to pay for their own commutation. Once commutation was suspended, the substitution fee rose as high as $1000. Those acceptable for substitution could not be eligible for the draft and included men between 18 and 20 years of age, veterans, aliens, and men from the South.

Advertisement

How to avoid the draft! On receipt of $1.00 will send instructions how to avoid the draft, or get exempt, if drafted, at the cost of just 37½ cents. Lawyer, 129 Spring Street, Station A, New York City.

(Cited in Werstein, 1971: 17)

Undoubtedly the fees of $1.00 and 37½ cents were a salespitch, to draw in potential clients. However, this ad reflects the variety of ways, beyond substitution, commutation, and legitimate exemption, to avoid the draft. Skilled workers, as well as the very rich, were able to stay out. Many trade associations formed Draft Insurance Societies, where members were assessed from $1.00 to $100. Any member who was drafted had his commutation paid by his society. This protection of the skilled workers placed further burdens on the poor — a burden they would not tolerate.

Seeds of Discontent

Resistance to the draft fomented across the union. Draft riots occurred in Boston, Massachusetts; Wooster, Ohio; Portsmouth, New Hampshire; and Rutland, Vermont; as well as Albany, Syracuse, Auburn, Buffalo, Utica, Troy, Tarrytown, and Yonkers, New York. Troops and artillery quelled disturbances in Ohio; military enrollment officers were killed in Rush and Sullivan counties, Indiana. Areas in Wisconsin, Pennsylvania, Missouri, Illinois, Maryland, Delaware, and Kentucky experienced active resistance to the draft (A. Cook, 1974: 52 and Marmion, 1969: 37). Joel Headley (1970 (1873): 136), a journalist who witnessed the New York City riots, made the following observation:

> The ostensible cause of the riots of 1863 was hostility to the draft, because it was a tyrannical, despotic, unjust measure — an act which has distinguished tyrants the world over and should never be tolerated by a free prople.

Resentment to the draft is viewed more broadly by many commentators. It is seen as one aspect of general discontent, deriving from political, social, and military upheaval converging at this point in history. President Lincoln's suspension of *habeas corpus*, allowing the practice of arrest without trial, was widely resented (A. Cook, 1974: 49–50; Milton, 1942: 112). Many of the New York City rioters, recently-arrived Irish immigrants, saw the draft as another form of the English tyranny they had long resented (Headley, 1970 (1873): 149). At a July 4, 1863, rally in New York City, the crowd remained silent during a reading of the Declaration of Independence until the clause condemning the abusiveness of the King, at which point the crowd reacted wildly. The comparison to Lincoln was the source of the cheers (McCague, 1968: 6–8).

Many other factors underlay the unpopular reception of a national draft. Foremost was that in the 1860's, conscription required involvement in an increasingly unpopular war. New York's Governor Seymour was elected on a conciliation platform, winning by a large margin in New York City (McCague, 1968: 8–9). By 1863, faltering support for the war, not confined to New York City or State, characterized sentiment throughout the Union. The war's fading popularity derived from resistance to the draft, the failure to win the expected quick victory, heavy losses, opposition to the Emancipation Proclamation and blacks in general, and rising inflation (A. Cook, 1974: 49–50; Milton, 1942: 127).

False claims of imminent victory were pervasive. The Battle of Gettysburg, fought only days before the New York City riots, was initially proclaimed as a major Union victory. This "victory" became increasingly tainted. The casualty figures rose with each newspaper edition until it was clear the North had actually lost more men than the South — 23,049 to 20,000 (A. Cook, 1974: 49–50; Headley, 1970 (1873): 140; McCague, 1968: 44).

Lincoln's perceived attitudes towards blacks, topped by the Emancipation Proclamation, added fuel to the fires of discontent. During the war, increasing numbers of blacks had been hired and exploited as laborers on docks in Chicago, Detroit, Cleveland, Buffalo, Albany, New York City, and Boston — many as strike breakers. After the Emancipation Proclamation, fear spread that large numbers of blacks would come North, further threatening job security (Fite, 1963 (1930): 189ff.; Man, 1951: 375ff.; Werstein, 1971: 49). This fear was incipient before the war, as illustrated by this quote from the October 1, 1860, *New York Herald:*

> Hundreds of thousands [of blacks] will emigrate to their friends — the Republicans — North, and be placed by them side by side in competition with white men. Are you ready to divide your patrimony with the Negro? Are you ready to work with him in competition — to work more than you do now for less pay?
>
> (Cited in Man, 1951: 378–379).

The economy in the large cities suffered throughout the war. Inflation mounted rapidly. By the time of the New York Riots, wages had risen only 12 percent, while prices had soared 43 percent. Economic conditions deteriorated to such an extent that the 4th and 6th wards of lower Manhattan, where most rioters lived, were described by the visiting Charles Dickens as worse than any of London's slums (A. Cook, 1974: 49–50; McCague, 1968: 20–35).

The factors cited above only intensified resentment of the Federal government and the draft. The draft's discrimination against the poor sparked the New York City riots. The inclusion of the rich on the draft rolls only heated the situation. This charade fooled no one. The well-to-do could buy their way out (Headley, 1970 (1873): 149; McCague, 1968: 70). A *New York Daily News* editorial charged that "the evident aim of those who have the Conscription Act in hand, in this state, is to lessen the number of Democratic votes at the next election" (Cited in McCague, 1968: 47–48).

The Riot

The first draft draw in New York City was on Saturday, July 11, 1863. The following Monday, two columns of men, women, and children rioted.* From lower Manhattan, the march began with shouts of anti-draft slogans. The columns moved north, halting street cars and cutting telegraph wires (which connected police stations), and in general, causing minor property destruction. The columns joined, and for a time gathered around the Central Park reservoir. Eventually, they proceeded to burn the draft office at 667 Third Avenue at 46th Street. The crowd then divided into smaller groups and throughout the remainder of the day, battled police, and burned, or tried to burn, public buildings.

By the end of the first day, the target of attack shifted from the draft. Attacks on blacks — adults and children — were numerous; they were burned, lynched, and shot. Rioters looted and burned blacks' homes, businesses which catered to them, and even the "Colored Orphan Asylum". The pro-Lincoln newspaper *The New York Tribune* and specifically, its editor, Horace Greeley, became another target of the crowds. There were repeated attempts to burn the paper's headquarters, and many of its reporters were beaten.

The rioting continued for three days, with an ever-growing list of targets: the draft; the armory; the blacks; the *Tribune* and much of the press; the police; the rich; and stores for general looting. Only several losing battles with 10,000 federal troops finally quelled the rioters. The draft served as only the initial spark for a segment of the population heavy with grievances spanning political ideologies.

The extent and seriousness of the riot can be assessed in the numbers killed. The estimates begin with 105 dead, but most place the figure much higher, with at least 1,000 and up to 3,903 killed. No accurate figure is possible to obtain, particularly because there was no real way to determine the number of blacks killed (Gates, 1970: 158; Headley, 1970 (1873): 271; Milton, 1942: 151–152).

Government Panic: Pay off the Poor

As a direct response to the riots, the draft was suspended in New York City and not resumed until August 19 of the same year. Once it had been resumed, few expected it to produce men directly. As a significant outcome of New York's and other cities' draft riots, large

*The description of the riots is drawn from the following sources: Headley, 1970(1873): 148ff.; McCague, 1968: 66ff.; Man, 1951: 375ff.; Murdock, 1967: 42–49; Schlissel (ed.), 1968: 88; Werstein, 1971: 49ff.)

amounts of municipal, state, and federal funds were ear-marked expressly to subsidize those who could not buy their way out of the service. All levels of government were caught up in buying off the poor. On July 15, 1863, New York's City Council approved approximately $2,400,000 to pay the commutation fee of all draftees. The mayor vetoed the ordinance, but approved payment for police, firemen, militia, and men of indigent families. Brooklyn, then a separate city, presented $300 to each draftee to use for whatever he wished — commutation, substitution, etc. Syracuse, Buffalo, and Albany led a long list of others in following suit for fear of future riots (Murdock, 1967: 20–22, 29). Murdock (Table 1-1) captures the degree to which this practice swept the nation.

Did it Work?

The Civil War draft failed in direct procurement of manpower for the military. Avoidance (exemptions and commutations) and resistance (no-shows and non-registrants) hampered the draft, which ultimately

Table 1-1 Commutation Money Paid By State

State	Amount ($)	Manpower Equivalent
Maine	$ 610,200	2,034
New Hampshire	208,500	695
Vermont	593,400	1,978
Massachusetts	1,610,400	5,368
Rhode Island	141,300	471
Connecticut	457,200	1,523
New York	5,485,799	18,286
New Jersey	1,265,700	4,219
Pennsylvania	8,634,300	28,781
Delaware	416,100	1,387
Maryland	1,121,900	3,773
D.C.	96,900	323
Kentucky	997,530	3,325
Ohio	1,978,087	6,593
Illinois	15,900	53
Indiana	235,500	785
Michigan	614,700	2,049
Wisconsin	1,533,600	5,112
Iowa	22,500	75
Minnesota	316,800	1,056
Totals	$26,366,316	87,887

(Murdock, 1967: *Patriotism Limited*, 31)

directly brought in only 46,347 men, so that, in a Union Army of well over 2,000,000 men, only 2.3 percent were draftees. Even after adding substitutes, that is, indirect draftees, to these figures, only 6 percent were draft induced (Gates, 1970: 159; Useem, 1973: 73). Murdock (Table 1-2) illustrates just how this process worked for the four draft calls during the war.

Widespread avoidance and resistance characterized this war. The former, exclusive to the rich or subsidized, included substitution and, until 1864, commutation. The latter involved the destruction of draft records; non-registration; no-shows for induction; desertion; and flight to Canada. Beyond these individual acts of non-compliance, widespread discontent, manifest in the draft riots of 1863, expressed the general movement of opinion.

Yet the 1863 Enrollment Act was effective (Murdock, 1971: 33ff.). The draft directly supplied few men. However, substitution and the over $700,000,000 paid out in Federal and state bounties made the difference. Indeed fear of further draft resistance prompted localities to conduct bounty pledge campaigns and bond drives, and even to levy bounty taxes to avoid a direct draft. Bounties induced volunteerism and made possible the meeting of local draft quotas, although the "margin of success was narrow" (Murdock, 1971: 33ff. and 344). Largely poor men, induced by bounties rather than patriotism, comprised the Union Army. This was enough to achieve victory.

Deserters, Evaders, and Canada

The draft riots provided the most vocal resistance to military service during the Civil War. "No-shows" signified a more covert strategy of evasion. Over 161,286 draftees, who held no exemptions and paid

Table 1-2 Total Draft Statistics (All Union States)

Call	Drawn	Did Not Report	Exempted	Held To Service	Commuted	Furnished Subs	Drafted
Summer 1863	292,441	39,415	164,395	88,171	52,288	26,002	9,881
Spring 1864	113,446	27,193	39,552	45,005	32,678	8,911	3,416
Fall 1864	231,918	66,159	82,531	56,005	1,298	28,502	26,205
Spring 1865	139,024	28,477	28,631	17,497	460	10,192	6,845
Totals	776,819	161,244	315,509	206,678	86,724	73,607	46,347

(Murdock, Ibid., p. 13)

neither substitutes nor commutations, simply failed to show up. Beyond this, hundreds of thousands simply failed to register at all (Milton, 1942: 139; Murdock, 1971: 356).

Desertions through bounty jumping have already been discussed. Deserters left for many others reasons as well. Desertion rates were so high that the army created a Deserter Branch to track these men down; 260,399 men deserted from the Union Army. Desertions in 1863 numbered 4,647 per month, rose to 7,333 per month in 1864, and were 4,368 per month in 1865 when the war ended (Lonn, 1928: 151–154; Milton, 1942: 138). At the end of the war more than 100,000 deserters remained at large (Baskir and Strauss 1978: 112).

Canada again provided a popular refuge. This time individual evaders and deserters traveled north without their families. In an effort to halt this traffic, an executive order, issued by President Lincoln in 1862, prohibited citizens subject to the draft from traveling outside of the United States. To help implement this order, Secretary of War Stanton ordered a cordon drawn at the Canadian border. Nevertheless, well over 10,000 Union deserters are estimated to have entered Canada during this war (Lonn, 1928: 201–203; Murdock, 1967: 52–53).

Several features of the Civil War became precedents for even the Vietnam Era. First, a national draft was established. Second, this draft reinforced systematic patterns of class discrimination. Third, avoidance and resistance to an unpopular war emerged concurrently in the civilian and military sectors. During the Civil War, the methods of procuring manpower, while strained, worked. One hundred years later, during Vietnam, the draft and military were again strained. This time the system came even closer to collapse.

WORLD WAR I: A TRADITION CONTINUES

The National Enrollment Act expired shortly after the end of the Civil War and received little attention until the First World War began. When it was reintroduced, Congress quickly approved a national wartime draft. The draft's old inequities, commutation and substitution, had been eliminated — but only in form, not in substance.

Prepared as a comprehensive draft law, the Selective Service Act of 1917 required that men be drafted into a federalized National Guard by county draft boards comprised of local citizens. Enlistments were forbidden in 1918, so as not to unbalance the conscription process (Gates, 1970: 159–160; Useem, 1973: 74).

Avoidance

Though this draft was proclaimed as fair, its loopholes indicate otherwise. The so-called "orderly process of selection" clause illustrates its inequities. Each registrant was evaluated in terms of his value to the war effort. Unskilled and blue collar workers, "assessed" as contributing the least, were drafted first. Thus, the "orderly process" really meant that "the poor inevitably bore a disproportionate share of the burden of service" (Gates, 1970: 160). On the other hand, those who qualified could legally avoid service through class-biased deferments. Over half of those first called received deferments, usually for family hardship or occupational reasons. All deferments were permanent, since no one was reclassified in this war (Baskir and Strauss, 1978: 18–19; Useem, 1973: 73–74).

Students stand out as one of the most conspicuous beneficiaries of favored treatment. The Student Army Training Corps allowed 145,000 men to drill for emergencies while they continued their studies. Although some students were finally "activated", the signing of the Armistice prevented their actual service (Marmion, 1969: 57).

The 1917 Selective Service Act had a provision for Conscientious Objector status (CO's) — for members "of any well-recognized religious sect or organization . . . whose existing creed or principles forbid its members to participate in war in any form. . . ." However, these conscientious objectors, unlike other exempted classifications, had to perform "in any capacity that the President shall declare to be non-combatant " (Chatfield, 1971: 68–69). By any "well-organized religious sect" the writers of the Act recognized the traditional Peace Churches: Mennonites; Quakers; Church of the Brethren; Jehovah's Witnesses; and Hutterites. The numbers of men applying for CO's rose from 1,500 in the Civil War to 64,693 in World War I, with 56,380 accepted by the government. Of these only 20,873 received calls to service, with 3,989 refusing to accept noncombatant status. Later about 1,300 did accept such assignments in the military; 1,200 were placed on farms, and 100 in Quaker War Relief Camps in France. "Absolutists" refused to cooperate in any way. Of these, 17 received death sentences (none carried out): 142, life prison terms; and 345, terms averaging 16½ years. It was not until 1933 that a Presidential pardon by Roosevelt secured the release of the last of these men (Schlissel (ed), 1968: 129–131; Sibley and Jacob, 1952: 12).

Evasion

Although scattered, opposition to the World War I draft did exist (Weinstein, 1959: 215 ff.). Estimates of the number of draft evaders during World War I range from 171,000 (Chatfield, 1971: 69) to more than 250,000 men (Gates, 1970: 160). There was also extensive stealing of draft lists in parts of New York City and in an entire Indiana county. Stalling tactics, the deferment game, gained in popularity. Seventy percent of all eligible men in New York City filed exemption claims. In Akron, Ohio, 4,000 men were "no-shows", in October, 1917; in Donora, Pennsylvania, 40 percent of all registrants gave false addresses.

Canada provided another option. The Canadian House of Commons estimates that between 30,000 and 60,000 men entered Canada during this war. More reasonable estimates fall substantially lower. These were primarily men with Peace Church backgrounds, particularly Mennonites and Hutterites. The men who fled World War I often took their families with them, and in one case, brought an entire community. Many Canadians deeply resented the migrants. The Canadian "Great War Next-of-Kin Association" recommended drafting U.S. Mennonites, while Methodists, Presbyterians and Veterans' groups wanted them deported (Epp, 1970: 13–14; Sibley and Jacob, 1952: 15–16). D.A. Ross, writing in the *Winnipeg Free Presss*, stereotyped resisters thus:

> . . . Last Monday anyone who witnessed the arrival of a number of settlers from the United States would have been struck by their extraordinary appearance. For the past 40 odd years, I have witnessed the arrival of settlers from all parts of the world, and in all that time, I have never seen such an undesirable lot. Physically they all looked as if they came from the same mold . . .
>
> (Ross, 1918: 1).

The Draft Succeeds: "An Orderly Process"

Despite undercurrents of avoidance and resistance, this draft worked. It was so successful that the military pay scale dropped below civilian rates. (This has lasted through to the present day all-volunteer force.) In all previous wars, money in the form of bonuses, re-enlistment, or high pay offered inducements to procure manpower. By 1918, with a reliance on a successful draft, military pay dropped well below that of civilian jobs for the first time (Gates, 1970: 160). The 1917 Act not only discriminated against the poor in the "orderly process of selection," but created conditions in which it was no longer deemed important to bribe them. The need for a bounty was dead.

The Selective Service Act of 1917 effectively realized its objectives, without major violence, bloodshed, or resistance. Of the 4.7 million men who served in World War I, 2.8 million (60 percent) were draftees

(Chatfield, 1971: 69), as opposed to the 6 percent of Union soldiers in the Civil War (directly or indirectly). The surface inequities of the Civil War draft had been removed. However, the 1917 Act was still stacked heavily in favor of the higher classes. Replacing the flagrant loopholes of commutation and substitution, a sophisticated deferment system was installed. The introduction of the "orderly process" refined and maintained the old ways.

WORLD WAR II: AN ALL-OUT EFFORT — FOR MOST

> . . . When the demand for manpower pushed conscription to very high levels during World War II, selective service approached universal service, and this tended to minimize class factors, at least in terms of who wore a uniform (the rank of the wearer was another matter).
>
> (Useem, 1973: 81).

Probably in the year 3000, heroism in World War II will remain a prerequisite for election to the office of the President of the United States. Americans in the main supported this war and as a nation like to remember it as good and just. However, even here, the trends of discriminatory procedure re-emerge. In World War II, the impact of discrimination fell not on who served, but rather where and when.

The extent of mobilization for this war can be quickly understood by looking at age-cohort participation during peak years. Table 1-3 reveals that for the primary birth dates, 1921–1927, no fewer than 73.8 percent served. Thus the margin for discrimination as to who wore a uniform was greatly reduced.

The "Orderly Process" Continues

The 1917 Selective Service Draft Act expired shortly after the First World War ended. At the approach of World War II, a new Selective Service Act was passed in September 1940. This law was significant as the first peace time draft in the nation's history (Clifford, 1973: 2; Gates, 1970: 161). Initially it specifically prohibited draftees from serving beyond the borders of the United States and reinstated the deferment system in the "National Interest" (Marmion, 1969: 57).

The draft boards served as the monitors of the "National Interest". At the time of Pearl Harbor, 6,422 boards, with three to five members appointed in various ways, assessed men's eligibility. With some flexibility in directing men both into and away from the military, the boards could exercise subjective interpretation of the selective service regulations. These interpretations were tinted by the boards'

Table 1-3   Percentage of Service in
Military of Males by Year of Birth

Year of Birth	Percentage Ever in Service
1929	62.3%
1928	69.7
1927	77.7
1926	73.8
1925	73.9
1924	75.6
1923	75.2
1922	75.3
1921	74.2
1920	68.5
1919	66.7
1918	55.8

(Winsborough, 1975: *Statistical Histories*, 1975: 23)

membership, which did not reflect the population of potential draftees: instead, the lawyer, dentist and physician assigned to each board
were joined by business and professional men, or well-to-do farmers;
many ex-officers in the American Legion or ex-servicemen participated as well (Sibley and Jacob, 1952: 57–58).

War manpower needs intensified and certain selective service
requirements became more rigid, as implemented by these draft
boards. One of the first changes permitted the shipping of draftees
overseas; another eliminated certain deferments, such as that for having a child. By 1944, even student and occupational deferments were
closed to most. College enrollments fell to one-third their prewar
levels (still, as the quote below illustrates, college was at least somewhat of a haven). The length of service permitted under the draft
was also expanded, aptly summed up in the changing of the title of
a song about the draft during the war from *I'll Be Back in a Year, Little
Darling* to *I Won't Be Back in a Year, Little Darling* (Baskir and Strauss,
1978: 20; Lingeman, 1970: 173; Marmion, 1969: 57).

> During World War II, people with some college were less likely to serve
> than those with 11 years of education, and college graduates were less
> likely still.
>
> (Segal, 1981: 32)

Despite the changes, those student and occupational deferments
which remained "in the national interest" were most accessible to

the upper class: those men more likely to become the doctors, engineers, and scientists. Even in a period of near-full mobilization, discrimination in procurement was by no means eliminated (Gates, 1970: 27) and discrimination in assignment, as we will see, intensified.

Conscientious objector status differed significantly from other draft exemptions in that it required alternative service. The number of CO's grew significantly during World War II, both in degree and in kind. The conscientious objector section of the draft law, more inclusive than any previously, allowed certain CO's to perform alternative service outside of the military in civilian public service camps (CPS). More importantly, the criteria for becoming a CO, while still religious, were broadened beyond membership in a Peace Church. Local draft boards again determined who fit the definition of a conscientious objector and whether the CO should serve in the military as a noncombatant or work for a CPS camp: 50,000 men served in the former capacity and 11,950 in the latter (Gory and McClelland, 1947: 250; Sibley and Jacob, 1952: 45–53 and 83; Schlissel (ed), 1968: 214–217; Wittner, 1969: 49).

The World War II CO's were also educationally elite compared to their age-peers serving in the army (Table 1-4). A comparison of test scores of CO's in CPS camps to those of army men shows that 70 percent of the CO's versus only 9 percent of the army men fall in the top category of the general classification test. When the top two categories are collapsed, the percentages compare at 97 versus 45.4 respectively.

In addition to the CO's discussed above there were 5,300 CO's convicted for Selective Service violations, including 5,000 Jehovah's Witnesses who served in prison rather than participate in any aspect of the draft process. Another 1,624 CO's failed to report for civilian

Table 1-4   CPS and Army Men Test Scores by Army Grade

Army Grade	CPS	Army
I	70%	9.0%
II	27	36.4
III	3	29.0
IV	0	17.0
V	0	8.0
Total	100%	100%
	N = 596	N = N.A.

(Gory and McClelland, "Characteristics of Conscientious Objectors in World War II," in *Journal of Consulting Psychology* [1947, 250].

public service jobs (Sibley and Jacob, 1952: 83–84; Schlissel (ed), 1968: 214ff.).

Safety in Uniform: World War II

Although some deferments remained legitimate means of avoidance, more significant in World War II was the class-related "safety in uniform". In the introduction to this chapter, the historic shifting of military needs was discussed. The proportion of ground combat roles dropped from 90 percent of enlisted men, as late as the Civil War, to 23 percent of all military enlisted men and 39 percent of army enlisted men in 1945 (Gates, 1970: 42–43; Lang, 1981: 41). Conversely, the percent of enlisted men in the safer positions rose dramatically from the level of the Civil War. For instance, those in technical and scientific positions went from .15 to 10.4 percent; administrative and clerical from .73 to 12.6 percent; mechanics from .95 to 16.6 percent (U.S. Bureau of the Census, *Statistical Abstract of the United States,* 1975: 326).

These figures suggest that wearing a uniform did not automatically mean high risk, even in an "all-out effort" like World War II. In World War II, the majority of enlisted men were sheltered in safer positions — in the national interest. Those with the least pre-service education, linked to social class, were placed in combat. The "orderly process" of World War I was used to justify both deferments and this systematic assignment procedure in World War II.

Dissent within Limits

> *"The Draftee's Prayer"*
>
> Dear Lord, today
> I go to war:
> to fight, to die
> Tell me what for?
> Dear Lord, I'll fight
> I do not fear
> Germans or Japs;
> my fears are here
> America.
>
> (Cited in Wittner, 1969: 47)

While this World War II poem lacked the punch of Muhammed Ali's statement that "No Vietcong Ever Called Me Nigger", it touched on the sentiment of some blacks who questioned their role in the U.S. military. Robert Weaver, a black member of the Roosevelt Administration, stated that his people's attitude toward the war was "certainly not enthusiastic support". Still, blacks accounted for only 4.4 percent of all draft evasion cases, and only 400 blacks out of 2,427,495 registrants were classified as conscientious objectors (Wittner, 1969: 46ff.). The former figure would rise geometrically during Vietnam; the latter would rise only arithmetically.

Despite this war's popularity, desertions occurred. During the peak year for desertion, fiscal 1944, the Army and Marines suffered losses of 63.0 and 6.9 per 1,000 men, respectively. Rates of desertion in World War II, overall, surpassed those of Vietnam. But any comparison across wars must be viewed in light of the military's juggling of records which promoted a deflated image of Vietnam desertions. That is, it was much easier to be classified as a deserter in World War II than in Vietnam. Nevertheless, as will be seen, Vietnam's peak levels of desertion surpassed those of World War II (Cortright, 1975: 10–13; Cooney and Spitzer, 1969: 53–62; Starr, 1973: 38–39; U.S. Bureau of the Census, *Statistical Abstract of the United States*, 1975: 327).

Draft evasion in World War II rose in absolute numbers from World War I — from 171,000 to 348,217 — but the total number of draftees rose from 2.8 to 10 million. The percentages of World War II evaders are not nearly as significant as those for their World War I predecessors or their successors in the Vietnam Era. World War II was, by and large, an accepted conflict and "unlike World War I, the second World War produced no great wave of disillusionment" (Wittner, 1969: 42 and 120).

The draft worked reasonably well in World War II. Ten million of the 16,500,000 men who served during this conflict were draftees (Gates, 1970: 161). Undercurrents of dissent, avoidance, desertion, and evasion were not disruptive during this war. Nevertheless, deferments to avoid the service and "dangerous" assignments in the military were still tied to social class. The use of the CO deferment by men not connected to Peace Churches and the power invested in local draft boards were two of the more significant World War II appendages added to a military procurement system designed for and by members of the upper classes. In this all-out effort, there was still room for discrimination inside and outside the military. This room was filled.

KOREA: UNDECLARED DISCRIMINATION

Assistant Secretary of Defense John A Hannah: There is too much validity in the statement that is often made that the son of the well-to-do family goes to college, the sons of some of the rest go to Korea.
(Cited in *U.S. News and World Report*, February 21, 1953: 18)

If World War II provided room for discrimination, Korea supplied a mansion. During the Korean conflict news commentator Edward R. Murrow said that the draft policies offered protection for the "intellectual elite" (Mayer and Hoult, 1955: 153). The channels through which men could escape the draft, the military, and even the Korean assignment were clearly defined. Because of our limited role, direct manpower needs in the Korean Conflict did not approach the mobilization of World War II. Draft exemptions were readily available. In particular, the social-class related tudent deferment received much broader utilization than in World War II (*U.S. News and World Report*, February 21, 1953.)

The types of men who acquired CO's in World War II re-surfaced during the Korean Conflict. They came from a broader base than the Peace Churches, and in greater numbers. In World War II, CO's numbered a tolerable 4 per 10,000. Early in the Korean War the number of men classified as CO's reached 13 per 10,000; at the end, the number fell to 5 per 10,000. The reduction at the end of the war reflects the more stringent review of the applicants by local draft boards. Nevertheless Korea marks a record rate of CO's (Smith, 1971: 233).

Korea also witnessed a return of the deferment game of World War I. Prior to Pearl Harbor, 26 per 1000 men once classified IA (top priority) appealed their status. By the end of the relatively popular World War II, that figure dropped to three per 1000. In 1950, before the start of the Korean Conflict, only one man per 1000 appealed his 1A status. By the end of the Korean War, this figure rose to 47 men per 1000 (Smith, 1971: 231–232). While some of the appeals, perhaps most, were legitimate, a knowledge of how to operate the Selective Service could obviously delay and perhaps avoid one's entrance into the military.

Safety in Uniform: Korea

In the Korean Conflict, the position of men in the service also reflected social class differences. The nature of in-service discrimination was modified as military needs deflected men away from direct ground combat. By 1953, only 35 percent of all army, and 18 percent of all military enlisted men served as ground combat troops (Gates, 1970: 43). As the military needs shifted away from these troops, men with greater skills and education were in demand; but not for combat. Enlisted men in technical and scientific positions now accounted for 12.7 percent of all positions — up from 10.4 in World War II and .15 in the Civil War; 18.1 percent were placed in administrative and clerical positions — up from 12.6 and .73, respectively; 15.3 percent were now classified as mechanics and repairmen — slightly down from 16.6 percent in World War II, but up from the .10 percent of the Civil War (U.S. Bureau of the Census, *Statistical Abstract of the United States*, 1975: 326).

Men with more advanced education were assigned to roles and locations sheltered from the greatest risk. These men generally can be assumed to have had a more privileged background than the combat troops. A study of Detroit residents supports this assumption:

> The number of Detroiter's who died, were captured, or were reported missing in Korea varied directly with the relative economic standing of the city areas from which the men stemmed. The variation was such that the data herein substantiate the charges made by a number of observers that Korea was a poor man's war.
>
> (Mayer and Hoult, 1955: 155)

Tables 1-5 and 1-6 illustrate the Detroit-specific conclusions of this report, which the authors maintain are representative of national trends. They found that the lower the economic status of the household, the greater likelihood for the person to become a casualty. Conversely, using education and technological skills as measures of social class, the higher the education or technical competence of a man, the more likelihood that he was stationed in a relatively less exposed combat area.

Desertion, Evasion, and Dissent

Although the Korean Conflict lacked the public support of World War II, the desertion rates were substantially lower. Army and Marine

Table 1-5 Korean War Casualty Rate per 10,000 Occupied Dwelling Units, by Median Income of Census Tract, Detroit, Michigan

Median Income	Casualty Rate per 10,000 occupied dwelling unit
Under 2500	14.6
2500–2999	10.8
3000–3499	9.1
3500–3999	8.6
4000–4499	7.5
4500–4999	6.6
5000–5499	5.8
5500 and over	4.6

(Albert S. Mayer and Thomas F. Holt, "Social Stratification and Combat Survival," in *Social Forces*, 34 [December 2, 1955], 157. Reprinted by permission, University of North Carolina Press.)

Table 1-6   Korean War Casualty Rate per 10,000 Occupied Dwelling units, by Average Value of Home, Detroit, Michigan

Economic Level As Given by Average Value of Home (dollars)	Number of Occupied D.U.s — Based on %5 sample	Number of Casualties	Rate per 10,000 Occupied D.U.s
Under 4000	5,480	9	16.4
4000–4999	13,520	21	15.5
5000–5999	40,600	53	13.1
6000–6999	71,380	108	15.1
7000–7999	88,620	82	9.2
8000–8999	120,320	63	5.3
9000–9999	72,100	38	5.3
10,000–10,999	31,740	17	5.4
11,000–11,999	23,740	17	7.2
12,000–12,999	19,540	11	5.7
13,000–13,999	13,020	8	6.1
14,000–14,999	10,360	7	6.7
15,000 and over	16,260	7	4.3
Totals	526,680	441	8.4

(Mayer and Holt, Ibid., p. 157)

desertion rates peaked in fiscal 1953 at 22.3 and 29.6 men per 1,000 (lower than World War II or Vietnam) (U.S. Bureau of the Census, *Statistical Abstract of the United States,* 1975: 327). However, as in World War II, the system easily absorbed these losses.

Draft evasion too was within absorbable limits in this conflict. The number of evasion cases *prosecuted* during the war, however, rose steadily. Table 1-7 shows the number of violators prosecuted under the 1948 Selective Service Act, applicable to this conflict.

As the Korean Conflict progressed, its popularity with the U.S. public diminished. At the beginning of the war, two public opinion polls indicated that 17 or 20 percent (respectively) of the American

Table 1-7   Selective Service Violation Prosecutions by Year

Year	Defendants
1950	43
1951	314
1952	659
1953	771
1954	1,015

(U.S. Bureau of the Census, *Statistical Abstract of the U.S.,* 1953: 148; 1955: 147)

public *did not support* our involvement. By the end, these figures rose to over 33 and 50 percent per respective poll. This contrasts with World War II, when the dissent figures fell from 34 percent to eight percent during the war (Smith, 1971: 223–225).

Korea, with its decreased direct manpower needs, produced extreme discrimination concerning who should serve and where. Class-related deferments and military assignments provide the most flagrant examples of this. The appeals game again offered an option only to those with the luxury of knowledge of and exposure to the deferment system. CO status, while not easy to obtain, remained virtually exclusive to the upper classes and Peace Church members.

Yet, despite these avenues of avoidance and some resistance, and despite the war's growing lack of support, the system again worked. The numbers of evaders and avoiders never seriously threatened the draft, which eventually accounted for over 1,500,000 men (27 percent) of the 5,800,000 men on active duty during the war (Gates, 1970: 121 and 162; U.S. Bureau of the Census, *Statistical Abstract of the U.S.*, 1975: 326). Nor did in-service resistance during this unpopular war threaten the functioning of the military. Such statements cannot be made about the Vietnam conflict.

SUMMARY

From prior to the American Revolution until the Korean Conflict — from commutation and substitution fees to deferments and in-service assignments — methods of raising and maintaining armies in this country have blatantly protected the higher classes, and discriminated against the less advantaged. However, undercurrents of avoidance and resistance, legal and illegal, emerged during each military conflict. After the Civil War, the form of and opposition to inequitable procurement procedures grew increasingly sophisticated.

From Colonial times onward, a number of patterns of procurement, avoidance, and resistance began to evolve, which would coalesce during the Vietnam Era. Overt methods of class discrimination — substitution and commutation — date back to the early colonies, and continued into the Civil War. After World War I these overtly discriminatory practices were replaced by a more subtle system of draft exemptions, continuing legal forms of avoidance. This "orderly process" was amenable to manipulation. Playing the so-called deferment game (stalling tactics) became popular in World War I and was evident in Korea.

Parallel to the growth of legal exemptions, men seeking the alternative of conscientious objector status are of great significance in the history of procurement. At first, by law and commitment, only members of the Peace Churches would attain this status. By the time of World War I the numbers who sought this classification leaped geometrically; in World War II and Korea the numbers grew in both degree and kind. These men began to question the concept of war itself, on moral grounds. Unlike men who avoided through exemptions, CO's who would no longer directly participate in the military process had to perform alternative duties.

Historically, the nature of the military's needs shifted, and internally the military itself developed in complexity. Assignment within the service grew complicated, affecting not only who served, but in what capacities they served. Social class was at the root of these assignments. This channeling of men within the military was most explicit during World War II and Korea. This tendency, as will be demonstrated, grew most pronounced during the Vietnam era.

Resistance, while varied in form and in quantity, was apparent across our history of military conflicts. The destruction of draft board records dates back at least to the Revolution, was very significant in the Civil War, and was in evidence in World War I. Draft evasion through nonregistration or not showing up for induction was rampant during the Civil War and widespread in World War I. Desertions reached nearly epidemic proportions in both the Revolution and Civil War, and for the length of the war, they were higher in World War II than Vietnam. The use of Canada as a refuge also dates back to the Revolution, was very significant in the Civil War, and noticeable in World War I.

The Civil War offers perhaps the clearest parallels to Vietnam. In both wars the military procurement system suffered serious challenge — often it was the symbolic scapegoat for other issues, such as lack of trust in the government, or a general frustration with the economy. Serious problems emerge both for the procurement and maintenance of the military.

The Vietnam Era marks neither the birth of discrimination in military procurement and assignment, nor the rise in avoidance/ resistance strategies. What distinguishes Vietnam from the past is that historically the system had worked. By the end of the Vietnam Era, this statement could no longer be safely made.

CHAPTER 2

Vietnam: The Well Ran Dry

Draft Dodger Rag	Deferment
Sarge. I'm only 18	1H/1S
I've got a ruptured spleen	1Y
And I always carry a purse	1Y/4A/4F
I see like a bat	1Y/4F
My feet are flat	4F
And my asthma's getting worse	1Y/4F
Oh, think of my career	2A
Of my sweetheart dear	3A
And my poor old invalid aunt	3A
Besides, I ain't no fool	1S/2S
I'm a-going to school	1S/2S
And I'm working in a defense plant	7A

Understanding the erosion of popular support for the Vietnam War places in perspective the procurement of men for this war, and resistance to it. In World War II, dissent against U.S. involvement dropped from a pre-Pearl Harbor peak of 34 percent to 8 percent. In Korea (depending on the poll used), dissent rose from 17 or 20 percent to 33 or 50 percent, respectively (Smith, 1971: 223–225). The proportion of Americans who objected to our participation in the Vietnam conflict (Figure 2–1), according to Gallup surveys,[1] rose steadily with time to 60 percent. Vietnam surpassed Korea in terms of public disapproval. It is only in this context of the war's growing unpopularity that the actions and non-actions of the men subject to military procurement can properly be understood.

This chapter explores the establishment and breakdown of the channeling process inside and outside the military during the Vietnam Era. The focus is on draft-eligible males because they were targeted by the procurement system. The procedures of procurement and assignment, and the unravelling of these procedures, recapitulate 300 years of history.

LIMITED MANPOWER NEEDS: LOTS OF DISCRIMINATION

Vietnam was a war which did not require full mobilization and thus permitted very selective channeling. The male eligibility pool, much deeper than during the Korean Conflict because of the post-World

Figure 2-1

**Percentage of Public Opposed to
U.S. Involvement in Vietnam**

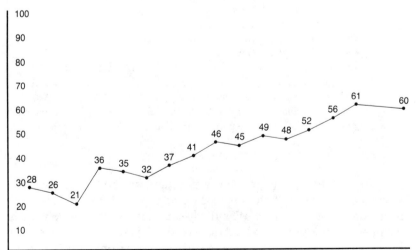

(The Gallup Poll, *Public Opinion 1935–1971*, Volume III; The Gallup Poll, *Public Opinion 1972–1977*, Vol. I.)

War II baby boom, enhanced the possibility of selective channeling of the 26,800,000 men of draft-eligible age during the Vietnam Era, 1964 to 1973. Less than one-third of these men, 8,615,000, served in the military, including the reserves.[2] Only 2,150,000 served in Vietnam — 8 percent of all eligibles and 25 percent of men who were in the service (Baskir and Strauss, 1978: 5). In other words, less than one-third of all eligible men entered the service and far fewer actually ended up in Vietnam. The actual number of men and women, of all ages, who served in Vietnam during the duration of the conflict, is generally accepted to be approximately 2.8 million (McFadden, 1981: A1). Baskir and Strauss, however, by their focus on age-eligible males, allow us to trace the extent and patterns of discrimination which characterize this period of military procurement and assignment.

> At the inception of the conflict, Selective Service policy worked to exclude two groups. On the one hand, it was government policy to defer young men who were pursuing higher education and entering occupations defined to be in the national interest. These were the sons primarily of upper- and upper-middle class families. On the other hand, it was also government policy to exclude young men who could not meet certain minimum mental and physical standards. Those excluded on these criteria were disproportionately from lower-class and minority backgrounds.
>
> (Starr, 1973: 6)

In the civilian sector, the guardian of the *status quo* was the Selective Service System — those who defined the methods of channeling (Chatterjee and Chatterjee, 1970: 288–290; Useem, 1973: 89–90). Through channeling the higher classes were protected and, at least early in the war, the very poor and least advantaged were no longer in demand.

General Lewis B. Hershey, Director of the Selective Service until well into the Vietnam Era, referred to local draft boards as "little groups of neighbors" who sat in judgment of their peers. Until 1967, when Congress enacted reforms, draft boards were very homogeneous and distinct from the pool of men eligible for military service. Veterans accounted for 66 percent of the members; about half of the members were over 60, with the average age over 50; 30 percent had four or more years of college, relative to the nationwide figure of 12 percent. Blacks composed only 1.3 percent of all 16,632 board members, with no blacks on the boards in Alabama, Arkansas, Louisiana, Mississippi, Kansas, Indiana, or New Jersey. After much adverse publicity the number of blacks rose to 6.7 percent — blacks at that time represented 12 percent of the nation's population (Davis and Dolbeare, 1968: 57–63; Murray, 1971: 120–130). A study in Wisconsin found that 66 percent of the board members had held public office (Davis, 1969: 66) and, on 16 boards in the Cleveland metropolitan area, almost 69 percent of the members held white collar jobs (Chatterjee and Chatterjee, 1970: 289–292). If draft board members represented "little groups of neighbors," the neighborhoods were very exclusive.

The draft board's staff, which held enormous power, was also nonrepresentative. Draft boards met twice a month, usually for no more than three hours. The meetings often involved discussions of the personal appearances of registrants, leaving the majority of the work to clerks, who were also not a fully typical sample of the general population. For example, after the "reforms" of the late 1960's, blacks held only 447 of the 6,527 Selective Service positions — 6.85 percent. Seventy percent (313) of these 447 worked in New York, Washington, D.C., Illinois, and California. The often powerful clerk was neither peer nor neighbor of the registrant (Murray, 1971: 130–131).

President Johnson's 1967 National Advisory Commission on Selective Service exposed the degree of selection discrimination by these nonrepresentative boards, which persisted throughout the war. The Commission found that although almost 50 percent of blacks represented were found "not eligible" for the service in 1967, the boards drafted 30 percent of qualified blacks versus only 18 percent of qualified whites. At the time, blacks comprised 1.3 percent of draft board membership (Cited in O'Sullivan and Meckler, 1974: 252).

The implementation of Selective Service regulations by local boards varied enormously and provided another means to exercise biases. In New York the Peace Corps was at one time considered a legitimate deferment. At the same time in Kansas it was not. Mortuary training was a valid "out" in Illinois but not in Alabama (Flacks, Howe and Lauter, 1967: 3; Lauter and Howe, 1970: 183–184).

These variations existed even within given localities. For instance, in Lake Charles, Louisiana, conscientious objector status was granted almost automatically by one board, rarely by a second, and on a case-by-case basis by a third (Baskir and Strauss, 1978: 26). In Saginaw, Michigan, one board was far more reluctant to grant CO's than the other boards in town.

The subjective judgments of the board of registration made a difference for many, and social class was the overriding determinant. Davis and Dolbeare, in an extensive study of the Selective Service from 1965 to 1967, concluded that early in the Vietnam conflict the working and lower middle classes were not being allowed out, and the higher classes were.

We see an intricate meshing of deferment policy and organizational characteristics which has the combined effect of offering alternatives to military service to the sons of the higher socio-economic strata while conferring the management of deferments and inductions upon community influentials drawn from the same strata.

(Davis and Dolbeare, 1968: 3–4)

Men not holding exemptions were eligible for the draft until age 26. If a man held certain temporary deferments, he could be eligible until age 35 — although this did not occur often. During the Vietnam Era, 1964 to 1973, 1,759,000 men were drafted. (As we will see, the threat of the draft played a significant role in forcing enlistments throughout the conflict.) Almost all draftees served in the Army: 3000 were channeled into the Navy, and another 44,000 entered the Marine Corps (U.S. Bureau of the Census, *Statistical Abstract of the U.S.*, 1975: 326 and 327).

During the Vietnam Era, 8,769,000 men were permanently excused with draft deferments (Baskir and Strauss, 1978: 28–31). While all deferments had a rationale, from channeling in the national interest to exemptions for family hardships, certain deferments reinforced class lines of avoidance. In this section, the more popular methods are discussed.

Deferments: Loopholes for the Rich

Men who attended college, whose family and/or class expectations and resources channeled them into school, "purchased" a head start in avoiding the draft. In school, under the protection of student deferments, these men enjoyed four extra years to formulate their opinions about the military. In 1966, prior to some limited reforms, almost two million men held student deferments (Useem, 1973: 88).

Those who chose to channel themselves away from the military had many options other than a student deferment. The occupational deferment was held by 300,000 men in 1966, and over the whole span of the war, 483,000 permanently escaped the draft through this deferment. As in previous wars, eligibility for occupational deferments was determined by what was "necessary to the maintenance of the national interest." Necessary occupations usually required college degrees, and included, at different times, high school teachers, missile scientists, chemists, geologists, scientific linguists, etc. (Baskir and Strauss, 1978: 31; Davis and Dolbeare, 1968: 88–89; Useem, 1981: 29–30; 1973: 88). In 1968, when the New York City draft boards confirmed teaching as a legitimate way to avoid the military, applications for teaching positions rose by 20,000 from the previous year (Baskir and Strauss, 1978: 32).

Medical and psychiatric deferments, allegedly equal for all, offered another means of escaping the system. Racial differences meant different access to these deferments. For example, in 1968 whites received double the rate of medical deferments given to blacks (Murray, 1971: 133; Useem, 1973: 87–88). Many were helped by knowledge of what types of medical or psychiatric problems served as "deferable," and by access to a physician, psychiatrist, or psychologist willing to defend or create a deferable problem. In Los Angeles, men paid between $1000 and $2000 for orthodontal braces — a legal deferment. From 1960 to 1973, 3,575,000 men were given physical deferments and another 255,000 were classified as psychiatrically unacceptable (Baskir and Strauss, 1978: 30ff.).

The conscientious objector (CO) status provided another available alternative — to more men than in any previous war. First observed in World War II, the trend toward accepting the better educated, non-Peace Church members grew most pronounced during the Vietnam Era. As in previous wars, the CO legally had to perform two years of service: as a non-combatant in the military, or (for most) two years of alternative civilian service beyond commuting distance from home. Thus, the CO status differed from other exemptions in that men so classified were still obligated to devote two years of their lives to some form of service — often in menial low-paying jobs (Baskir and Strauss, 1978: 41).

Two important Supreme Court decisions, *U.S. v. Seeger* — 1965 and *Welsh v. U.S.* — 1970, opened the doors for many previously unclassified CO's. The Seeger case, a landmark, considerably broadened the basis on which one could claim CO status. While a CO claim still had to be rooted in "religious training and belief," the court's definition of "religious" went beyond traditional usage to include agnosticism: belief in a God was no longer required as long as religious belief occupied "a place in the life of its possessor parallel to that filled by orthodox belief in God." Five years later, the Welsh case broadened the criteria even further. The court ruled that CO claims no longer had to be called religious at all. What remained critical was a deeply held conviction that participation in combat (1-AO) or the military (1-0) violated one's "religious" *or* "moral" beliefs (O'Sullivan and Meckler, 1974: 229; Seeley, 1981: 54ff.).

These decisions reflected the serious pressures on "the system" during the Vietnam Era. Young men actively took stands against combat participation, or any participation, in the military. Public consciousness progressed well beyond the Peace Churches and organized religion. The number of civilian CO's grew from 17,900 in 1964, to 40,600 in 1970, to 61,000 in 1971. The ratio of men holding CO's rose: out of 10,000 men, there were 4 CO's during World War II; 5 at the end of Korea; 6 in 1964; 7 in 1968; 8 in 1969. By 1970, 10 men out of 10,000 were conscientious objectors. During the last three years of the draft, almost 145,000 claims succeeded. In fiscal 1971 alone, 125,000 men applied for CO status (Baskir and Strauss, 1978: 41; Cortright, 1975: 5; Smith, 1971: 233; Useem, 1973: 131).

Obtaining a CO deferment required a class-related ability to read and write, in the particular judgment of a generally upper-class draft board. Exposure to the types of belief supporting conscientous objection, and access to an attorney or even a counselor to help in such cases are also matters associated with social class. To repeat, however: unlike the other class-linked deferments, a CO classification required two years of alternative service — distinguishing CO's from the other class-privileged exemptions.[3]

All deferments, legitimate or not, involved some legal manipulation of a very manipulatable system. The extent of legal maneuvering is perhaps most evident in the rising numbers of men who appealed their 1-A (most vulnerable) draft classifications. Again it must be noted that the ability to appeal involved class-related knowledge and resources. During World War II, the number of men appealing 1-A classifications fell from a pre-Pearl Harbor level of 26 per 1000 to 3 per 1000 by the end of the war. In the less popular Korean conflict the numbers rose, from beginning to end, from one to 47 per 1000. In Vietnam from July 1965 to July 1969 (even before the highest degrees of both resistance and avoidance), the numbers soared from 4 to 102 per 1000. (Smith, 1971: 230–231). The more unpopular the war, the more popular the appealing process became.

Deferments: Rejection of the Poor

> . . . . The very poor tended to be disqualified from service, whereas the rich were more easily able to obtain *de facto* exemption through a complex deferment system.
>
> (Useem, 1973: 174)

The limited warfare in Vietnam allowed the military to be very selective in procurement and assignment. We have already witnessed how the upper classes had options to escape the draft. The least advantaged in our society, particularly early in the war, were also "selected-out" through rejection. As stated earlier, the military no longer needed massive numbers of unskilled personnel, particularly as ground combat roles decreased; instead it required better educated and more highly skilled personnel.

One measure designed to screen men's alleged qualifications was the Armed Forces Qualifications Test (AFQT). Test scores, divided into five categories, distinguished men in Categories I, II, and III as acceptable; those in IV as marginal; and those in V as unacceptable. Men scoring in Category V and, depending on the time, Category IV, were declared mentally unsuitable, and therefore exempted from the draft (Baskir and Strauss, 1978: 30–31 and 122–131; Kapinos, 1967: 36).

That the AFQT, like general intelligence tests, contained built-in racial and class biases comes as no surprise. From 1950 to 1966, 54.1 percent of blacks and only 18.6 percent of whites failed the exam (Murray, 1971: 133). During 1968, blacks were five times more likely than whites to fail the test (Useem, 1973: 88).

The AFQT's class biases are quite obvious. A special assistant for manpower in the Department of the Army notes

> The examinee's score on the tests depends on several factors: on the level of his educational attainment; on the quality of the school facilities; and on the knowledge he gained from his educational training or otherwise, in and outside of school . . .
>
> (Karpinos, 1967: 39)

Educational attainment and the quality of school facilities are almost inevitably linked to racial and class background in this nation. Poorer youth are more likely to drop out of school. Wealthier children enjoy the luxury of choosing among private schools and the "better" public institutions. The rejection of men through the AFQT translates into a general rejection of those with the least privileged backgrounds.[4]

These avoidance and rejection patterns produced a military disproportionately comprised of men from the lower-middle/working classes. The rich were protected through the complicated maze of avoidance exemptions, under the guise of channeling. The poor were rejected initially because they did not fit into the perceived manpower demands of the modern military. The lower-middle/working classes were sufficiently skilled and politically dispensable to be channeled into the military (Segal, 1981: 31; Starr, 1973: 6; Useem, 1973: 134 and 1981: 29–30; Williams, 1971a: 21).

Reforms or Classism?

As a result of the loopholes for the more privileged, systematic rejection of the poor, and increased manpower needs for Vietnam, by the mid-1960's the draft faltered in its ability to meet its objectives. Two strategies were employed to get more men in uniform. First, the AFQT standards were lowered, putting formerly "unfit" men into uniform, and disproportionately into the front lines of combat. Second, a series of selective service reforms channeled more men of higher social class into uniform, but not necessarily into combat roles, in Vietnam.

Secretary of Defense Robert McNamara:
The poor of America have not had the opportunity to earn their fair share of this nation's abundance, but they can be given an opportunity to serve in their country's defense and they can be given an opportunity to return to civilian life with skills and aptitudes which for them and their families will reverse the downward spiral of decay.

(Cited in Starr, 1973: 190)

The base of available men had to be broadened by eliminating deferments, lowering standards, or both. The solution was to get more men from all classes into uniform, and more men from certain classes into combat. Toward the latter end, "Project 100,000" surfaced as one answer. Under the banner of liberalism, Defense Secretary Robert McNamara announced in mid-1966 a program to induct, annually, 100,000 "new standards men". "Project 100,000" offered a thinly rationalized effort to fill the military and combat quotas by dipping the ladle deeper into the lower classes for both draftees and volunteers. By 1970, only 29 percent of blacks (down from 54.1 percent) failed the now-lowered AFQT standards, and 5.3 percent of whites (down from 18.6) could not pass the exam (Helmer, 1972: 9; Murray, 1971: 133–135; Starr, 1973: 190–197; Useem, 1973: 140).

Project 100,000 marked the beginning of three major lowerings of AFQT Category IV's "bottom line". Forty-one percent of the first 240,000 men brought into the military between 1966 and 1968 — as compared to 12 percent of the total military population — were black; 75 percent came from low-income families; 80 percent had dropped out of high school, and 40 percent read at less than a sixth-grade level (Baskir and Strauss, 1978: 129). Compared to others in the service, these men did not have the skills to fit low-risk jobs. While during the war only 23 percent of all military personnel were assigned to combat positions, 37 percent of "Project 100,000" men found themselves in combat roles (Useem, 1973: 140). Not only did they fare badly in this respect; they often failed to receive honorable discharges. Category IV soldiers were courtmartialed at two and a half times the rate of the rest of military personnel. Approximately 80,000 received undesirable, bad conduct, or dishonorable discharges; and 100,000 received general discharges (Baskir and Strauss, 1978: 129; Starr, 1973:

95). For these men, military service hardly fulfilled McNamara's promise of "an opportunity to . . . reverse the downward spiral of decay."

"Project 100,000" amounted to an effort to fill the ranks with the poor, disproportionately exposing them to danger. When the needs for personnel were reduced, "Project 100,000" ended. Although unique to Vietnam, this program reflected a consistent theme in the long tradition of raising manpower in the United States: dealing from the bottom of a stacked deck.

Channeling the Rich

Largely as a result of unfavorable publicity about the draft's discriminatory nature, some loopholes were eventually plugged. Marriage exemptions were eliminated early in 1966. Prior to this, marriage had offered yet another avenue for avoidance, with one of every eight married men in the Notre Dame study reporting an early marriage to avoid the draft. The head of the Georgia Selective Service acknowledged that in one week 46 men who had been ordered to induction centers got married (Baskir and Strauss, 1978: 33). Married men could, after 1966, still seek student or occupational deferments, although these deferments were also curtailed.

New occupational deferments were eliminated in 1970 (Useem, 1973: 77). However, men already holding this exemption could still maintain it, e.g., the college-educated New York City teachers, engineers, doctors, etc., mentioned earlier.

In 1967 the student deferment was modified to exclude certain graduate students, although those in their second year (or further advanced) remained exempt. Most incoming undergraduates received deferments until December 1971. In 1972 incoming freshmen were vulnerable to the draft, no longer protected by student deferments. By this time, however, draft calls had dropped dramatically. These reforms disrupted plans for a college education for only a few men, reducing their four-year headstart on avoidance of the military (Baskir and Strauss, 1978: 27–28; Useem, 1973: 76–77 and 99). After these reforms, more former college students eventually entered the military, and even went to Vietnam. The number of former college students in the military increased threefold between 1965 and 1970 (Useem, 1973: 109 and 134). Nonetheless, "[they were] still underrepresented in relation to the civilian population [and] probably underexposed to the battlefield" (Ibid., 109). Shortly we will see just how safe these men were.

The most famous of all draft reforms came in 1969 with the

introduction of the lottery, a random selection of men by their birth date. The "impartiality" of the lottery was, nevertheless, compromised by the residual deferments — occupational until 1970; undergraduate students until 1972, as well as CO's and cases of family hardship[5] (Useem, 1973–81).

These reforms had questionable impact. By the time most reforms were instituted, the war had wound down. Draft calls were reduced to 156,000 in fiscal 1972 and to less than 27,000 the following fiscal year. These totals may be compared to 340,000 in fiscal 1966; 299,000 in fiscal 1967; 340,000 in fiscal 1968 and 265,000 in fiscal 1969 (U.S. Bureau of the Census, 1975: 327). Indeed the deferment game made it quite possible for a young man with patience, knowledge of the system, and financial resources to delay induction, sometimes for the duration of the war. As the war dragged on, this game gained in popularity.

> . . . More and more draft-age men began to realize that they could outlast the war by exercising their legal rights and slowing down the processing of their cases.
>
> (Baskir and Strauss, 1978: 27)

On the other hand, the reforms served as a rude awakening for many within the classes that before had been largely protected. With the loss of draft deferments, the so-called "club of induction" encouraged tens of thousands to enlist before they were actually drafted. Enlistment often gave these men a greater choice of military branch, and placement within that branch, than being drafted would allow. How these men, often designated as "reluctant volunteers," were channeled (compared to draftees) is the subject of the following section.

SAFETY IN UNIFORM: VIETNAM

> *1967 — U.S. National Advisory Commission on Selective Service:*
> . . . White middle class college educated Americans are likely to escape the mud and death of Southeast Asia, while those who are poor and "unsuitable" for college die in battlefields at a rate double that of their proportion in the population.

Even after more members of the higher classes eventually entered the military, the working class and the poor still paid the greatest price. In-service "channeling" continued to protect the rich: "Once in uniform, the higher a person's social class standing, the more likely to be placed in non-combatant roles" (Useem, 1973: 134).

The channeling of higher numbers of the upper classes into the military or military reserves in the late 1960's occurred directly through the draft, and more frequently, indirectly through the threat of the draft for "reluctant volunteers". At no time during the Vietnam War did draftees comprise more than one-third of all enlisted men (U.S. Bureau of the Census, *Statistical Abstract of the United States,* 1975: 327). The threat of a draft, however, led increasing numbers into uniform. Indirectly the draft swelled the military ranks. Helmer (1974: 3) estimates that "reluctant volunteers" comprised 50 percent of all Army and Air Force enlisted men in 1970. Pentagon studies estimate that among enlisted men, the number of "reluctant volunteers" rose from 38 percent in 1964 to 54 percent in 1968. Among officers, they increased from 41 to 60 percent (Useem, 1973: 78). This section deals with reluctant volunteers, who often served up to two extra years in special programs to avoid Vietnam. The large numbers of non-draft motivated volunteers also joining the service are of course a separate group.

"Reluctant volunteers" were often attracted to and sought after by the "safer" branches of the service: Coast Guard, Navy, Air Force, Reserves and National Guard, as well as non-combat programs in the Army and Marines. The Notre Dame study estimates that during the Vietnam Era 15 million men took steps to avoid combat; of these, almost half did so by carefully choosing their pathways in the military (Baskir and Strauss, 1978: 7). The sophisticated stratification demanded by the modern military steered those with higher education — who had had the most opportunities to achieve a higher education — to safety. Thus, even after the proportion of ex-college students in the military tripled, "those who arrived overseas were less likely to see front line service" (Useem, 1973: 135).

Critics of the Vietnam Era draft charge that the rich could escape while the poor were forced to serve. This notion reflects only partial accuracy: the higher classes did retain their historic claims to the most options for avoidance — inside and outside the service; however, our now specialized military no longer targeted the poorest of the poor.[6] This was especially true after the reforms of the mid-1960s. Many of the new targets became the reluctant volunteers.

By the 1960's the nation and military had become so complex that "channeling", *nee* "the orderly process" in World War I, could be defended as serving the national interest. The deferment system permitted the "mentally qualified" (a euphemism for the higher classes) to be channeled away from the military to fulfill their "special order of patriotism." Less consistently with history, however, the military grew so specialized that it required manpower with skills and education more advanced than those accessible to our lowest classes. This trend had been developing with modern warfare needs shifting away from the combat infantrymen. It became very pronounced with the high technological specialization of the military in Vietnam.

As illustrated in Chapter 1, fewer and fewer men were assigned to combat as the military became more complex. By 1963 (the dawn of the Vietnam Era) only 14 percent of all military enlisted men, and 29 percent of army enlisted men, were assigned to ground combat units in which minimal skills were required (Gates, 1970: 43). (These percentages would rise slightly during the war.) Table 2-1 reflects the historic rise in non-combat duty assignments for enlisted men. The draft or threat of a draft was used to meet the new requirements. Men from the working and lower-middle class became the prime targets. During the Vietnam years, the rich preserved their traditionally greater opportunities to escape the military, while the heaviest burdens of service no longer pressed the poorest classes; instead, "people from the lower-middle rather than the very lowest strata served disproportionately" (Segal, 1981: 31). Once in the service assignment and risk would once again reflect class lines.

The safer military programs had much stricter entrance requirements than those the Selective Service boards used for draftees. Those requirements often followed racial and class lines. The Reserves and National Guard, the safest, obligated a man, unless activated, to four to six months of active duty, plus summer and monthly meetings lasting for six years. A variety of studies show that the 1,040,000 Reservists and National Guardsmen during the Vietnam Era "were better connected, better educated, more affluent, and more often white, than their peers in the active forces." In 1969–70, blacks ac-

Table 2-1 Rise in Non-Combat Assignments for Enlisted Men

	Technical and Scientific	Administrative and Clerical	Mechanics and Repairmen
Civil War	.15%	.73%	.10%
Spanish/American War	.52	3.13	.95
World War I	3.66	7.99	8.49
World War II	10.4	12.6	16.6
Korean War	12.7	18.1	15.3
Vietnam War	22.1	14.7	18.6

(U.S. Bureau of the Census, *Statistical Abstract of the United States*, 1975: 326)

counted for only one percent of the National Guard (Baskir and Strauss, 1978: 49–53).

Studies show that in 1966, 71 percent of all Reservists were in the Reserve to avoid the draft; in 1968, 80 percent. By 1970, the President of the National Guard Association placed this figure at 90 percent (Baskir and Strauss, 1978: 49–51; Gates, 1970: 114; Useem, 1973: 78).

Active duty in the Navy, Coast Guard, Air Force, and the safety programs in the Army and Marines, like the Reserves, involved less risk, even if a man was sent to Vietnam. (This is certainly not meant to imply that men channeled to the "safer" noncombat programs in Vietnam were in a danger-free situation. In this type of war, there were no truly safe areas, as the shelling of our embassy and the Tet Offensive in early 1968 prove rather convincingly. On the other hand, men in these programs, compared to draftees and combat-assigned volunteers, had a much lower risk of becoming casualties in Vietnam.) There were over 46,000 battle deaths during the Vietnam Era. The Coast Guard lost a total of seven men. The Navy suffered 1,000 deaths: Navy men were generally on ships offshore, much safer than the ground-based forces. Three-quarters of the Air Force's 1,000 deaths involved men over draft age, including pilots and navigators: men who were in the military because they chose to be. Compared to the Navy and Air Force, the Marines (13,000 killed) and the Army (31,000 killed) involved a 19 times greater likelihood of dying in Vietnam (Baskir and Strauss, 1978: 54; U.S. Bureau of the Census, *Statistical Abstract of the U.S.*, 1975: 326).

Men with the right credentials could avoid Vietnam altogether. Helmer (1974: 34) found a substantial relationship between education levels and reasons for enlistment. On the evidence of Department of Defense surveys of the motivations of men who enlisted and were stationed outside of Vietnam in November 1968, reluctant volunteers — those who were draft motivated — were more likely to be college educated than non-draft motivated volunteers.

Men who were "draft motivated" tried for the most advantageous branch of service, entry time, and/or status. They would not have been in uniform, had there been no threat of a draft. Men motivated by "non-draft" reasons sought career opportunities, travel, and the opportunity of learning a trade.

Table 2–2 reports findings by education for men not assigned to Vietnam. For Army enlistees, level of education predicted who ended up in Vietnam: college graduates had a 42 percent likelihood of Vietnam assignment; high school graduates had a 64 percent chance, and high

Table 2-2   Education by Reasons for Enlistment

	Less than HS Graduate	High School Graduate	Some College or More
Draft Motivated	31.0%	43.8%	62.0%
Non-draft motivated	60.3	50.1	31.6
Other	8.7	6.1	6.4
TOTAL	100 %	100 %	100 %

(John Helmer, *Bringing the War Home: The American Soldier in Vietnam and After*, p. 34. Copyright © 1974 by John Helmer. Reprinted by permission of The Free Press, a Division of Macmillian Publishing, Inc.)

school drop-outs had a 70 percent chance (Baskir and Strauss 1978: 10). College education was highly related to volunteer status (reluctant or not), and ultimate assignment.

CONVERSELY: DANGER IN UNIFORM

Draftees, disproportionately drawn from among the poor and working class, bore the brunt of the fighting and death in Vietnam. Their casualty rate was 50 percent higher than that of volunteers.

(Useem, 1981: 30)

The disproportionate assignment of "Project 100,000" men into combat roles represents only the tip of that iceberg. In 1969, draftees accounted for 88 percent of infantry riflemen in Vietnam; 10 percent were first-term volunteers, and 2 percent career men (Glass, 1970: 1747). Starr (1973: 10) calculates that in 1969 Army draftees were "being killed and wounded at nearly double the rate of non-draftee enlisted men." Reporting on a study by the Army general staff (Table 2–3), he cites astonishing statistics which reflect the gravity of the discrimination in Vietnam.

Although a higher *percentage* of draftees than volunteers were

Table 2-3   Army Casualty Rates

	1965-1970 (March)		1969	
	Draftee	Volunteer	Draftee	Volunteer
Killed	2.44%	1.58%	3.1%	1.7%
Wounded	10.54	6.84	20.3	12.0
TOTAL	12.98	8.42	23.7	13.7

(Starr, *The Discarded Army: Veterans after Vietnam*, p. 11. Copyright © 1973, Paul Starr. Reprinted by permission of the Center for Study of Responsive Law.)

killed or wounded during the Vietnam Era, in absolute numbers almost twice as many volunteers were killed as draftees — 30,760 to 15,403. However, the ratio of draftee deaths to total deaths increased each year from 16 percent in 1965 to a peak of 48 percent in 1971 (Table 2-4). The draftee casualties were disproportionate to the numbers of draftees in the military, and the percentage of draftee deaths grew as the war intensified.

Casualty risks correlate intimately with social class for both draftees and volunteers. Baskir and Strauss, in their 1978 study at Notre Dame, surveyed a sample of 1,586 Vietnam Era age-eligible men in South Bend, Indiana; Ann Arbor, Michigan; and Washington, D.C. They found that "poorly educated, low-income whites and poorly educated, low-income blacks together bore a vastly disproportionate share of the burdens of Vietnam — men from disadvantaged backgrounds were twice as likely as their better-off peers to serve in the military, go to Vietnam, and see combat" (p. 9).

A community study by James C. Clayton and Jerry S. Smith provides evidence that a disproportionate number of Salt Lake City men from the working class families — with annual incomes of $4,000 to $8,000 — were killed in Vietnam (cited in Useem, 1973: 108). Similarly, in a study of Wisconsin war dead (killed prior to January 1, 1968) Zietlin et al. (1973: 320) found that "the sons of the poor and of the workers have borne by far the greatest burden of the war in Vietnam, in the measured but unmeasurable precision of death."

Badillo and Curry (1976: 397–406) provide an in-depth analysis of 101 communities in and around Chicago which reflects similar findings. They arrived at two related conclusions which support the notion that men of higher class were safer in uniform: first, "a community's wartime losses are shown by these results to be not significantly related to the level of military participation"; and second, "the

Table 2-4 Ratio of Draftee Deaths to Total U.S. Military Deaths by Year

Actual year	Percentage
1965	16%
1966	21
1967	34
1968	34
1969	40
1970	43
1971	48

(U.S. Bureau of the Census, *Statistical Abstract of the U.S.*, 1976: 325)

policy question of 'who shall serve' became not nearly so important as 'who shall serve how'." Table 2-5 reports their findings of casualties by income, education, and occupation levels of community. While they are admittedly limited geographically, these studies of the draftee-versus-volunteer casualty rates as well as the evident channeling of reluctant volunteers away from danger, underscore the undisputable finding: men with the most options for avoiding combat in the military, and with the most class-related skills prior to entry into the service, established greater safety in uniform.

In the Vietnam Era, class discrimination in procurement focussed on the lower middle and working classes rather than the poorest, as in earlier times; within the military, class discrimination in assignment channeled men with the most advantages into the least dangerous roles.

Table 2-5 Social Stratification of Combat Casualties: Cook County Communities

Indicator		Number of Communities	Casualty Rate per 10,000 Age-Eligible Males
Income (median family)	$ 4,000– 7,000	11	17.19
	7,000– 9,000	7	16.01
	9,000–11,000	22	15.38
	11,000–13,000	33	14.15
	13,000–15,000	17	13.41
	15,000–17,000	6	8.17
	17,000 or more	5	6.27
Education (median for population)—no. of years	Less than 10	18	19.64
	10.00–10.99	19	17.21
	11.00–11.99	20	13.94
	12.00–12.99	39	12.51
	13.00 or more	5	5.79
Occupation (% of male labor force in white collar)	Less than 20	11	18.41
	20.00–29.99	23	16.81
	30.00–39.99	26	15.57
	40.00–49.99	15	14.26
	50.00–59.99	7	10.95
	60.00 or more	19	8.72
		(N = 101)	

(Badillo and Curry, in *Armed Forces and Society*, Vol. 2 (3) 1976: 403).

RESISTANCE: CIVILIAN STANCES

Earlier in this chapter we discussed men who actively channeled themselves away from the military through legal deferments, as well as those "reluctant volunteers" who purposely minimized their chances of either Vietnam or combat assignment. In a very real sense, the men who intentionally chose these routes can be described as resisters to the war. Unlike their counterparts in the popular World War II and the unpopular Korean War, these men — in unprecedented numbers, each in his own way — would not passively submit to the military procurement and channeling procedures. They resisted, however, within acceptable legal *mores;* the term "avoiders"[7] describes them appropriately. Avoidance has existed since colonial times as an option linked tightly to the higher social classes. Resistance is another matter.

Resistance at the beginning of the war was individual or confined to small, isolated groups. (This was also true of avoidance, as demonstrated by the rise in men appealing their 1-A status from 4 to 102 per 1,000.) In 1964, three Missouri men refused induction, and served up to 23 months in jail. In the same year, twelve men burned their draft cards in New York City and received scorn from across the nation (Baskir and Strauss, 1978: 64–65). These actions would eventually snowball into "the national movement with an abundance of muscle" in which hundreds of thousands marched in protest against the conflict (see Colhoun, 1981a, b, and c for an excellent overview).

Throughout the war, both the Justice Department and Selective Service were determined to squash dissent. For instance, the latter attempted to reclassify anti-war protesters, e.g., in 1965, 35 University of Michigan students. Such reclassifications were eventually rejected by the courts (Baskir and Strauss, 1978: 25).

The government's hard-line policy was progressively formalized. In 1967, the Justice Department ordered that draft-related cases were to receive top priority in Federal Courts, encompassing violations of the Selective Service law and activities of such resistance figures as Benjamin Spock, William Sloane Coffin, Michael Ferber, the Berrigan brothers and others (Baskir and Strauss, 1978: 54; O'Sullivan and Meckler, 1974: 225–228; Useem, 1973: 128–129).

Prosecutions were only the beginning of the Government's response; sentences for draft evasion lengthened during the peak war years. In 1965 the average prison term for a convicted evader was 21 months; it rose to 26.4 in 1966, and to 32.1 in 1967, peaked at 37.3 in 1968, and then dropped to 36.3 in 1969, 33.5 in 1970, 29.1 in 1971,

22.0 in 1972, and 17.6 in 1973 (U.S. Bureau of the Census, *Statistical Abstracts of the United States,* 1976: 340). The decrease in length of sentence after 1969 was due in part to the anti-war sentiments of what had become a majority of the American public.

Partially as a result of increased numbers of violators and partially as a result of increased government priorities to prosecute, the number of cases completed per year rose steadily: 341 in 1965; 516 in 1966; 996 in 1967; 1,192 in 1968; 1,744 in 1969; 2,833 in 1970; 2,973 in 1971; 4,906 in 1972; and 3,495 in 1973 (U.S. Bureau of the Census, *Statistical Abstract of the United States,* 1976: 340). By 1970, draft evaders accounted for ten percent of all federal cases, ranking fourth behind auto theft, immigration law violations, and narcotics (Useem, 1973: 127–128).

Selective Service and Justice Department officials tried to camouflage the rise in the number of draft resisters as simply a result of larger draft calls. That is a distortion; in fiscal 1966, four legal complaints per 100 inductees compare to 12.9 in 1970 (Useem, 1973: 127–128). Since these figures represent only those cases completed, they grossly understate the actual number of men who resisted the Selective Service. Altogether, 209,517 men were formally accused of draft offenses; at least 360,000 were investigated but never charged. The Justice Department and the courts became so overloaded with draft cases that only a small proportion were actually charged and even fewer prosecuted. Between 1967 and 1970, nationwide only 11 percent of all formally charged draft violators were prosecuted (Baskir and Strauss, 1978: 69, 81, and 84; O'Sullivan and Meckler, 1974: 225–226). During the entire war, of the 209,517 accused draft offenders, only 25,000 were indicted.

An even more striking fact is that only 8,750 (slightly more than one-third of those indicted) were convicted; fewer than 4,000 served time in jail. Indeed, as the war grew increasingly less popular, prosecutors were less willing to pursue these cases; fewer juries were willing to convict and fewer judges willing to punish severely. We have already seen how length of sentences dropped after 1969. Dismissals and probation became more popular as well. In Milwaukee, for instance, in 1970, 46 out of 50 draft resisters received federal prison terms — but for the remainder of the war, only one of 24 was sent to jail (Baskir and Strauss, 1978: 73–82). Figure 2-2 demonstrates that it became progressively harder and harder to obtain a conviction in these cases.

Two predominant methods of draft resistance typified the Vietnam Era: refusal to register, and refusal to cooperate at some point

Figure 2-2

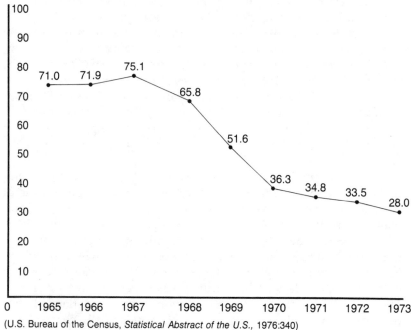

Percentage of Convictions in Selective Service Cases

(U.S. Bureau of the Census, *Statistical Abstract of the U.S.*, 1976:340)

after registration. The latter strategy was elected frequently by men who ultimately went into exile. The former, refusal to register, characterized the actions of less advantaged draft-eligible men.

> Muhammed Ali's struggles with the Selective Service, chronicled on every sports page in the nation, have educated more young men in how to evade the draft than all anti-war organizations put together.
>
> (Flacks et al., 1967: 4)

Flacks, Howe, and Lauter recognize that the "anti-war organizations" too frequently remained isolated from the less advantaged. Ali's refusal to step forward at his induction reached an audience distinct from the activists who were from the privileged classes, and generally white. Although the poor could not pursue successful Ali-type court fights to obtain CO status, his actions, as well as those of Julian Bond and other black leaders, did much to legitimize non-participation. For many this non-participation took the form of non-registration, in preference to the dangers of military channeling. Estimates on the number of non-registrants during the Vietnam Era vary widely, from 250,000 to 2,000,000 men. The vast majority of these men came from less affluent backgrounds than the men who elected avoidance or resistance after registration (Baskir and Strauss, 1978: 86–87; Ferber and Lynd, 1971: 283).

The second form of draft resistance, popular across all social classes, was the refusal of induction. Here the figures soared by the end of the war. Between September 1969 and March 31, 1970, in Oakland, California, over half the men slated for induction did not show up and another 11 percent, once there, refused induction (Cortright, 1975: 5; O'Sullivan and Meckler, 1974: 225–226). For the state of California, the draft quota from October 1969 to May 1970 was 7,800. With a system so badly shaken by this time, 18,000 men were called for induction in order to meet this quota. Only 40 percent showed up (Useem, 1973:143).

Earlier in this chapter, the unprecedented rise in civilian "avoidance" of the draft during the Vietnam War was examined. In a similar way, resistance to the draft became so high that the Government could neither prosecute nor convict the overwhelming majority of cases. In the past, the numbers of (legal) avoiders and (illegal) resisters were always tolerable, so that the system could work. This time the astronomical growth of draft resisters and avoiders severely diminished any possibility of the continued participation of a large land military force in Vietnam by the United States. Perhaps the largely upper class avoidance could be absorbed; but the inclusion of large-scale resistance across class lines was beyond functional limits.

MILITARY UNRAVELLING

Colonel Robert Heinl: Armed Forces Journal, June 1971:
The morale, discipline and battle-worthiness of the U.S. Armed Forces are, with a few salient exceptions, lower and worse than at any time in this century and possibly in the history of the United States.
(Cited in Colhoun, 1977:11)

Dissent against the war went beyond the civilian sector. The Vietnam Era set the stage for what many view as a breakdown of the United States Armed Forces. Waterhouse and Wizard (1971: 55) suggest that, historically, military dissent was never so politically oriented as during the Vietnam Era. In the past, for the most part, troops had expressed unhappiness in apolitical ways; in the Vietnam Era, this ceased to be the case. Cortright (1975: 52–75) and Hayes (1975: 125–139) categorize G.I. resistance during the 1960's and early 1970's into three phases of dissent. A general period of individual dissent lasted from 1965 to 1967. In 1968 a rapid growth of the G. I. underground press, coffee-houses and the American Servicemen's Union emerged. This second phase merged into the third by 1969, with comparatively widespread mutinies, disobeying of orders, AWOL's and desertions.

Paralleling the civilian authorities' attempts to suppress dissent, the military brass came down extremely hard on those who tried to protest. Beyond KP or extra sentry duty, these men suffered transfers, imprisonment, and court-martials (Waterhouse and Wizard, 1971: 104–142). A former military lawyer wrote that servicemen suspected of being against the war were followed by military intelligence agents to such an extent that in Fort Sill, Oklahoma, in 1967, the agents outnumbered the dissenters (Sherman, 1968: 24). The fate of the early dissenters is best described by a former G.I.: "Given the general passivity within the ranks and the tight control exercised by the brass, these first acts required a clear willingness for self-sacrifice . . ." (Rinaldi, 1974: 52).

This first phase is illustrated through the case of Lt. Henry H. Howe, Jr., who in November 1965 joined an anti-war demonstration while off duty in El Paso, Texas. He received one year at hard labor and a less than honorable discharge. In June 1966, the first formal cases of direct military resistance to the war occurred when three men at Fort Hood, who had refused orders to Vietnam, received three to five years' hard labor plus dishonorable discharges. Two black Marines stated in the barracks that blacks should not fight in Vietnam; one received six years of hard labor, and the other ten (Cortright, 1975: 52; Hayes, 1975: 127).

Dr. Howard Levy, who refused to train Green Beret medics, was perhaps the most famous of these early dissenters. At Levy's court-martial his officers admitted that they ordered him to train the Green Berets knowing that he would refuse. This violates Article 90 of the *Manual for Court-Martials* which states,

> Disobedience of an order which has for its sole object the attainment of some private end, or which is given for the sole purpose of increasing the penalty for an offense which it is expected the accused may commit, is not punishable under this article.
>
> (Cited in Sherrill, 1970: 110–111)

Many feel that Captain Levy was framed in order to provide an example to potential dissenters. Captain Levy, who became a national symbol of the military dissenter, received a sentence of three years at hard labor plus a dishonorable discharge (Cortright, 1975: 51; Sherrill, 1970: 110–111).

The second phase involved dissenters no longer acting individually or through symbolic acts of resistance. By 1968, groups of G.I.'s expanded resistance within the military; there were three overlapping developments: the widespread appearance of underground newspapers; the growth in the number and popularity of coffee houses; and the founding of the American Servicemen's Union (ASU).

The coffee houses and newspapers, sometimes lasting no more than a single weekend or edition, were very popular at bases in the United States and Germany, but also appeared at installations throughout the world, including Vietnam. While the format varied, the content persisted: a forum was created for grievances against the war and the way the military treated men (Colhoun, 1977: 33; Waterhouse and Wizard, 1971: 75–88).

The American Servicemen's Union was founded on Christmas Day, 1967, by Private Andrew Stapp, with the help of 14 representatives from 14 United States bases. By January 1969, 4,500 members had joined the ASU and by July of that same year, the number had risen to 6,500. These men circulated the union's paper, *The Bond*, to tens of thousands of military personnel. ASU demands went beyond the immediacy of Vietnam and dealt with the very fabric of the military structure. They included an end to saluting officers; a federal minimum wage; collective bargaining; election of officers by enlisted men; and a right to disobey illegal orders (Cortright, 1975: 55–58; Stapp, 1970: 88–100; Waterhouse and Wizard, 1971: 133–136).

The coffee houses, underground newspapers, and the ASU represent a historic turning point. The Captain Levys no longer stood alone; attempts to isolate them did nothing to stop their increasing support. The number of newspapers and coffee houses skyrocketed. In 1971, on United States bases alone, 26 coffee houses and 144 underground papers could be counted (Hayes, 1975: 131–135). By 1972, the Defense Department placed the number at 259 (Cortright, 1975: 55). However, the dissent went far beyond these signs of discontent, including

> . . . high desertion rates, drug addiction, mutinies, and the "fragging" or assassination of officers.
>
> (Savage and Gabriel, 1976: 344–345).

This analysis of the army in Vietnam as of 1969 holds good, to a large extent, for the entire military, inside and outside of Vietnam.

The most mild forms of military dissent have already been discussed: large numbers of servicemen avoided Vietnam and combat by channeling themselves elsewhere. Military applications for Conscientious Objector status emerged as a more direct way to take a moral stance against participation. The rigors of obtaining a CO while in the service magnify the problems civilian applicants encountered. Beyond the class-related difficulties in articulating and gaining a hearing for moral beliefs, the in-service applicants were judged by military officers, including psychiatrists and chaplains. The numbers of men who pursued this strategy increased from 829 in 1967 to a peak of 4,381 in 1971. Approval rates rose from under 30 percent to over 75 percent in 1972 (the higher approval rate is in large part related to Federal Court decisions that the military had to follow the Seeger interpretation, which broadened acceptable CO criteria) (Baskir and Strauss, 1978: 57; Cortright, 1975: 16).

A much more serious form of military dissent involved "fragging" — physical attacks with weapons on officers. During World War I, when 4.7 million men served, 370 cases of violence directed at officers resulted in court-martials. In Vietnam, from January 1970 to January 1972 alone, when only 700,000 troops served, there were 363 cases which involved explosives; another 118 cases were listed as possible fragging — these figures omit cases in which only rifles or knives were used (Linden, 1972: 11–17). The Chief of the Psychiatry Division at Fort Leavenworth, Kansas, where many men convicted of fragging served, documents 800 incidents, again excluding cases involving guns and knives, from 1969 to 1972 (Bond, 1976: 1329).

Unlike fraggings in both World Wars and Korea, which generally occurred in field situations, in Vietnam rear echelon fragging emerged as the dominant form. Bounties on officers and noncommissioned officers were occasionally raised. In one incident, an underground G.I. paper reportedly offered $10,000 for the elimination of an officer who had ordered a particularly disastrous attack (Colhoun, 1977: 34; Linden, 1972: 12–17). In another case, $350 was offered (Baskir and Strauss, 1978: 61).

Refusal by enlisted men to follow orders, including going into combat, provides further evidence of open dissent during Vietnam (Baskir and Strauss, 1978: 112 and 143). Cortright (1975: 35–39) has found that of these refusals, the majority aimed toward "purposely evading enemy engagements"; however, late into the war, he reports ten major incidents of field mutinies. These became more frequent and widespread as the war wore on. Savage and Gabriel (1976: 350) sum up the growth in degree and kind of these mutinies:

> . . . Unlike mutinous outbreaks of the past and in other armies, usually short-lived events, the progressive unwillingness of American soldiers to fight to the point of public disobedience of orders took place over a four-year period between 1968 and 1971 . . . Mutinies in Viet Nam fell into patterned behavior and did not occur as sporadic events.

The severe problems within the military can be seen in the enormous numbers of Vietnam Era men who failed to receive Honorable Discharges. Of the five forms of discharge from the military (Honorable, General, Undesirable, Bad Conduct, and Dishonorable), the last two require a court-martial and the last three — called "bad paper discharges" — indicate that the person is released "under less than honorable conditions". To avoid bottlenecks, the administratively-granted Undesirable Discharge became the most frequently utilized. If a person holds *less than honorable discharge* by court-martial he/she is barred from health care, education, and other Veterans' Administration (VA) programs; if it is administratively granted, most often the case, then the decision to grant or deny benefits remains entirely with the VA. Not only can a bad paper vet be denied benefits; he will no longer be legally entitled to reclaim his pre-service job and will face difficulties in obtaining a new one (Baskir and Strauss, 1978: 152–162; Starr, 1973: 167–168).

The numbers of bad paper discharges rose in all branches of the service during the Vietnam Era, as the war and resistance to it progressed. The vast majority were administratively granted. In 1965 and 1966, bad papers accounted for only 2.1 and 1.7 percent of all discharges. Another 3.5 and 2.8 percent received the somewhat stigmatized but not directly punitive General Discharge. To put it another way, during these early years 94.3 and 95.5 percent of all discharges were Honorable. In 1971, 1972, and 1973, bad paper discharges constituted 3.4, 4.6, and 4.5 percent, and General Discharges had gone up to 4.0, 5.1, and 5.7 percent. In other words, the number of men receiving Honorable Discharges fell to 92.7, then to 90.3, and to 89.8 percent by the end of the war (U.S. Bureau of the Census, *Statistical Abstract of the United States*, 1979: 376).

Starr (1973: 170) inspected the Defense Department's figures and found a dramatic growth in the number of Undesirable Discharges, in particular, after 1969, paralleling the public shift towards opposition to the war. Until 1969, these discharges averaged about 11,500 per year. In fiscal 1970, the number rose to 22,537, and by 1972 it reached 40,018. Starr correctly points out that the 1972 increase is especially striking because Undesirable Discharges were then no longer issued to many identified drug users.

While the total number of those not receiving Honorable Discharges during the Vietnam War remains a bureaucratic mystery, a conservative estimate stands at 563,000, of which 529,000 were administratively granted (Baskir and Strauss, 1978: 155). These men, depending on the type of discharge, carry stigmas for life. They can be deprived of old and new jobs, denied crucial benefits and social acceptability. Admittedly, some of these discharges result from crimes; however, they all took place in a military structure which was unraveling in the context of a war that the U.S. public could no longer support. Martin Agronsky notes:

> In making such comparisons, it is important to keep in mind that, unlike those of World War II, most Vietnam Era desertions did not take place under fire, indicating that servicemen took off not because of danger, but because of disgust.
>
> (Cortright, 1975: 10–11)

Desertions and men Absent Without Official Leave (AWOL) stand as the most recognizable form of the military's loss of control. It is useful to make comparisons with Korean and World War II rates; however, the Vietnam Era desertion figures have been deflated by the Pentagon, by definition and design. During Vietnam, to become officially a deserter, one had to be both AWOL for 30 days or more, and classified as a deserter (by court-martial or administratively) on the basis that he had no intention to return. During the Vietnam Era, the marked tendency to categorize soldiers as AWOL's, even after 30 days' absence, reduced the desertion rates (Helmer, 1974: 36–37; Musil, 1973: 495–496).

Government officials like to argue that the Vietnam Era had rates of desertion lower than those of World War II and not much higher than Korea. While this is technically accurate overall, Vietnam desertion rates peaked at higher levels than either war (the fiscal 1971 Army rate was three times that of Korea's peak (Cortright, 1975: 9–10; Musil, 1973: 496; Useem, 1973: 132). Army desertion rates rose almost 300 percent from 1968 to 1971 (Cortright, 1975: 11). Table 2–6 indicates the steadily increasing incidence of desertion per 1000 men during Vietnam, through contrasts with Korea and World War II.

Members of those branches expected to carry the bulk of the fighting (the Army and Marines) most dramatically refused to stay. Those deserting from the Army in fiscal 1971 represent the equivalent of six full divisions (Musil, 1971: 496). The growth in the number of desertions (Figure 2–3) parallels the loss of public support for the war.

The desertion rates were linked to the unprecedented rates of military men going AWOL. In the Army, the number of AWOL's rose from 60.1 and 57.2 per 1000 men in fiscal 1965 and 1966 to 176.9 and 166.4 in 1971 and 1972 respectively. While earlier figures are not available for the Marines, the rates of AWOL'S in 1971 and 1972 were 166.6 and 170.0 (U.S. Bureau of the Census, *Statistical Abstract of the*

Table 2-6 Desertion Rates per 1000 by Military Branch per Fiscal Year

	Army	Marines	Navy	Air Force
World War II				
1944	63.0	6.9	3.0	*
1945	45.2	5.4	3.5	*
Korea				
1951	14.3	10.1	3.1	NA**
1952	22.0	19.7	6.3	NA**
1953	22.3	29.6	8.7	NA**
1954	15.7	NA**	6.9	NA**
Vietnam				
1965	15.7	18.8	6.7	0.4
1966	14.7	16.1	9.1	0.4
1967	21.4	26.8	9.7	0.4
1968	29.1	30.7	8.5	0.4
1969	42.4	40.2	7.3	0.6
1970	52.3	59.6	9.9	0.8
1971	73.5	56.2	11.1	1.5
1972	62.0	65.3	8.8	2.8

(U.S. Bureau of the Census, *Statistical Abstract of the United States*, 1975: 327.)
*Part of Army
**Not available

United States, 1975: 327). The numbers of AWOL's during Vietnam are 23 percent higher than in World War II and 36 percent above Korean rates (Helmer, 1974: 38).

The frequency of such actions of dissent cannot obscure the fact that the vast majority of deserters returned to military control, either voluntarily or involuntarily; the Pentagon places this majority at 90 percent (Musil, 1973: 495–496). Significantly, for this work, most deserters did not become exiles. Approximately 90 percent remained in the United States (Baskir and Strauss, 1978: 169). However, the fact that most deserters returned seems less important than their effect as a disruptive factor. Service personnel in and out of Vietnam were actively defying the military by at least temporarily leaving. Altogether, almost one million years of military service were lost due to absentee offenses (Ibid.: 122).

A more detailed description of the Vietnam Era deserters follows in other chapters, but one misleading assumption deserves rebuttal here. The vast majority of Vietnam Era deserters did not leave directly from Vietnam or from combat-related situations (Bell and Houston, 1976: 17; Cortright, 1975: 11). In direct contrast to World War II, where 20,000 soldiers were convicted for combat desertions, in Vietnam only a few thousand were court-martialled for deserting from *combat*, with

Figure 2-3

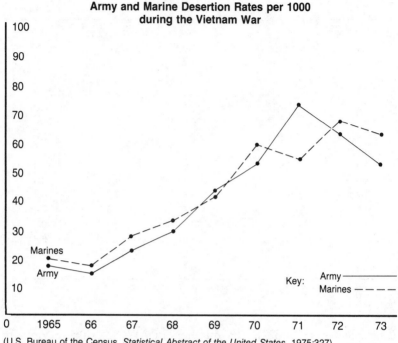

Army and Marine Desertion Rates per 1000 during the Vietnam War

(U.S. Bureau of the Census, *Statistical Abstract of the United States*, 1975:327)

only 24 actually convicted. Only 12,000 individuals left the military while serving in Vietnam or under orders to go there (Baskir and Strauss, 1978: 112–114). In the Army, only 3 percent of all deserters left from Vietnam and only one percent from combat (Bell and Houston, 1976: 17).

While it is difficult to determine accurately the numbers of men who actually deserted or went AWOL during the Vietnam Era, at least 1,500,000 incidents of absence without leave are documented. However, many went over the hill more than once (Baskir and Strauss, 1978: 122). The Pentagon puts the number of deserters at slightly under 500,000 (Musil, 1973: 495); others suggest at least 550,000 (Baskir and Strauss, 1978: 115).

SUMMARY

By the end of the Vietnam Era, the U.S. military was rapidly losing control over its men. The legal in-service avoidance, the fraggings, mutinies, bad paper discharges, AWOL's, and desertions all reflect a progressive breakdown of military legitimacy within the Vietnam Era. Indeed this breakdown paralleled the growing ineffectiveness of the Selective Service System. Baskir and Strauss (1978: 110), using data acquired while serving as members of President Ford's Clemency Program, write that by 1971, if "a random group of 100 army soldiers" was examined one would find 7 desertions; 17 AWOL's; 20 frequent marijuana users; 10 using narcotics regularly; 2 disciplinary discharges; 18 lighter punishments; and 12 complaints to Congress.

At the same time as largely upper-class draft avoiders were being joined by resisters of all social classes in the civilian sector, avoidance and resistance spread within the military. Just as the harsh reactions of civilian authorities failed to quell dissent, the military's efforts to "get tough" did little to discourage protest. None of this is surprising in view of the growing belief by the public that the U.S. should not have been in Vietnam.

The protection of the upper classes from military procurement and dangerous assignment in earlier wars characterizes the Vietnam conflict as well. For much of the war the "legitimate" loopholes permitted channeling of some civilians out of the service, e.g., exemptions for students; those in key occupations; those with medical, dental, or psychological "problems"; and even CO's, although the latter required two years of alternative service.

In the military, safer branches and programs including the Reserves, National Guard, Coast Guard, Navy, Air Force, and European assignment sheltered many of the educational and occupational elite. Conversely, the growing trend of military sophistication placed the heaviest burden on the working and lower-middle classes. The parallels between casualty figures and income reflect the in-service reinforcement of the class system.

In these first two chapters, 300 years of procuring and maintaining the military forces were shown to perpetuate class discrimination. Until this system met severe challenge during the Civil War, the higher classes enjoyed open protection. After that conflict, the discrimination grew more subtle, with a maze of deferments and safety-in-uniform programs. With the exception of the Civil War, resistance and avoidance, while present, stayed well within tolerable limits. In the Civil War, the system survived, but barely. By the end of the Vietnam War — indeed a major contribution to the end of the war — these limits had been assaulted by members of all social classes.

Avoidance and resistance often carried a heavy price. We must not lose sight of the men who were channeled through deferments into professions they might not have preferred; the men who dodged Vietnam by enlisting in certain programs and who wound up serving another year as a result; the men who married or had children in order to escape the draft; the men who never registered for the draft, or did not show up for induction and spent years living in fear of knocks at the door; the deserters who stayed underground in this country; and the men who served in prisons or stockades as a result of evasion, desertion, or dissent. There are also the bad paper veterans who are still being denied their rights, often for beliefs no different from those of the men who escaped the draft by the class-centered deferment system.

These two chapters have addressed the military-based demands on draft-eligible males and their varied responses. The remainder of this book focuses more narrowly on military and draft resisters who chose exile in Canada as their response. However, dissent, legal and illegal, was not restricted to the male gender or age eligibles. The hundreds of thousands of men and women, old and young, who attended anti-war demonstrations participated in national resistance to Vietnam. Arrest records, for acts ranging from sit-ins to burning draft board files, present a militant example of widespread reaction to the Vietnam War. Men and women of all ages took a stand against the war.

Beyond everything discussed above, the Vietnam War damaged an entire nation. The country still has not truly recovered from that incredible decade. The stories of the men who went to Canada, told in the next six chapters, bring into focus just how deeply the war divided the United States.

NOTES

1. The Gallup Organization had two wordings of this question. Until November 1965 it asks, "Some people think we should not have become involved with our military forces in Southeast Asia, while others think we should have. What is your opinion?" After that time, the question reads, "In view of the developments since we entered the fighting in Vietnam, do you think the United States made a mistake in sending troops to Vietnam?"
2. Reservists could be activated. During the *Pueblo* incident of 1968, 37,000 guardsmen and reservists were activated, with 15,000 sent to Vietnam (Baskir and Strauss, 1978: 50).
3. In actuality, not all CO's were assigned alternate service jobs, and some did not complete their full two years. The majority did both (Baskir and Strauss, 1978: 41).
4. Starting points for a more detailed discussion on the implications

of intelligence testing include: Samuel Bowles and Herbert Gintis, *Schooling in Capitalist America* (New York: Basic Books, Inc., 1976); Leon Kamin, "Heredity, Intelligence, Politics, and Psychology: II," in *The IQ Controversy*, ed. N. J. Block and Gerald Dworkin (New York: Pantheon Books, 1976); Otto Klineberg, *Negro Intelligence and Selective Migration* (New York: Columbia University Press, 1935); and Marshall H. Segall, *Human Behavior and Public Policy: A Political Psychology* (New York: Pergamon Press, Inc., 1976).

5. The family hardships deferment basically exempted men whose families were in serious need of their presence. The well publicized case of millionaire/actor George Hamilton, who received such a deferment, revealed it to be yet another easily manipulated escape hole — for some.

6. Dr. Robert Laufer of the Vietnam Era Research Project was essential in clarifying this issue, both in terms of who was targeted, and the complexities of the modern military.

7. The usage of "avoiders" in this context must be credited to Baskir and Strauss, 1978.

PART TWO

FROM THE CRADLE TO CANADA

Chapter One provides a historic context for understanding the patterns of military procurement and resistance. Chapter Two extends this analysis to a generational context — examining military demands and methods of avoidance and resistance during the Vietnam Era. The draft and military resisters who exiled themselves to Canada, the focus of the remainder of this book, must be placed in both contexts in order to be fully understood.

While the remainder of this work deals solely with draft dodgers and military deserters, it must be understood that these men did not emerge spontaneously, nor were they the only dissenters of this generation. For the most part, the men who went to Canada either before entering the military or during their military career, decided that both the war in Vietnam and the U.S. itself were not worth fighting for. The pathways these men traveled to Canada were diverse: some were rocky, others were smooth. Some felt encouraged by their families to seek exile; others came from families fraught with difficulties. Most feel these family experiences contributed to their ultimate choice of Canada.

The decision to go to Canada was routine for some and difficult for others. They all underwent a sometimes rapid and often radical political transformation in a time span ranging from days to years. The break they made forced them to leave their families behind. However, they felt their country offered them no alternative.

Part II, "From the Cradle to Canada", deals specifically with these men, by exploring the transition from "all-American" (albeit privileged "all-American") boys to exiled draft and military resisters. Through early childhood experiences (Chapter Three) and the politicization process (Chapter Four), these men are followed to their departure for Canada.

CHAPTER **3**

Family Backgrounds:
Privileged and Diverse

[*In Part One of Shakespeare's* Henry IV, *the fat knight Falstaff — though himself a lover of life — is nevertheless given a commission to draft a company of men for a war. He chooses, first, men who can afford to buy their way out; then he "presses" into service men who are too poor to buy him off. Falstaff cheerfully admits, "I have misused the king's press damnably" (IV.ii.13). When Prince Hal enters, there is the following exchange:*]

Prince. *I did never see such pitiful rascals.*
Falstaff. *Tut, tut; good enough to toss; food for powder, food for powder; they'll fill a pit as well as better: tush, man, mortal men, mortal men.*

(IV.ii.70–73)

The paths these men followed "From the Cradle to Canada" can be traced from early socialization to a politicization in early adulthood. Many young people, during the Vietnam Era, underwent a politicization in which they redefined themselves in relation to a society which was itself undergoing rapid and bitter transformation. The nature and pace of this politicization process of course reflects early childhood and adolescent influences. In this chapter we concentrate on the socialization of these men in their families, exploring demographic and quality-of-life characteristics.

The first half of this chapter presents factual background data on the men in this sample: how they compare to each other, to other draft and military resisters, and to their age peers who remained in the United States. The second half explores their backgrounds qualitatively from the perspectives and through the words of the men themselves.

The consequences of the sampling techniques employed in this study have been discussed in the introduction; one point should be re-emphasized. These men should not be considered typical draft and military resisters. Because of the relatively active social networks demanded by our technique (interviewing friends of initial resisters) these men are probably more connected to each other than most. Not reached are those dodgers and deserters who assimilated beyond resister circles, those who went to other countries, those who have returned to the U.S., and those who never went into exile — the vast majority of the draft dodgers and military deserters. The men who returned to the U.S. and those who never left are largely from the lowest social classes, and were accordingly least able to "make it" in Canada (Bell and Houston, 1975; Emerick, 1972; Kasinsky, 1976, Williams, 1971a). The term "survivors" is used to describe those men who somehow remained in Canada, and connected to each other there.[1]

Although these "survivors" derive from more privileged pasts than other resisters within our survivor sample, the deserters and draft dodgers differ in substantial ways. Military deserters who remained in Canada encountered many more problems than the men who had gone there to avoid the draft. The origins and implications of this are discussed in later chapters.

Throughout this work, the extensive reference to the literature on resisters in Canada is essential for a number of reasons. The literature provides a context for the present study. First, it helps specify how well this sample represents the general population of resisters. Second, it provides a valuable time perspective; this study was undertaken much later than most works on the subject. Third, it offers necessary supplemental information for the data here, which are based on a study of 11 deserters. Other data-based analyses of the resister community which are referred to include works by Adams (1970), Emerick (1972), Kasinsky (1976), and Williams (1971a).

EARLY ENVIRONMENT: SOCIAL CLASS

The environment — family and family values — in which a person is raised is critical to understanding his life course. Social class of origin was a critical early influence on the lives of these men. As a factor in determining access to information and resources, social class influences the extent of control one can exert and the breadth of options he can utilize. To explore the backgrounds of men in this sample, three standard indicators of socioeconomic status (SES) are utilized: *parental education, parental occupation, and family income*. These resisters are examined first relative to national norms.

Patterns of *parental education* epitomize the distinctions between resisters who went to Canada and other men in their age group. Draft dodgers' parents were educated well beyond national levels, and military deserters' parents were at least slightly better educated. Table 3-1 confirms these observations, comparing national levels of education with data from three studies on resisters and their families of origin (Kasinsky, Adams, and our own sample).

While resisters, in terms of parents' education, are a class of men privileged from early in life, the present sample is further advantaged, relative to other resister samples. These draft dodgers' parents (Table 3-1) were slightly more likely to have had four years of college or more, than those in Adams' sample — 35 percent and 30 percent versus 24 percent and 17 percent for father and mother respectively. (It is not possible to compare with Kasinsky since she chose the highest education completed by either parent). Again, comparing this sample of military deserters to Adams', 46 percent of this sample's fathers had at least some college, compared to 35 percent of Adams'; 19 percent of these mothers had at least some college education, compared to Adams' 26 percent.

Table 3-2 reports on the Vietnam Era Research Project (VERP) Northeast sample. When viewed internally, the channeling of men into the military directly conforms to social class of origin. As expected, veterans' parents lack the educational achievements of parents of men who could afford college — the college nonveterans and most of the draft dodgers. Non-college nonveterans' parents fall close to the veterans' on this measure: they too lack the educational backgrounds of the more privileged groups. This last group comprises a range of men including, but not limited to, the poorest classes of men — many of whom were systematically excluded from the Vietnam Era military.

That the draft dodgers' parents rate highest on this measure substantiates the findings of Table 3-1. In terms of education, they were most advantaged. Deserters' parents were still above average in educational achievement, and higher than other veterans and noncollege non-veterans. Unlike military deserters who stayed in or returned to the U.S., the Canadian survivors are drawn from relatively elite family backgrounds.

Like education, *parental occupations* contribute significantly to early home environment, and again to sons' choices into/out of the military. Using national norms as a benchmark, Table 3–3 suggests that resisters' parents had noticeably higher-level occupations. Kasinsky (1976: 285) concurs, with 61 percent of her dodgers' parents and 37 percent of her deserters' parents in the highest category. (Her

Table 3-1 Educational Attainment

Heads of Household — U.S. National Sample of Households; Parents in Kasinsky's Sample of Draft and Military Resisters; Fathers and Mothers in Adams' and Northeast VERP Samples of Draft Dodgers and Military Deserters.

	U.S. House holds (1963)[2]	Kasinsky Sample		Adams Sample				VERP Sample			
				Dodgers		Deserters		Dodgers		Deserters	
		Dodgers	Deserters	Fa	Mo	Fa	Mo	Fa	Mo	Fa	Mo
Four Years[3] of College or More	11%	47%	28%	24%	17%	14%	6%	35%	30%	0%	18%
Some College or Post High School Vocational Training	9	15	11	20	20	21	20	14	18	46	0
High School Graduate	28	38	33	28	45	40	53	31	42	18	55
Less than High School Degree	52	0	28	22	13	22	18	20	10	27	18
Not Applicable/No Response	—	—	—	6	5	3	3	—	—	9	9
Total	100%	100%	100%	100%	100%	100%	100%	100%	100%	100%	100%
	(N=47,436,000)	(N=47)	(N=36)	(N=110)		(N=72)		(N=49)		(N=11)	

(U.S. Households; U.S. Bureau of the Census, *Historical Statistics of the United States, Colonial Times to 1970, Part I,* 1976: 289; Kasinsky, 1976: 284; Adams, 1970: 52–53).

Table 3-2 Percentage of Education Completed by Parents of Northeast VERP Sample

	Vietnam Veterans		Vietnam Era Veterans		College Nonveterans		Non-college Nonveterans		Draft Dodgers		Military Deserters	
	Fa	Mo	Fa	Mo	Fa	Mo	Fa	Mo	Fa	Mo	Fa	Mo
Four Years of College or More	9%	5%	7%	5%	18%	12%	7%	5%	35%	30%	0%	18%
Some College or Post High School Vocational Training	13	6	16	13	14	18	12	16	14	18	46	0
High School Graduate	15	44	23	43	24	35	27	35	31	42	18	55
Less than High School	61	41	50	35	44	34	50	41	20	10	27	18
No Answer/Not Applicable	2	4	4	4	0	1	4	3	0	0	9	9
Total	100%	100%	100%	100%	100%	100%	100%	100%	100%	100%	100%	100%
	(N=82)		(N=101)		(N=102)		(N=95)		(N=49)		(N=11)	

Table 3-3 Occupational Levels U.S. Households; Fathers in Adams' Sample and VERP's Sample

	U.S. Household (1963)	Adams' Sample		VERP Sample	
		Dodgers	Deserters	Dodgers	Deserters
Professional/Executive/ Managerial/Owner	26%	40%	27%	65%	46%
White Collar/Sales	11	19	19	15	18
Blue Collar/Craftsman/ Semi-Skilled/Farm	41	23	33	20	27
Retired/Unemployed/Deceased/ No Answer/Not Applicable/ Other	22	18	21	0	9
Total	100%	100%	100%	100%	100%
	(N=47,436,000)	(N=110)	(N=72)	(N=49)	(N=11)

(U.S. Households, U.S. Bureau of the Census, *Statistical Abstract of the U.S.*, 1965: 344; Adams, 1970: 51).

data are not included on this table because her other categories are not comparable).

Fathers of draft dodgers held a substantially higher percentage of "professional" jobs than the national norm; fathers of military deserters were slightly higher than national levels. An analysis of the six cells of the Northeast VERP sample (Table 3-4) reconfirms military-related class discrimination. For the draft dodgers, military deserters, and the college non-veterans, fathers' occupations are well above the national level.

In an analysis of employment, Adams reports that 40 percent, and Kasinsky that 61 percent, of the draft dodgers' fathers fall in the highest category. The sample here shows over 65 percent at this level, again suggesting a more elite background. Thirty-seven percent of military deserters' parents in Kasinsky's study, 27 percent in Adams', and 45 percent of this sample are at this level. While again recognizing that our number is small, it appears that these men too came from slightly higher status backgrounds than other military deserters.

The third major component of SES is *family income*. Table 3–5 reflects the national distribution of family income as well as data on this sample (comparable data on other resister samples are not available).[4] Compared to national figures, draft dodgers' family incomes are over-represented in the highest bracket. In contrast to the occupational and educational data, the military deserters are over-represented in the *low* income bracket.

This pattern of findings on "SES" reinforces the major point advanced in Chapter Two: the higher classes have the most options for avoiding the military (draft dodgers and college non-veterans); the working and lower classes are most likely to be channeled into the military (veterans), and the poorest are often systematically excluded from service (a segment of the non-college non-veteran sample).

Homogeneous through Class

This sample of resisters derives from more privileged backgrounds than their age peers as well as fellow resisters — probably because this research was conducted later than the other studies. Those resisters who did not fit well in Canada, in part as a result of class background, often returned to the U.S. The later the research was conducted, the more likely that the respondents were from a higher social class.

The resisters who remained in Canada, the draft evaders in particular, before their common act of resistance, were homogeneous in

Table 3-4 Occupational Level of Fathers (or Heads of Household) of Northeast VERP Sample

	Vietnam Veterans	Vietnam Era Veterans	College Nonveterans	Non-college Nonveterans	Draft Dodgers	Military Deserters
Professional/Exec/Managerial/Owner	22%	23%	31%	20%	65%	46%
White Collar/Sales	4	14	9	10	15	18
Blue Collar/Craftsmen/Semi-Skilled Farm	69	57	57	66	20	27
Retired/Unemployed/Deceased/No Answer/Not Applicable/Other	5	6	3	4	0	9
Total	100%	100%	100%	100%	100%	100%
	(N = 82)	(N = 101)	(N = 102)	(N = 95)	(N = 49)	(N = 11)

(U.S. Households, U.S. Bureau of the Census, *Statistical Abstract of the U.S.*, 1965, 344; Adams, 1970: 51).

Table 3-5 Family Income for U.S. Households and Northeast VERP Sample

	U.S. House-holds (1963)	Vietnam Veterans	Vietnam Era Veterans	College Nonveterans	Non-college Nonveterans	Draft Dodgers	Military Deserters
$10,000 or More per Year	20%	46%	35%	60%	37%	80%	36%
$7,000-$9,999	23	24	35	18	26	14	9
$5,000-$6,999	21	17	16	13	21	6	55
Under $5,000	36	9	13	9	12	0	0
No Answer	0	4	1	0	4	0	0
Total	100%	100%	100%	100%	100%	100%	100%
	(N = 47,436,000 households)	(N = 82)	(N = 101)	(N = 102)	(N = 95)	(N = 49)	(N = 11)

(U.S. Households: U.S. Bureau of the Census, *Statistical Abstract of the U.S.*, 1965: 345).

terms of social class. Using all three SES indicators as a composite, these men come from families relatively privileged compared to the norm for their age groups. High parental social class correlates with sons who eventually opted for, and survived in, Canada. In this sample and others, draft dodgers were clearly from a higher social class than deserters.

Homogeneous through Race

A black resister:
If you leave Watts or the Black Bottom in Detroit and get into this; it's like jumping into a pitcher of buttermilk. It's all white . . . the music on the radio, the pictures in the papers and magazines and on television.

(Cited in Emerick, 1972: 13)

In terms of race, resisters in Canada are extremely homogeneous. Those who went to Canada were mostly white; those who remain are almost exclusively white. This sample of 60 had just two blacks — one military and one draft resister. The former has since returned to the United States to accept a bad paper discharge with all its negative consequences, rather than live with the isolation and discrimination he found in Canada. The latter, at last contact, remains uncertain about whether he will remain in the climate of "racism" he has encountered in Toronto.

Estimates are that only between 500 and 1000 black draft dodgers stayed in Canada with not many more military deserters (Williams, 1972a: 339–341). Blacks were safer, and felt less alienated, by either staying in or returning to the United States, where they had "the viable alternative of going underground in the ghettos to avoid military service." Blacks felt further alienated in Canada from other resisters, to the point of forming their own separate resister groups, (Emerick, 1972: 13; Kasinsky, 1976: 100).

Blacks who exiled themselves to Canada also felt alienated from blacks who resided there. The black deserter interviewed in this sample commented:

The — the blacks here are different. They — I guess — I learned that people of the same race have different backgrounds, have different cultures. That affected me. West Indians are most — 90% of the West Indians here are totally different. In a lot of ways.

Religion

Emerick (1972: 13) reports Catholics to be overrepresented among his military deserters and underrepresented among his draft dodgers.

"High" Protestants (Episcopalians and Presbyterians) are underrepresented; "Middle" Protestants (Methodists) are overrepresented. Jews appeared only in his sample of draft dodgers. In our sample (Table 3-6) Catholic military deserters are also overrepresented. A number of Jewish draft resisters and no Jewish military deserters were included. In contrast to Emerick's findings, High Protestants are well represented.

Family Composition

Adams (Table 3-7) and this work (Table 3-8) concur that draft dodgers came from intact two-parent families more frequently than military deserters. Adams found fewer differences. Since his is a significantly larger sample, our comparison should be viewed cautiously. Examining Table 3-8 internally, one finds that the draft dodgers were most likely to come from two-parent families. The composition of these families may have been a significant factor in socialization: more likely, the levels of family cohesiveness (despite its composition) influenced these men, as the discussion which follows emphasizes.

QUALITY OF FAMILY LIFE

The demographic data establish a clear profile of these men's backgrounds: relatively wealthy, educated, and highly professional. The-

Table 3-6 Religious Backgrounds of VERP Sample

	Draft Dodgers	Military Deserters
Catholic	27%	55%
"High" Protestant (Episcopalian, Unitarian, Presbyterian)	37	18
"Middle" Protestant (Methodist, Lutheran)	6	9
"Low" Protestant (Baptist, Fundamentalist)	8	18
Jewish	14	—
None	8	—
Total	100%	100%
	(N = 49)	(N = 11)

Table 3-7   Family Composition for Adams' Sample

	Draft Dodgers	Military Deserters
Both Parents Present	73%	69%
Divorced or Separated	13	15
Parent(s) Deceased	11	13
Other	3	3
Total	100%	100%
	(N = 110)	(N = 72)

(Adams, *American Refugee Study*, 1970: 50).

Table 3-8   Family Composition for Northeast VERP Sample

	Vietnam Veterans	Non-Vietnam Veterans	College Nonveterans	Non-college Nonveterans	Draft Dodgers	Military Deserters
Both Parents Present	72%	70%	79%	74%	88%	64%
Other	28	30	21	26	12	36
Total	100%	100%	100%	100%	100%	100%
	(N = 82)	(N = 101)	(N = 102)	(N = 95)	(N = 49)	(N = 11)

matic material follows, providing descriptions of how these men interpret their socialization during childhood and adolescence, and how they relate these experiences to their decision to resist. Draft and military resisters tell their own stories, revealing their own memories of "growing up": memories of families, positive and negative, credited with helping these men develop into self-described independent, free-thinking individuals with moral foundations for their actions.[5]

The themes discussed below were generated from responses to an open-ended question about growing up from childhood through adolescence. The question was ours; the responses were their own and could go in any direction. The three predominant themes are as follows; concern with interpersonal home life; the role of religion within the family; and family political attitudes.

Interpersonal Homelife

When these men discuss their families, most often they reflect on "interpersonal relationships." In 56 of 59 responses (an Act of God destroyed part of the 60th taped response), respondents identify these relationships as a key aspect of growing up. The responses range from warmth to serious conflicts, with little overlap.

Positive Homelife

(312): [The family] tended to stay together, try to help each other out.

Thirty-seven men report warm recollections of their home lives. They often assert that through these relationships they learned to be independent, and take responsibility for their actions. Thus, (606): "I was given a lot of individual freedom . . . I was generally encouraged to do what I wanted to do"; (402): "[I] was basically taught to think for myself and, you know, be aware of the consequences."

They were encouraged to think and participate in important family decisions by their parents:(413) ". . . sort of consulted on how we felt," or (305) . . . "they treated the children as equals . . . almost everything we experienced, we experienced together."

Beyond family decisions, many enjoyed memories of joint family activities. Thus, (615): "We did a lot of things together, like keeping a garden, a lot of work with the lawn, landscaping and I think it was pretty good." For others, this meant (308), ". . . weekend trips or go fishing, go for boatrides, amusement parks, just out in the country and picnics." Others (e.g., 407) ". . . got along with my parents well, especially my father [who] was quite active in sports and drew my brother and I into that quite a bit. That was really a major part of growing up."

These families are characterized as having few arguments, even good friendships; (606): "My brothers and I got along fairly well. My parents didn't seem to have any serious disagreements." For another, (404), his "best friends were [his] brothers and sisters." And one of those brothers (305), who followed him to Toronto, puts it, "We went through some hard times and that tends to get people together."

Parents are viewed as (613) "well informed"; these parents encouraged an interest in world events. For instance, (404): "I remember we used to sit up and watch the late night TV shows together and if an interesting guest would come on . . . we would discuss what he had to say."

These men share positive memories of their families. They remember their families helping to shape them into responsible, thinking adults, aware of the world around them. They feel they were raised to think independently; they were involved in family decisions and activities. Credit is given to parents for helping to shape them into self-directed adults.

Negative Memories

> (313): I guess the earliest thing is . . . a lot of fighting . . . my father and mother fought a lot over ridiculous little things . . . I got freaked out 'cause I knew there was a revolver in the bedside table in my parents' room and I emptied it because they were fighting . . .

Not all who talked about interpersonal relations describe their families in positive terms. Nineteen men, almost one third of the sample, picture their early home lives negatively. These men connect the lack of family harmony to their act of resistance, as others credit their positive family experiences.

Many describe major flaws in at least one parent. One (420) describes his mother as "not very nice", adding "neither of my parents were." Another (609) says his father was "maybe one of the most selfish people I've ever met," while the thing that got to another (417) about his father was "the hypocrisy of him." One resister (614) remembered his father as "rather shallow" and his mother as a "rather inept intellectual."

Portraying their parents so negatively, these resisters remember frustrations. As one (614) puts it: "I felt I couldn't get satisfaction from either of my parents." From another (418), "It's always too difficult for me to relate to [my mother]."

The absence of warmth, the failure to interact with parents, forms one type of negative recollections; and many families suffered from severe marital problems. Some of these memories reflect very deep scars.

> (410): . . . shouting fights and physical once in a while. I remember running out . . . of the kitchen one night with a baseball bat to get him [father] because he had her [mother] up against the window wth a knife at her throat.

Another (307) reveals:

> "My mother drank quite a bit . . . and my father worked a hell of a lot . . . by the time I went to school it was — grab your dinner in the kitchen and go watch TV."

For yet another (700), the memories were as bitter:

> My father was an alcoholic and that caused a lot of trouble. It got to the point where there were one or two years I suppose, where there wasn't much income coming in."

Alcoholism was but one of many problems described. One (419) describes his "physically violent" father, and another (610) his mother who, with a heart condition, "spent half of a year in bed." For these men, independence was necessary for survival rather than a result of parental encouragement.

Some resisters who came from homes with step-parents cited other problems. One (409) pictured his step-father as "a big southern guy . . . I didn't hate him — but I didn't like his stern mentality." Another (622) depicted his step-father as a man who "had difficulty showing compassion."

These negative memories propel an early move toward independence. These men often felt pushed into positions of autonomy for reasons of survival. They were forced, rather than encouraged, to act on their own.

An Empty Bag

(611): My father was in a way mildly detached . . . He was a good father, I never remember him beating us or abusive or having any negative qualities, but neither do I remember his being warm and fatherly.

Interpersonal relationships, for 10 resisters, are described only by their absence. This void is associated by these men with their eventual act of resistance. One (318) notes: "I would say that they [his family] may have not been really close, but lots of involvement," and another (611) comments that "we did a fair number of things together as a family although I was never very close with my brother and sister, or my parents."

These men remembered their families as being involved — without emotions. Involvement was expressed largely through parental concern. Parents showed (318) "definitely a lot of concern, a lot of pressure," and (408), "they were concerned about us children and our going to school."

These men felt that one of the most important aspects of their childhood, was the lack of definite emotion within their families. As opposed to the resisters who picture positive or negative families, these men describe a void. Once again this void is spoken of as a factor which accelerated their independence.

Most resisters, whether describing interpersonal family relations as positive, negative, or devoid of emotion, try to link their acts of resistance to early family relationships. They try to clarify how childhood and adolescent experiences contributed to their resistance, a decision that would deprive them, at least by distance, of family relations. A range of early experiences are seen as leading or pushing them to Canada. Concern for interpersonal relationships is a salient and natural issue for these men, who left their families behind — not always on the best of terms.

Religion: More Secular than Ecumenical

> (314): [Mother] had an idea of what she thought I should be as a man —
> very moralistic, believing in God — my father was the same way.

Religion is described by 21 men as another major theme in early socialization. Many choose to define their families with religious labels. For instance (413) describes his parents as "upright Catholics"; (700) sees his family as "typical Irish Catholic", and (621) comes from a "typically Jewish" background.

Two points are evident. First, a number of men appear to seek a catch-all label to define their families. Second, it was the children of Catholics, over-represented in the military deserters, and Jews, over-represented in the draft dodgers, who were more likely to use religion by itself as a means to define their families. Both religions deeply permeate other aspects of family life, in ways which go far beyond the church or synagogue.

Many men recall their family lives as immersed in religion. One dodger (700) recalls "heavy involvement of the Catholic church. And our friends all revolved around the church." Another (414) notes the influence of the priest: "If the parish priest said something it was paid attention to." A military deserter (421), a member of the fundamentalist Church of God, recalls that "all our activities were centered around the church . . . there was church twice on Sunday, prayer meetings on Wednesday night, youth fellowship groups, youth fellowship parties."

Religious involvement provoked two types of memories. Most frequently, religion influenced the moral fiber of families. One man (410) was "raised with the morals that I had learned in Catholic school," and another (422) remembers "teachings of Sunday school as important" when he was a youngster. While the men do not necessarily toe the religious line, they identify a type of religious morality as a significant influence in their early experiences.

The second type of memory of religion appears more negative. To these men, all-encompassing religion smothered and constrained their independence. The man who belonged to the Church of God (421) "started to resent it when I was first in high school because I felt . . . alienated from — from my peers . . . they would have proms, and — and guys would go out drinking on Saturday night and I couldn't get involved in that." Another (407) remembers Catholicism as "forced on us . . . attending mass and attending benedictions and so forth. Things of this nature and this was something I was involved in until I got to an age where I could get out of it!" Those who felt smothered by the church argue that this repression led to a general process of seeking alternatives. Canada later became such an alternative for the Vietnam situation.

The vast majority of men who raise the matter of religion as a major socialization theme do so to label their families or to provide a context for family activities. Most view religion as an aspect of moral development; others express resentment over the degree to which religion dominated their home lives. Religion is also intertwined with political activism. This is explored as the final theme of family background, political orientation.

Political Influences: Blood Redder than Politics

> (309): [My parents were] Midwestern Republicans. Fairly conservative and very much into the work ethic, education ethic, achievement, motivation, etc., that kind of thing.

> (613): [My parents were] very liberal, progressive, well-informed.

Twenty-two men raise the theme of politics as an important ingredient in their family backgrounds. Initial expectations were that many would identify far-left households of origin. This was substantially incorrect. While a few men mention left-wing parents, most do not. This, in part, is due to the fact that Canada was not the only alternative for potential resisters. Men could avoid Canada through manipulating the selective service system and many children of the political left were encouraged to do so. But it is also true that children do not always conform to the politics of their families.

Of these 22 men, half describe their parents as conservative to right-wing and half used liberal to left-wing labels. Those discussing conservatism do so, in the main, without reference to any actual political ideology. Conservatism is expressed instead in terms of lifestyle or personality. For instance, one draft dodger (620) refers to his father as "basically a decent man, very conservative, very materialistic." A military deserter (402) saw his parents as "very patriotic, conservative," and another (605) depicts his "conservative" family as "about the cheapest family that I ever saw."

Conservatism is often tied to religion. A draft dodger (406) whose parents are in the fundamentalist Christian Reform Church, sees his family as directed by "religious beliefs which were complete obedience to one's superiors." The military deserter (421) from the Church of God, describes his father as a man who "really studies the Bible and . . . looks to religion as a — as a way of totally guiding his life." These men view their families as governed by religious conservatism.

Only a few men placed the conservative label squarely in the political arena. One (307) describes his father as a "supporter of Joe McCarthy when he was in the Senate and [he] was very wary of all sorts of liberal ideas. We were sort of brought up to believe that Franklin Delano Roosevelt was . . . marked the beginning of the downslide of American society and so forth." Another (412) remembers an atmosphere where "a Communist is all pfff — simply because they're Communist, things like that." Few resisters from conservative families see their parents' views as ideologically grounded. Those who were from the fundamentalist churches came closest to this explanation of their parents' beliefs. Conservatism was universally depicted as negative. These men express disdain for, and separation from, these views of their parents.

By contrast, resisters who describe their families as liberal/left generally tied this to specific social issues, through the use of examples or contexts representing a clear position. One (414) describes his neighborhood as all white, with his parents not minding "if blacks had moved in, which for Flushing was, at that time, pretty liberal. I remember them talking about Castro . . . and they were in favor of him." Another (316) describes his father as "somewhat liberal . . . civil rights and so forth."

As is the case with some of the men who describe their families as conservative, some of these, particularly those with Jewish or Catholic parents, closely link their families' politics to religion.

> (401): My father was a Catholic liberal . . . he knew a lot about the Catholic Workers and he knew Dorothy Day . . . he helped start this magazine called *Crosstown* . . . it was kind of a radical, Christian, not Catholic but Christian, magazine.

Unlike their conservative counterparts, men from the liberal/left families try not to distance themselves from the political labels they place on their parents. In fact, most of these descriptions seem calculated to show that they adhere to early political teachings, crediting such attitudes as major influences.

Resister Status

Some interesting patterns distinguish the reported socialization experiences of military deserters and draft dodgers. Table 3-9 illustrates that the two groups are equally likely to report positive family relationships, but the military deserters are substantially more likely to report negative relations. Whether these negative reports accurately reflect early family life, or derive from exile-related family tensions (much more characteristic of the military than the draft dodgers' families), remains a question. (See Chapter Seven).

Table 3-9 VERP Resister Status by Family Characteristics

		Draft Dodgers	Military Deserters
Interpersonal	Positive	62%	64%
Relationships	Negative	29	45
	Absent	15	0
Religion Influential		35	36
Politics	Left/Liberal	21	9
	Conservative	10	55
		(N = 48)	(N = 11)

More interesting are the political orientations of the families of these men. Draft dodgers tend to describe liberal families; military deserters report more conservative upbringing. Whether this factor is compounded by social class, religion, or both, conservative families tended to encourage their sons to join the military, to fight for America.

SUMMARY

The first half of this chapter provided a demographic profile of the men in this sample, relative to each other, to studies of other draft and military resisters, and to age-equivalent nonresisters. Our data indicate that this sample constitutes an elite group of survivors. The draft dodgers come from families whose parents are much better educated, hold far better jobs, and earn more money than the median American family. The military deserters' parents, while not as privileged as their counterparts, are still above national SES norms. These draft and military resisters' parents are also of higher SES than parents of resisters from other studies. Those who are able to remain in Canada and connected to other exiles seem to have greater SES advantage than those who have returned to the U.S. or who never made it across the border.

The three themes discussed in the second half of this chapter are of course the result of filtered hindsights. Despite enormous diversity in family backgrounds, many respondents focus on an explanation of how they got to be *who* and *where* they are today. They allow for little ambivalence in their responses.

Men from close liberal/left and/or moral-religious families talk of being encouraged to develop a personal independence, a willingness to commit to moral, political action. These men present their families as positive role models. Men from families depicted as not close explain that they had to become independent. From a smothering of family religion, they had to break away. Men from conservative families espouse views which are the antithesis of their parents'. Families portrayed as negative role models propelled these men toward independent adulthood.

Common to these explanations is the fact that childhood and adulthood experiences paved the way to Toronto. One road was smooth: the other rocky. One group was aided in developing the critical thinking that enabled resistance; the other had little choice but to develop it, despite family views.

Finally, there is very little recognition by the respondents of their privileged class backgrounds: an interesting omission. None commented on their economic or educational advantage as it eased the path of resistance. Many may have difficulty admitting that they had a headstart over their age cohorts, men who were not able to take advantage of, or survive in, Canada.

The following chapter explores the ways in which these men from somewhat diverse family backgrounds, albeit basically from a privileged class, arrived at one place — Toronto.

NOTES

1. Discussions with Dr. Robert Laufer helped me understand the sample in this context.
2. 1963 was chosen as the benchmark for all parental background tables. This decision was based on the fact that the questions were asked in terms of when you were growing up — ages 14–17. For those men who ended up in Toronto, 1963 is the mean year in which they were 16. Dr. George Rothbart suggested that I utilize this method of comparison.
3. Adams defines "four years" to include any post-secondary degrees, while the other surveys use the more conventional definitions of actual college work.
4. All sample groups have higher than normative income levels. A telephone contact method may have biased the groups in this direction. Nevertheless, internal comparisons bear out predictions about relative advantages.
5. Dr. Charles Kadushin's reassuring guidance laid the groundwork for the transformation of what at first seemed "unworkable" transcripts into thematic categories — a strategy used throughout this work. The interpretations are my own.

CHAPTER **4**

New Perspectives:
Goodbye America

I just wanted to be free
To be all that I was promised
By the fathers of our fathers
Long ago.
But it's gettin' kind of scary
And it's gettin' harder breathin'
And I think it's gettin' time
For me to go.

He was almost to sweet Canada's border
He was almost to sweet Canada's border . . .
(From "Peacemaker," a song by Hoyt Axton, © 1972 *Lady Jane Music*).

This chapter focuses on the politicization process which occurred during the years immediately preceding the men's departure for Canada. For most, radical changes occurred in perceptions of, and attitudes toward, the military and the nation; and the changes were combined with varied involvement with anti-war activities. For a minority, few changes in perceptions occurred; Canada was a natural phase in the life cycle.

DIFFERENT STARTING LINES:

(405 — military deserter): Oh . . . like any 18-year-old, I think I probably would have expected to serve.

(419 — draft dodger): It was just an aspect of reality that I wasn't ready to choose to have anything to do with. Because as far as I knew at that point I would go to the university and be exempt forever and ever after.

These responses to a question concerning attitudes at age 18 toward military service reflect the extremes. The former speaker came from a home in which he was expected to serve; the latter was expected to attend college and pursue a career. For one, military service was considered a matter of course; for the other, the military was considered a course for others. The military deserter saw no alternatives at 18; the higher SES draft dodger was already aware of options.

Social class helps to explain these differing perspectives. At the time of draft registration, men in the Northeast VERP Sample report expectations to enter the service which vary by social class:[1] 63 percent of Vietnam veterans (generally from the lowest social classes) thought when they registered that they would eventually serve; compared to 54 percent of Vietnam Era veterans; 54 percent of non-college non-veterans; 31 percent of the higher social class college non-veterans; and 31 percent of the even higher class draft dodgers. Of our small sample of military deserters, 36 percent, at the time of registering, expected to go into the military when called.[2] At the time of draft registration, those from the lower classes had greater expectations of serving. (412): "I never knew anyone that didn't get drafted."

Despite the fact that most of the men who went to Canada did not expect to serve in the military, the majority did not, at age 18, harbor negative feelings toward the service. Feeling either neutral or positive toward the military, at 18 these men viewed service as an obligation, or an opportunity. One military deserter (304) saw no options: he said that going into the service "was sort of like going to the university — you didn't think about it. It was next — you just did it. If you were told to do it, you did it." A draft dodger (615) concurs: "It was something they told me I had to do . . . I'm 18 — I don't know anything." Others put it as (416) "inevitable" and (415) "something that had to be put up with."

These men saw the military as something that they would eventually face. No options were considered; neither was there much enthusiasm. Others viewed the military as an opportunity — (406) "a way to get an education, a good education. And, yeah, a chance to travel, etc., the old dream." Another (606) while not particularly positive about the Army, saw potential in the Air Force since later he "would be able to use the experience." The military was seen by one (414) as an opening for "opportunities for myself that may not come as easily or at all through other channels, like school." To another (420), who eventually enlisted, it gave "a sense of belonging . . . everything was taken care of so nice and neatly."

For others at 18, the military offered a chance to fill a "patriotic obligation" (402); as a military deserter (307) says, "I was brought up to believe that it was one of the duties of the citizen." And a draft dodger (610) describes his feelings at that time: "I guess I was pretty straight . . . I recognized that we needed an army and that it won a lot of wars and saved the world for democracy." These men accepted the military as necessary if not inevitable. This uncritical acceptance would be altered radically in a short time.

Others did not see uniforms in their futures. For these men, the military was (407) "somewhat removed." They did not regard it as a looming reality, often because they were going (305) "to college . . . I thought no, it's not going to bother me, I'll think about it four years after this." One just said that he (408) "didn't feel that I'd have to serve."

These men viewed the military as something that they would never have to deal with: others (616) did not even "think about it . . . no, not when I was 18." This group "had no feelings at all" (625) about the military. They were so sure of their distance from the military, that (317) "at that time, I felt nothing about it" and (605) "Well, when I was 18 — I tell you, I didn't think a hell of a lot about it."

These men, at 18, were secure in the belief that they would not have to face the military. Another group, a distinct minority in this sample, recall negative opinions about the military. Some saw it as rather comical, "something like PE on all the time . . . kind of combination Boy Scouts, Physical Ed" (312). Another (310) recalls that "the recruiters came to our high school and stuff and wore their fancy uniforms, I always thought it was kind of a joke . . . a little strange parading around in those Halloween costumes and stuff with all those braids in their caps."

A very few maintain that they developed fairly rigid rejections of service by this time. The military, one claims, already represented (609) "a total infringement on my freedom. I looked at myself as a person," and another (620) claimed to be "repulsed by it . . . the whole purpose of it. The dehumanized aspect, the murderous aspect." A third (618) "didn't feel that it was a place where I belonged." One draft dodger (623) puts it in more rigorous political terms, stating that "the existence of the military . . . as outlined and defined by the U.S. Department of Defense was criminal."

Social class affected attitudes toward military service, and also influenced the actions taken by these men. The war resisters and men in the VERP Northeast sample were asked, "Did you ever do anything to try to change your draft status — like seeing a doctor, or lawyer, getting married and having children, seeing a draft counselor, or anything else?" Affirmative responses varied by implicit social class.

Of Vietnam veterans (those who served in Vietnam proper) — nine percent "did something"; Vietnam Era veterans — ten percent; non-college nonveterans — 15 percent; college non-veterans — 24 percent; draft dodgers — 47 percent; and military deserters — 36 percent. The higher the social class, the greater the likelihood of action to channel oneself away from the draft. The discrepancy between college non-veterans and draft dodgers is in large part explainable by the fact that draft dodgers, when they lost their deferments, scrambled for new exemptions. Conversely, when men from the lower SES backgrounds were faced with the likelihood of being drafted, they were much less likely/able to take action to avoid the military.

THE BUBBLE BURSTS

> (416): The war crushed my reliance on the good will, intelligence, integrity and sanity, when you come right down to it of — of the United States.

Just a few years after generally accepting, if not always approving of, both the military system and the world role of the U.S., these men began to radically reconceptualize their views. In the years prior to exile, the *status quo* had become no longer tolerable. For instance, views of the military changed (312) "from almost like neutrality — like something that's expected, I'd say to something everybody was hostile to." Another (607) describes his transformation of feeling "from one of mild distaste to one of extreme repugnance."

While these two men had been initially neutral or slightly critical of the military, others had once been quite positive. One (406) defines his new views as a "complete reversal . . . okay, initially I looked at the military as again a source of education, a source of discipline, a chance to broaden my horizons, the American dream and it turned out to be a nightmare." Another (318) recalls, "When I registered I had the attitude that the services were all right and that you needed to have them. And I guess my attitude now was that they were a pretty sick part of society." A deserter (305) underwent a similar metamorphosis, concluding that "the U.S. Army was . . . just a bummer . . . I don't want to say immoral or sound kind of corny to say that but . . . that's what I feel."

For most of these men the war in Vietnam precipitated this shift in attitudes toward the military; although some mention other events of the turbulent 1960's.[3] It is hard to find statements by men in this sample supporting the war. However, a few resisters do express a certain amount of ambivalence about U.S. involvement in Vietnam;

for example, (311): "I think I felt that it was far too aggressive and at the same time too wishy-washy . . . if they're there I wish they'd either shit or get off the pot." Another (402) saw a no-win situation and "felt fighting a war that couldn't be won . . . was wrong." Some reasoned that "it was a war that was impossible to win from the very start . . . there was no chance of winning it" (612).

Others felt that the United States should not have been in Vietnam, but that America was not the only aggressor. A military deserter (409) makes this point: "If they [the U.S.] didn't belong there, then the communists didn't belong there either." Another (610) agrees, "Well, I was slightly mixed. I mean I could see the domino theory . . . the Vietnamese were certainly under their influence [the communists'] to some extent. They were imperialistic too."

Others "thought they (U.S.) shouldn't be there . . . it was an internal problem, a civil war" (609). One (420) maintains, "It doesn't behoove the United States or anyone else to be involved in a civil conflict." Or simply, as a draft dodger (422) puts it, "We had no business being there whatsoever . . . it was not our conflict." These men report fairly mild or ambivalent opposition to the war. While this represents a major change from the perceptions they held at age 18, they still had not reached the final stage of politicization which would take them to Canada.

Recognition that the war was wrong marks the political starting point for many. One (419) went from "thinking it was silly, a mistake, a waste of time and progressed to the point of view that it was actively immoral and willfully wrong." Another (611); "Initially [I] just felt that we shouldn't be there. And as time went on I became more and more opposed." The view of another (417) began with "feeling that it was a mistake [and] eventually turned into the feeling that it was a horror." And the one military deserter in our sample who had served in Vietnam (421) remembers that "when I first went there I didn't know. At the end . . . I was definitely . . . totally against it . . ."

Others depict the war as (401) "absolutely inexcusable — absolutely morally terrible" and see (415) "no reason, no justification for being there." The war (612) was "corrupt from top to bottom" and is described as (513) "indefensible, it was just — just wasn't defensible at any level."

A few resisters maintain that by this period in their lives, they conceived of the Vietnam War in a broader context of U.S. foreign policy. The war (615) "was wrong, completely wrong and it's not just, you know, one shot, it's part of a pattern," and another (608) "began to see what I considered to be the true face of U.S.

policy . . . imperialism." A theme which would develop further once these men became settled in Canada is expressed below.

(416): It was crazy. I felt that the U.S. was being self-righteous. Megalomaniac. Chauvinistic, I didn't know that word at the time . . . the whole thing was crazy. It was just a piece of madness.

From mild dissent to moral outrage, these resisters-to-be were reaching a stage when cooperation with the military and with the war would no longer be possible. These resisters report substantial changes of feeling from the time when they expected to enter the service, expressed indifference to those who did face military service, or were too far removed to even consider the issue.

Vietnam: The Horror Show

(317): Defoliation and the extensive use of napalm and God knows what all was being used, the testing of new equipment.

The aspect of the war which caused most concern was its brutality, the (614) "bombing and burning . . . the land it looked like the surface of the moon." The extent of this "destruction of natural resources of a country," and the "mass destruction and the fact that the country wouldn't be able to recover for decades from the destruction we were wreaking" (417) proved particularly repulsive. The men could no longer support a nation (412) "dropping bombs from B-52 bombers, shelling, fire-bombing, napalm."

Many note the (313) "atrocities . . . you know, the beheading people, you know, just inflicting terror." The weapons led to (617) "the complete destruction of harmless villages," and (404) "random death." The war was seen as so brutal that (406) "some of the barbarity that was perpetrated . . . you just couldn't believe the extent of it."

Many viewed the war as senseless, which furthered the outrage; (612): "We were destroying so damn much to accomplish so damn little." Another (609) describes his reaction to the fact "that there are people being killed here and what's more insane, they're being killed for no reason." There was (308) "no logical explanation for Vietnam. It just didn't make sense."

Part of the war's illogic was revealed in the type of government the U.S. was grooming for South Vietnam. A draft dodger (404) felt that our own leaders "were propping up dictators against the people's democratic wishes." Another (607) was outraged by "not only the military actions which I found reprehensible in the extreme but the attempts to manipulate public opinion in Vietnam to support of the

South Vietnamese government, the pacification program, I found repulsive, obscene."

Some mantain that they were afraid of even further escalation. One (608) feared "the possibility of using nuclear weapons . . . extending the war even further, heavier commitments, things of that nature." Another (413) worried "that the war would spread, perhaps the Chinese would be involved, perhaps the Russians would end up being involved."

Disillusionment with U.S. actions in Vietnam undermined any commitment to the dubious adage, "My country right or wrong".

Uncle Sam Wants You!

> (311): It was frustrating me and demoralizing me. I couldn't go to graduate school which I wanted to very badly, I wanted to go straight on. I was considering a Ph.D. perhaps, considering medical school and all kinds of considerations that you have in your last years as an undergraduate, things that you want to do and things that you want to try. And at the time you couldn't do anything. You were either an undergraduate or you were a schoolteacher or you were a soldier or a criminal.

> (414): The more realistic the situation became, and still thinking of it in egotistical terms, the more concerned I became for my own welfare and the less I could envision myself as being a part [of the service].

By their own admission, many resisters gained a full awareness of the Vietnam situation only when the war became a possibility for them. For most draft dodgers, their cocoon of deferments began to unravel. During this "period of greatest concern",[4] 88 percent of all draft resisters in this sample lost their deferments. Only 26 percent of the Northeast VERP non-veterans lost theirs. This, of course, was a major factor in determining who became a draft dodger and who remained simply a non-veteran.

Identifying the factors that altered their perceptions of the war, resisters openly agreed that it was their (621) "approaching participation." That is (422), "The war was getting warmer than anyone thought it would . . . it was really going to touch my life which I hadn't thought before." The possibility of serving made the war an immediate issue (306): "it affected me so much personally"; and (618): "the fact that I would have to serve is what, you know, made me sit down and think about it."

The encroachment of the selective service into their everyday lives overwhelmed many men. In attempts to beat the system, many tried the old moves in the deferment game. Table 4-1 reveals the

Table 4-1   During your Period of Greatest Concern, Did Potential Service Alter Plans For:

	Draft Dodgers	College Nonveterans	Non-college Nonveterans
Education	47%	25%	10%
Career	41	21	5
Marriage	14	20	6
Plans for Children	6	7	2
	(N = 49)	(N = 102)	(N = 95)

percentage of draft dodgers and non-veterans who responded positively to the question "Would you say that the possibility of your serving in the military affected any of the following?" (education, career, marriage, plans for children). In each area, certain actions could serve as deferments at some point during the war. (There are no comparable data for deserters or veterans.)

Draft resisters, despite the many deferment loopholes, eventually ran out of options. That they ended up in Canada rather than in the military points to an avenue of avoidance that lower-class veterans were unaware of or unwilling to take. Table 4-1 reveals how the likelihood of being drafted affected the personal plans of many men. One (317) began seeing the draft "as more and more of an inconvenience . . . I had goals — like, if I wanted to be a doctor, if I wanted to be a success in business, I couldn't." Another (700) spoke of how the threat of Vietnam had become "a dominating factor in thinking about the future."

Buddies and Budding Awareness

Combined with selective service pressures, peer group supports fostered a growing awareness among these men. One (610) describes his reaction to ideas he heard expressed by peers encountered at college: "The Midwest was a very conservative united front and being presented with all sorts of different ideas in a liberal environment was startling." Another (312) credits his new awareness to exposure to "different people." A third (612) lost his attitude of "indifference" when "friends of mine got involved in various ways in the war and as the war became a reality . . . it dawned on me that the military had a function [which I couldn't condone]." A draft dodger received graphic letters from a friend who was in Vietnam:

> (419): During 1967 we corresponded and . . . I began to get letters from him in Vietnam, very detailed letters about what he was doing and

what was going on . . . what his unit did, and what happened to them . . . you could describe it as farcical basically. What they seemed to do was go out and camp in the jungle and get shot at . . . and then direct large amounts of artillery, airplanes and whatever against where they thought they were being attacked from, which seemed to have no discernible effect on their being attacked. In between this they would be bombed by their own planes or [they] went over their own mine-fields. Rape a few women and children. Just crazy stuff. Didn't correspond to any picture I had of either the military or war or even existence in any manner.

A military deserter who "split" from San Diego while awaiting orders for Vietnam began truly to see the war as an activity.

> (410): My brother was home and on leave from Vietnam — he had obviously changed as a result of his year there . . . a lot more violent, a lot more moody. Quite a bit quieter . . . I started realizing that the war was very real — there were people back on base who had been to Vietnam and they told me real stories . . . it was all of a sudden becoming very real . . . I was definitely heading for something that was real and not just a TV show. Not a John Wayne movie. It was real.

The influence of friends is best illustrated in friendship patterns. Eighty-five percent of those draft dodgers who responded report that at least half of their closest friends were against the war, and 60 percent say that all their closest friends during this period opposed it. Only 45 percent of the military deserters report that half their friends were against the war, but 45 percent state that their friends felt positive about their desertion.

Besides personal apprehensions and personal contacts — undoubtedly the most significant routes to a new awareness — the availability of information about the war heightened critical perspectives. There were (413) "teach-ins and lectures," and (414), "the underground newspapers . . . questions being raised and that was the same period of time when the first legislators were starting to have qualms about the whole thing." One man (607) even had his budding anti-war attitudes "reinforced by working in a defense company." The war's continual exposure in the straight media forced many to ask questions. They deduced that the war was wrong.

NEW AWARENESS

> (610): It [Vietnam] forced me to focus attention on all ethical issues more than I probably would have if it hadn't been there . . . it was

difficult to be neutral or wishy-washy in those times . . . it forced me
to more commitment than I would have [made] before. Basically I'm
a compromiser and so I'm sure that without something that strong I
would've been a compromiser then. But instead, I ended up going out
on a limb.

The ultimate outcome of this new perspective was Canada. In the
short run, a critical world view evolved — a world view which might
not have occurred without the war. As one resister (621) says, "It
was throwing a monkey wrench in my personal bourgeois existence . . . it was making me confront a moral question that I would
have otherwise . . . glossed over." Another (417) puts it in these
terms: "I had to, in effect, grow up and live in the real world instead
of in my ivory tower"; a third (305) saw the war as "making me more
of a human being, awakening me from slumber."

   Through anti-war activities, this new awareness was translated
into action. Table 4-2 shows the proportion of draft dodgers who took
part in a variety of such activities and presents comparisons with the
nonveterans in this sample. (Comparable data are not available for
veterans.) It should also be noted that anti-war activities are much
more prevalent among college, as opposed to non-college, nonveterans — a point established in Chapter Two.

   Draft dodgers were substantially more active than nonveterans,
with a total of 65 percent of them (vs. 28 percent of nonveterans)
participating in at least one of these anti-war activities. Since their
activities exceeded what was needed for self-preservation, their politicization witnessed a conversion from personal concerns to moral
and political commitments.[5]

   It has been demonstrated that these three groups represented in
Table 4-2 arise from distinct backgrounds. It is safe to speculate,

Table 4-2   Anti-War Activities During Period of Greatest Concern

	Dodgers	College Nonveterans	Non-college Nonveterans
Attended local anti-war demonstrations	47%	35%	11%
Leader in anti-war organizations	16	3	0.0
Attended national anti-war demonstrations	29	11	4
Participated in acts of civil disobedience against the war	16	5	1
Went to jail for anti-war activities	6	1	1
	(N = 49)	(N = 102)	(N = 95)

accordingly, that anti-war activities were related to social class standing. The higher one's social class, the more likely one would be to engage in anti-war activities. Despite many claims to the contrary, these anti-war activities were generally campus-based, class-biased. Resistance, on the other hand, as shown in Chapter Two, crossed class lines.

When Push Came to Shove — Draft Dodgers: Time to Leave

(419): One day I got, you are now 1A, and a couple of days after that I got Greetings. But what happened was that the day I got the induction notice, I was just stunned by what had happened . . . not knowing what to do . . . [A friend] said "Holy fuck, what are you going to do?" and I hesitated and then I said, "Go to Canada". And as soon as I said that, there was a kind of aah — solution.

Given the emergent political perspectives as well as personal apprehensions, when push came to shove, these men chose Canada over the military and Vietnam. Draft dodgers remained in the U.S. until they had to leave: until they received their induction notices, were reclassified 1A or, for a few, until after they refused induction.

Of the draft dodgers, only eight were under indictment when they left the U.S. By the time of these interviews, most of the sample had been indicted, almost exclusively for failing to report for a physical or for induction. Most of the indictments occurred after exile because men usually left before they had been processed in the courts. As one (414) puts it, "I was faced with the absolute inescapable reality of the draft. I was called, I got my notice, they made the ludicrous mistake of giving us up to 30 days to get our papers in order." Some men sat on the fence (417), "until I got my draft notice. That's — that's when I made the decision."

While these draft dodgers stated that receipt of a draft notice propelled them toward Canada, most left before the notice actually arrived. They saw themselves as running out of time. Like (403), they simply "did not think I'd be able to continue legal deferments until age 26." Alternatives diminished until "the only real option was to leave the country" (404). Canada in fact had become "my only option to serving in the military" (418). As one concluded (611), "The only avenue of avoiding the military and war that . . . really made sense to me was to leave the country."

This spark toward Canada coincided with the explicit end of deferments. One dodger (407) headed north upon receiving his "second notice to go for a physical." Another (404) knew it was time to go when he "was classified 1A from 1S or 2A." And some were multiple losers at deferment roulette; as (411) puts it, "My Conscientious Objector (CO) application was denied and I had an application for a medical deferment and it was denied." This was often echoed; (611): "My phony condition at the physical failed, my CO was turned down, my student deferment was taken away." Trying a deferment option bought these men additional time to make a final decision, time which was lacking for those who entered the service at 18, who had never heard of a CO or who had no access to sympathetic doctors willing to create a "phony condition."

What these men share, beyond often militant anti-war stands, is the fact that they did not leave until their hands were forced.

> (422): Well, we were hoping against hope. We had Canada as our out. But then when LBJ came on the air one night and said graduate students get it in the head, well, then we knew. So we kept hoping right up until the physical they'd find something wrong and they didn't, of course . . . and as soon as we knew that — that our physical had been passed and we were going to be 1A then that was it. Canada for sure.

A few men who refused to step forward at induction or simply failed to show up, waited even longer, until things got really tight. The sequence for one (408) was, "I was drafted and supposed to report . . . and I didn't go . . . about six months from that . . . finally I heard from the FBI . . ." and to Canada he went. Another (406) publicly refused induction and was told, "Well, okay, you might as well go home, but you know that the sheriff is going to come . . . At that point I started making serious plans to leave and it took three weeks for that to happen and during these three weeks, I just didn't open, answer, the door."

Options for these men ran out or were running out. Others still had options open but decided for a variety of reasons not to proceed with them. Many recognized conscientious objector status as a potential deferment which they did not pursue. This type of deferment, while admired, required two years of alternative service. It was described by some, e.g. (613), as "sort of going along with the whole thing . . . being a CO in effect was supporting the system"; or (422): "I didn't want to get stuck doing some shit job for no money for two years as [a] kind of penance because I figured there's no penance involved from my point of view."

In this sample, men who entertained thoughts of protesting the war by serving in jail far outnumbered those who talked about a CO. However, this may be partially attributed to selective hindsight.

Prison was eventually dismissed as an option because, in the words of (417), "no purpose would be served by my going to jail other than losing my civil rights and having a miserable time for some years." Another (413) talked of "serving time and then leaving the country." Perhaps more honest was the rhetorical question one (412) asked himself: "Would it be more fruitful for me as a person to leave the country as opposed to going to jail?"

Several men mentioned reading about or talking to draft resisters who had been in jail for draft evasion. One (610) found "that just about every one of them said if they had to do it over again, they wouldn't . . . that was probably the deciding factor of why I ended up in Canada." As another (700) puts it, "I think the only one who thought it was worthwhile. . . . was Joan Baez's husband. Of course, he had someone to promote him."

Many of these draft dodgers, despite their relatively high class backgrounds, indeed lost in the deferment game. This may seem to contradict the position that men from privileged classes could avoid the military or Vietnam. The reality is that men from the higher classes had the most options; however, these options were not infinite. These men had a greater knowledge of, and access to, deferments, or preferred programs if they decided to become reluctant volunteers; and they usually had extra time, through college, to consider their choices. Their final class luxury was time, to decide, over a period lasting months or years, when to leave. Lower-class military deserters lacked this alternative; they had to leave in a hurry.

Military Deserters: A Quick Exit

Contrary to popular mythology, the military deserters were generally not in Vietnam, or even under orders to go there, at their point of alleged "desertion." In this sample, just two were under orders to go to Vietnam; six were at other duty stations, two were slated to report for active duty as a result of ROTC commitments, and one had already served in and left Vietnam. This distribution is probably fairly representative of military deserters who remained in Canada (Baskir and Strauss, 1978; Bell and Houston, 1976; Kasinsky, 1976; Williams, 1971a).

In this sample, 57 percent of the draft resisters thought about Canada for at least six months prior to leaving; 37 percent planned for over a year in advance.[6] (One was living in Canada already and just never bothered to return to the U.S.). On the other hand, 73 percent of the military deserters (8) planned for less than six months.

Few had even six months to spare. This difference in time for planning generalizes beyond the present sample (Kasinsky, 1976.)

The military deserters were generally younger than the draft dodgers when they actually left for Canada. These men, coming from a class where options were less available or known about, often went into the military at 18 or 19 while the draft dodgers were safely deferred in college. Military deserters' hands were forced much earlier than those of draft avoiders, who often held deferments into their twenties. In our sample, 57 percent of the draft dodgers, compared to 45 percent of our military deserters, were 22 or over when they left. Omitting two ROTC candidates who were in college, only 33.3 percent of the military deserters were over 22. Although the actual numbers in our sample are small, the trend is documented throughout the literature (Baskir and Strauss, 1978; Colhoun, 1977; Kasinsky, 1976).

The reasons given for military desertion and for going to Canada parallel those of the draft dodgers. Some tried legal channels for separation from the military without success; (420): "My last opportunity to get things changed failed, which was the psychiatrist . . . my company commander didn't . . . think it was important enough." One considered (405), "feigned suicide, feigned psychological problems," but opted against these as unrealistic solutions.

Two saw the writing on the wall. For them the writing read Vietnam, not entry into the military. One (308) said: "The unit I was in, I think . . . there were 35 guys in the unit and 33 of them went to Vietnam . . . the odds weren't very good." Another (410) talked of a friend of his who had been caught AWOL and had agreed to go to Vietnam, where he was killed — "All of a sudden it was real. It was close."

Others mention exposure to people who alerted them to options — options of which they had been virtually unaware when they first entered the military. One (314) dated a woman whose brother was a draft counselor "and I was talking to him about it and I guess it started from there." Another (409) heard from a friend who had avoided the draft by going to Canada "and . . . he worked for the anti-draft program and I got it from the horse's mouth. All I needed to know . . . in order to take off."

The emotional impact of being in the military often drained these men. One (304) saw "no other alternative as far as I could see for saving my last bit of sanity . . . at least I'd have peace of mind." Another echoes the same sentiments, saying (405): "I began to worry about my mental health."

Resistance: A Political Statement

(402): Nixon invaded Cambodia and . . . the street fights, the tear gas, the national guard helicopters . . . I was chased by a whole platoon of deputy sheriffs [in Madison, Wisconsin] and if they'd caught me, they would have — they would have beaten me up and I would have spent 30 days in jail for resisting arrest . . . I just figured if I went to jail in Nixon's America when Nixon and Agnew were acting as cheerleaders for the National Guard at Kent State and Jackson State, it was just futile. Totally.

Military and draft resisters went to Canada not only for personal but for moral reasons. No matter what was at stake, the war was so wrong that resistance was the only feasible response. A military deserter in no danger of going to Vietnam (307) "realized that it could not be supported at all" and a draft resister (415) states that for him "it was unacceptable to go into the military." Another (608) left "mainly because I wasn't interested in going to Vietnam, fighting and being a member of the U.S. Army." The consensus is expressed by a military resister (308), "I didn't want to participate in Vietnam — in war, period."

Others were propelled to leave by an event or series of political occurrences, many not even directly involving Vietnam. Abrupt accelerators included (413), "Kent State . . . the point it brought home to me was . . . that [a] whole military psychology was — was spreading . . . it began to hit with it close to home, they started shooting white middle-class students." Another (316) recalled the violence by authorities at "the Democratic Convention of Chicago. That just sealed my fate, the results of that." To others (621) it was when "Martin Luther King was shot." The following reaction to that event shows how it could accelerate the decision to leave.

(305): That was the last straw. It seemed that somebody that taught non-violence and stuff, I could see how they did him in and I thought if they could do something like that, that way . . . there was no hope for the States.

These men personify a fact too often overlooked. Resistance, through exile, was by itself very much of a political statement.[7] Just as these men's antiwar actions exceeded the self-protective device of seeking deferments, their decision to enter Canada went well beyond avoiding orders to report for induction or to go to Vietnam. Exile was to these men the ultimate antiwar act — they refused to participate in the military or with a nation involved in Vietnam abroad or with

Kent or Jackson State at home. Whether the reasons were personal, political, or both, one theme unified all motivations to leave: these men saw no reason to fight for America. Their country was wrong at home and abroad.

America: Not So Beautiful

(612): You grow up in the United States and you say the pledge of allegiance every morning and . . . in the United States you can't help but grow up patriotic if you're middle-class and your family has two cars. We won the world wars and we've been the saviors of American or world peace and all that and I went through a real period of disillusionment.

Disillusionment with America was rampant. Events in Vietnam and at home were a major catalyst for this change; personal apprehension joined with political distaste to bring forth a new awareness in these resisters. However, both these explanations for exile are somewhat wanting. Political options other than exile were available and men have been in more personal danger in previous conflicts, with fewer exiling themselves.

Beliefs about American greatness, reinforced at home, in school, in the media, and in church, could no longer be sustained. This disillusionment was shattering: (625) "all-out lying that the U.S. was doing," or (305) "We saw the Senate hearings on the war and you could see these officials lying, getting caught in lies." The myth of America was replaced by a new reality: (401), "the American government was putting out stuff about the wonderful things they were doing for the Vietnamese — all this horseshit propaganda . . . it was all horseshit."

Disappointment with the U.S. government spread to include the people. One man (616) describes his feelings: "I was disappointed that the United States had really, could really, prosecute war at that time. And I was disappointed that the American people were so willing to be misled." A draft dodger (616) echoes this: "The American people were misled and wanted to be misled." And another (607) talks of becoming "more and more disillusioned with Americans in general and what I felt was their failure to recognize the true nature of the war."

These men changed from trusting to very mistrusting individuals. The war led one draft dodger (620) to "question lots of things about our government that I'd never questioned before." They were suspicious of everything, including (322) "the so-called Establishment at the time, the universities I guess, and the corporations and everything, the courts." Another (316) describes his change: "Well, I think when I was younger I probably had more faith in authority — I wasn't cynical at all . . . but as time went on these people just didn't seem to live up to that trust and I became real cynical and just wouldn't let them make any decisions for me."

SUMMARY

Socio-economic class affected men's attitudes toward the military, their expectations for serving and their knowledge of and willingness to use options out of the military. As an important determinant of the alternatives to service that people were aware of at age 18, class predicted who could get out and who could stay out.

Class paved different paths for the draft and the military resisters. The higher class draft dodger did not have to leave until his hand was forced by induction, impending reclassification, or rejection of other options. Time to plan was possible and cushioned the transition. Military deserters generally were politicized only after they were in the military, and enjoyed less time, fewer alternatives, and little room to respond.

With politicization, both groups of men experienced a shift in their views. Indifferent, or even patriotic, at age 18, these mena rrived at the strong conviction that our involvement in Vietnam was immoral, the military was reprehensible, and exile was the only viable option. These views were cultivated by a combination of moral commitment and personal self-interest. Apprehensions, contact with friends, and general exposure to the war opened many eyes. With awareness, an activism beyond the call of self-preservation emerged.

Exile in Canada was selected as an act of resistance against a nation involved in an indefensible war. Coupled with events at home, these men realized that the war was not the only thing wrong with America. This indeed is the saddest commentary on what the Vietnam War did to this nation. Most of these men gave up on America:

> (609) I went through this evaluation process in my head about what I'd be losing leaving and I came to the conclusion — I wouldn't be losing very much.

NOTES

1. Arguments presented in earlier chapters establish that college non-veterans and draft dodgers are generally from the higher social classes.

2. This last figure is consistent with the observation that these particular military deserters in Canada come from a slightly higher class
than other veterans. However, the number is so small that this finding
must be viewed rather cautiously.

3. Undoubtedly, had we interviewed more blacks, the Civil Rights
Movement would have been suggested as at least a second major
politicization factor. We didn't and it wasn't.

4. "Period of Greatest Concern" is that period when non-
veterans/dodgers were most strongly aware of the real prospect of
military service, and veterans/deserters most aware of the real nature
of service.

5. Periodic discussions with Dr. Robert Laufer helped me to place
resisters in this perspective.

6. In creating the computer programs to determine the age at which
men left and time spent in planning to leave, Dr. George Rothbart,
Joe Jamison, and Herb Phoenix provided valuable assistance.

7. Several conversations with Jack Colhoun were essential in arriving
at an understanding of this issue.

PART THREE

CANADA: REFUGE OR HOME?

Once the exile decision had finally been made, these men entered a nation about which they knew little, and which itself had ambivalent responses to their presence. Just as it was useful in Part I to connect the draft and military resisters to the past, it is also important to examine Canada from a historic perspective in order to understand the resisters' reactions to Canada, and Canada's reaction to them.

Chapter Five, "Canada: Uneven Welcome", examines the context to which these men arrived. Critical here are the selective emigration/immigration trends which historically involved a "brain drain" out of Canada, and increasingly selective entry standards into Canada. Varying Canadian attitudes toward draft dodgers and military deserters (as well as toward the U.S. in general) constitute much of this "uneven welcome." The War Measures Act, and the extent of Canada's involvement in Vietnam influence the interaction of these men and their new country. A general discussion of how relationships between resisters and Canadians evolved over the years concludes the chapter.

Chapter Six, "Impressions: The Canada They Found", centers on developing perceptions of Canada. Canadian and resister attempts to define the "ethos" of Canada, to understand Canada's development, and to decipher U.S. and British influences are given particular attention. Finally, favorable and unfavorable comparisons offered by the resisters to the United States are critically analyzed.

The complex relations between Canada, Canadians, and the resisters are examined in these two chapters. However, it must be made clear that this is a study of resisters. It has no pretensions to being an ethnography or history of Canada. The discussion is limited, rather, to issues directly affecting resisters in Canada.

CHAPTER 5

Canada: Uneven Welcome

Man for man the draft dodgers probably are the best educated immigrants we've ever had.

(Fulford, 1968: 11)

Confession to An American Friend

the day I became a nationalist
you were reading
with your rasputin's voice
warnings from Melville
I told you
I was tilling prairie fields
with your old man's tractor
while you gushed your nihilism
to a gathering of hungry exiles
disguised in our northland
as conscience-stricken noblemen
from the South

You like it in the provinces
provincial towns, provincial people
here you're self-important
you've come to save us
with talk of jazz and existential angst
how old-fashioned!

I lied
about who we are
I seemed meek and ignorant
a loyal dog

I wore the mask of a century of blacks
I lied
I am no peasant.

I am a rage and wolf-buffalo man
an ugly Metis a pemmican hunter
looking for a ritual kill
your tongue

I lied playing safe
you stayed
believing the name I gave
but I ran from your
self-made place

I ran to my mother's teeth
to her knife and gun
to her stones
to her trees and soils
but you were hidden everywhere
a hungry universal eye.

now I lie armed
with waiting.

(George Melnyk, in *Our Generation*, 1973: 23)

CANADA AND IMMIGRATION

Toronto Mail — 1887:

> There is scarcely a farmhouse in the older
> provinces where there is not an empty chair
> for the boy in the States.
>
> (Cited in Lipset, 1971: 34)

This statement, made nearly 100 years ago, reflects a twofold problem which still exists: first, Canada's serious underpopulation; and second, the fact that the United States looms as a hungry giant ready to devour Canadian resources, including people. In the first century in which statistics were accurately kept, 1851–1951, Canada lost nearly as many people as it gained — 7,100,000 entered Canada, and 6,600,000 left (Porter, 1971: 38). Among those leaving, particularly for the United States, Canada's better educated middle and upper class young adults were overrepresented. The "brain drain" in Canada reached its zenith in the early 1960's (Ibid.; Fulford, 1968: 11; *Hansard*, Second Session, 27th Parliament, IV, 1967: 3538; Levine, 1972: 431). Table 5-1 reflects the cross-border traffic. The column "From the U.S." includes exclusively Americans. During these years it can be safely assumed that the majority were resisters. The ratio of "From the U.S." to "From Canada" historically resulted in Canadian losses. By 1972, the emigration loads were equivalent for the two countries. In fact, the U.S. figures can be assumed to be deflated because while they include only legally landed Americans, they exclude illegally landed resisters, often military deserters, whose numbers, while unknown, are substantial (Kasinsky, 1976: 19).

Canada historically has relied on a significant immigrant population. In 1968, the mid-point of the Vietnam resister influx, one out of every nine Canadians was an immigrant (Jones and Lambert, 1968:

Table 5-1 Immigration to Canada from the United States and Immigration to the United States from Canada during the Vietnam Era

	From the U.S.	From Canada
1962	11,643	44,272
1964	12,565	51,115
1966	17,514	37,273
1968	20,422	41,716
1970	24,424	26,850
1972	22,618	23,000

(*Canadian Pocket Encyclopedia*, 1977: 321)

95). However, the anti-war resisters need to be distinguished from most other immigrants to Canada. These men, as a group, were substantially better trained and educated than other newcomers. Table 5-2 displays levels of resister education at time of arrival compared to other immigrants and Canadians. (The comparison year used for Canadians and general Canadian immigrants is 1967.) Immigrants in general were slightly better educated than Canadians; resisters were better educated (Fulford, 1968: 11; Kasinsky, 1976); and the resisters in the VERP sample were far better educated than male Canadians and male immigrants.

Canada has always relied on immigration to replace outgoing emigrants, but its economy never required the waves of newcomers needed in the United States during periods of economic expansion. This afforded Canada a certain amount of selectivity: since World War II, its immigration policy fostered relatively elite recruitment (Colhoun, 1977: 16; Porter, 1965: 56). The *Immigration Act of 1967* installed a point system virtually eliminating working and lower-class immigrants (Kasinsky, 1978: 6; Levine, 1972: 431–432; Wilcox, 1970: 51). Fifty points were required for legal entry as a landed immigrant. Points were allocated as shown in Table 5-3.

Under this system, undesirable newcomers could be stopped at the border and turned back. Pressure was applied from some quarters to relax the standards for American war resisters. This would benefit, in particular, the lower class military deserters, who had trouble making the fifty points. (Such exemptions were not without precedent: previous standards had been relaxed for 36,000 Hungarians in

Table 5-2 Education Levels of Canadians, Male Immigrants, Resisters

Education	Male Native-Born Canadians	Male Post-War Immigrants	VERP Dodgers	VERP Military Deserters
Elementary School or Less	39%	37%	0%	0%
Some High School	36	26	0	9
Completed High School or Attended Some College	20	28	47	64
University Degree or More	5	9	53	27
Totals	100%	100%	100% (N=49)	100% (N=11)

(Data on male Canadians and post-war immigrants from Richmond, *International Migration Review.* (Center for Migration Studies of N.Y.), 1969: 14)

Table 5-3   *Immigration Point System* (50 points needed for Landed Status)

	Maximum	
Education	20	(one point per year)
Personal Quality	15	(based on border interview)
Occupational Demand	15	
Age	10	
Occupational Skill	10	
Employment Arrangements	10	
Speak English or French	10	
Relatives	5	
Area of Destination	5	
Total	100	points

(Kage, *International Migration Review* (Center for Migration Studies of N.Y), 1967: 47–48.)

1956, and later for Chileans, South Vietnamese, and Czechoslova-kians.) These efforts to get special status for deserters failed, in part because deserters were not the U.S. immigrants Canada most wanted (Kasinsky, 1976: 62). For the most part, the draft dodgers were welcome; however, military deserters (and for a segment of the Canadian population, even draft dodgers) were not readily accepted. The following sections deal with the reasons why.

Selecting Resisters

Canadian woman living with military deserter:

I think Canadian immigration activity discriminated against certain types of people, quite definitely, especially more as times got worse in Canada . . . this discrimination was especially against the working class Americans, the deserters, who tried to enter the country legally.

There is evidence to back charges by military deserters, and their sympathizers, that the Canadian government discriminated by excluding them and encouraging the immigration of draft resisters. In one effort to expose official discrimination against military resisters, five Canadians from Toronto's Glendon College went to five different border crossings and tried to re-enter Canada posing as "William John Heintzelman," Air Force deserter. Despite the use of background details that would guarantee a *draft resister's* successful immigration, "Heintzelman" was rejected for entry at all five points. This widely publicized case demonstrated that Canada actively discriminated to keep military resisters out (Colhoun, 1977: 17; Kasinsky, 1976: 119–120; Wilcox, 1970: 43 and 53-54).

Even more damning evidence of active government filters was

found in a leaked confidential memo from the Ministry of Immigration in 1968. The memo reminded border stations to exercise a great deal of discretion in allocating points for entry, particularly with respect to "personal quality." This "discretion" should be aimed at three types of individuals: men with excessive debts; men involved in marital desertions; and military deserters. The government had to confess the origins of this memo, when it was read during a parliamentary debate. (*Hansard,* First Session, 28th Parliament, VI, 1969: 5845; Kasinsky, 1976: 120; Wilcox, 1970: 51). Deserters could legally be turned back under the ambiguous criterion of "persons who are likely to become public charges" (Baskir and Strauss, 1978: 176–177).

Men in this sample recognized and experienced this discrimination at the border. For instance: (407 — a draft dodger) "There was never any real question about whether dodgers could become landed immigrants or not. There was quite a bit of argument over deserters"; or (405 — a military deserter) "It was all right for middle class resisters [draft dodgers] to come but as soon as there were lots of deserters coming, they stopped it. They closed the border." Numerous commentators also provide descriptive evidence that military deserters were less welcome than draft dodgers. (For details see Baskir and Strauss, 1978: 176–177; Colhoun, 1977: 17; Franks, 1974: 74; Hawkins, 1972: 41; Kline et al, 1971: 80; Wilcox, 1970: 52).

Discriminatory treatment of military deserters was not restricted to the point of entry. Well-documented charges, some made on the floor of Parliament, accused the Royal Canadian Mounted Police (RCMP) of cooperating with U.S. authorities to illegally deport military resisters. While this practice never became widespread, it made life very rough for deserters, who had harder times from the beginning. Some RCMP harassment was directed at all resisters; however, the military deserters bore the brunt of those actions. (See Campbell, 1970: 18–19; Cocking, 1970: 28–30; Franks, 1970: 97–98; *Hansard,* 28th Parliament, Second Session, II, 1969: 1257; *Hansard,* 28th Parliament, Second Session, III, 1970: 2967; *Hansard,* 28th Parliament, Second Session, IV, 1970: 3401–3403; Kasinsky 1978: 1–2 and 217–218; Wilcox 1970: 52).

At times, legislation which would formally close borders to deserters was seriously considered (Kasinsky, 1976: 116). The debate raged frequently in Parliament from 1966 to 1970. Arguments against entry were twofold: first, Canada should be selective about the quality of its immigrants; and second, "desertion" in particular was undesirable. M.P. Scott championed the first point, and frighteningly for the resisters, Prime Minister Lester Pearson spoke to the latter issue. Scott's 1970 comments cited an immigration panel study:

. . . A large percentage of draft dodgers and especially deserters coming into this country are poorly educated. Many of them lack trade
skills or professional training and consequently, a large percentage of
these people have found it difficult to find jobs.

(*Hansard*, 28th Parliament, Second Session, VI, 1970: 6470)

Pearson's comments support the Immigration Department memo
cited earlier.

It is very difficult to take action in individual cases, but we would
certainly not do anything to encourage admission to Canada of this
category of United States citizens.

(*Hansard*, 27th Parliament, First Session, XII, 1967: 12523)

Obviously, these viewpoints never carried the day in parliament. But
often the issue was in doubt.

A Small Welcome Mat

(304): The draft dodger, he left before he was ever drafted, so since
there wasn't a draft up here, they didn't consider it illegal action, you
see. But desertion is illegal up here, and it's illegal down there, so they
had that and they still considered it, you know, a wrong thing to do.

The treatment of military deserters was usually negatively compared
to the treatment given draft dodgers. For instance (615): "I feel that
in terms of resisters, draft dodgers were generally treated better. They
were from a higher economic class and all that . . . "; or (402): "Well,
Canadians feel very positive about draft resisters. In fact, there was
a famous editorial [quoted in part at the beginning of this
chapter] . . . that American draft resisters with their . . . higher education were the most highly educated group ever to hit Toronto.
But when it came to deserters who didn't have the education — didn't
have the job skills — they just didn't get landed." Finally charges of
institutional discrimination went beyond the border; (406): "Deserters
tend not to be so middle class . . . as a result, official institutions
tended not to be so helpful."

Some of the Canadian women living with, or married to, draft
dodgers initially harbored hostility toward military deserters. They
traced their prejudice to the class biases with which they grew up.
For example, "It was inconceivable to me that every army aged individual did not realize that there was an alternative [in] Canada. My
background, my entire contact, had been with middle and upper
class Americans. I only learned later that my background was sheltered." Another woman said, "I was led to believe that deserters
were different. I learned that deserters just woke up a little bit later."

And a third told me, "When I first met him [the man she lived with] it seemed strange he had gone into the army rather than come up to begin with . . . that was my middle class background."

Some Canadians are seen as rejecting military deserters because of their emphasis on honoring commitments. For instance, Canadians (316) "would look upon deserters a little bit more harshly . . . it's almost like maybe they made a commitment and didn't follow through with it or something." Others concurred, saying (611), "Canadians felt that if you got involved in the military, it was somehow your obligation to follow it through and not to — not to desert." Many draft dodgers felt, like (616), that to Canadians, "the word deserter has a bad connotation."

While they are legitimate reflections of how draft dodgers saw Canadian attitudes, these comments also betray sentiments harbored by some draft dodgers themselves. A moral righteousness in some draft dodgers is evident in the following remarks:

> (603): I think [draft dodgers] were viewed as people that came up for moral reasons. Deserters — people that were frightened . . . they thought they might not be coming for let us say morally pure reasons.

> (609): Well resisters [draft dodgers] were people who left for ideals, this is the impression I got, and deserters were people who couldn't hack it. It was almost like a sign of weakness whereas resistance was a sign of strength . . .

CANADIAN SKEPTICISM OF THE UNITED STATES

> When are they going to set up draft dodger seminar groups to learn about Canada from Canadians? When are they going to begin asking what they can do for Canada, for Canada's primary problems, because the Vietnam War is not the only nor even the primary Canadian problem.
>
> (Mathews, 1970: 10–11)

A large faction of Canadians resented not only the deserters but any exiled Americans on Canadian soil. Allowing Canada to be used as a sanctuary was considered a way to prolong the war. Professor Robin Mathews, a spokesman of the anti-exile school, wrote that by ridding itself of potential troublemakers, the U.S. could continue to run its war smoothly. The " 'Freedom Train' is necessary if the war is going to continue without serious civil disruptions" (Mathews, 1970: 10). Mathews argued that by channeling these men out of the country, the U.S. government saved a considerable sum of money. He speculated that it would cost $14 daily to imprison resisters; when this was multiplied by 60,000 (Mathews' estimate of the number in Canada) the total came to savings for the U.S. of $300,000,000 per year. (Ibid).

Other Canadians considered the resisters cowards and phonies. A Canadian writer states, "The 'religious pacifism' of many of the U.S. draft dodgers currently hiding out in Canada (many of the student activists on our university campuses) is not only phony, but they are of little value to Canada as citizens or patriots" (Young, 1969: 7).

> In recent years U.S. citizens have increasingly taken over posts that should have gone to Canadians. That is where the U.S. draft dodger is today. He is part of U.S. imperialism in Canada.
> (Robin Mathews, cited in Kasinsky, 1976:141)

Probably at the heart of the matter was a widespread resentment of any form of United States incursion into Canada. For some this meant the loss of jobs to these white collar immigrants. A faculty member at York University in Toronto, a Canadian, described a growing sense of nationalism which began in the sixties and remains very much alive today. He said, "A lot of your people come up here on their white horses, with their good school degrees, and push us into the bush. For a while our colleges wanted your guys more than they wanted our own and even though it's less true now, we can't get those jobs back. And it's not just here [the universities] . . . " An article in the *Toronto Daily Star*, January 25, 1971, represented this viewpoint by accusing the resisters living in Canada of "grossly aggravating the unemployment situation" (cited in Levine, 1972: 431–432).

A frequent charge against U.S. resisters was that they typified U.S. attitudes toward Canada. Resisters remained "only slightly concerned with Canada" (Mathews, 1970: 11). The *Toronto Daily Star* (December 17, 1970: 4) ran a piece on AMEX — a major exile organization — in which that group's five priorities were printed. The last item was "to try and fit into Canadian life." The *Star* warned, "Unless the young Americans for whom AMEX speaks revise their priorities and put Number Five first, they risk arousing a growing hostility and suspicion among Canadians."

Some of these feelings derive from legitimate responses to resister insensitivity to Canadians. This is evident, in caricature, in a radio talk show farce. The CBC presented a national broadcast debate between Dr. Mathews and a resister named Woodward. Connections were confused, and a resister from our sample ended up on the air. The resister picks up the story from that point:

(309) . . . and Mathews laid down his ridiculous rap . . . and Calloway [the host] turned to me and said, "Well, Mr. Woodward," who I wasn't, so I could say anything I wanted to, "I guess there's a lot of room for disagreement here." I said not at all. Dr. Mathews just doesn't realize what's happening politically. What's happening politically is us draft dodgers — this may give you an idea of the rap it was in relationship to this — we're latter-day Empire Loyalists who are organizing guerrilla bands to go back and overthrow the revolutionary regime established in Washington, in 1776, and reclaim the colonies for the monarchy. And we went on to point out how that would corrupt the Quebec issue by giving Quebec French Louisiana . . .

A first reaction to this story might be laughter; however, what it reinforced to Canadians was the condescending attitude so many Americans had towards them. Canadian charges about U.S. resister insensitivity were grounded to some degree in reality.

Combined with arrogance, resisters' lack of knowledge about Canada heightened the bitterness felt by many Canadians. One Canadian woman living in a commune of young Canadians and Americans, including a draft dodger, states, "There is a very basic ignorance about Canada among Americans. They don't know we have a Prime Minister and that we don't live in igloos." Some resisters readily admitted to a naive view of Canada before arriving. Among the examples, (307): "Especially being from the South, I thought it was . . . it had dog sleds and things like that."

Many Canadians contended that these men should try to fit in, forget the past. As one resister (Williams 1971a: 65) wrote: "Canada was glad to have them, but they must forget whence they came. They must not be political exiles." Another resister (Gosselin, 1969: 12) suggests the root of Canadian resentment was against Americans' holding on to an "exile mentality"; he adds, "The Canadian viewpoint is rarely if ever considered by those who would have the Americans maintain an exile identity."

This issue did not subside over the years. An article in the magazine section of the *New York Times*, January 2, 1977, illustrates its longevity. In anticipation of President Carter's amnesty, the article (written by Steve Grossman, one of the leaders of AMEX) points out that a number of resisters planned to return to the U.S. This article became the center of a controversy which exposed long-harbored Canadian bitterness. The *Toronto Globe and Mail* (January 7, 1977: 6) angrily responded, "Canada appears little more than a mailing address, a way station, a base of operations from which to pursue political activity all of which is directed southward." Another of the women living in the commune mentioned above bitterly commented on the article that "too many [resisters] never planned to stay. To them Canada is — just the ultimate camping trip."

One American woman (Kane, 1977: 13) who came to Canada with a military deserter and decided to stay on her own, wrote a response to the *Times Magazine* piece: "I can imagine how dismaying it must be for a Canadian to notice his or her country mentioned only as a convenience . . . " Referring to Grossman's statements directly, she added, "It is purgatory of his own making, as is apparent from his terming himself an 'exile.' Funny, I thought it was Lot's wife who was punished for looking back."

The *Times* article reactivated the bitterness of those who felt resisters used Canada as a way station. These responses fail to recognize that many resisters remained political refugees, rather than voluntary immigrants, throughout their stay in Canada. They came to Canada as a protest against the Vietnam War. The article intended not to insult Canadians, but rather to reassert that some resisters planned to return to the U.S. just as, for example, many Greek exiles harbored earlier by Canada planned to and did return to Greece when the military regime fell in that country. The fact that the refugees from other nations were granted relaxed immigration standards, and Vietnam Era refugees from the U.S. were not, remained a major bone of contention for some resisters. These refugees contend that they were singled out for not putting down roots, while other political refugees were not subject to such scrutiny (Personal communication with Jack Colhoun of AMEX, May, 1981)

IMPROVED RELATIONS

> (606): As people began to realize that the war in Vietnam was actually wrong, they began to be more sympathetic to Americans who came to Canada to avoid the war.

The preceding pages focus on the negative feelings some Canadians held toward some resisters. These negative attitudes never won majority support; a great deal of ambivalence characterized the Canadian response to these men. The government never really was able to arrive at any open official policy — another reflection of this ambivalence (Fulford 1968: 11; Williams, 1971a: 124). As the war wore on, Canadian attitudes toward resisters improved (Walz, 1969: 5). Two polls by the Canadian Institute of Public Opinion, taken in 1968 and 1969, revealed an increase in levels of sympathy by Canadians for resisters, rising from 32 percent (Colhoun, 1977: 15) to 52 percent (Kasinsky, 1978: 117–118).

Men in this sample offer three major explanations for their improved standing among Canadians. First, there emerged Canadian realization that U.S. involvement in Vietnam was a huge mistake. This, of course, parallels shifting attitudes in the U.S. shown in Chapter Two. Resistance was no longer viewed as immoral. That is, (615): "I think as Canadians got more and more against the war in Vietnam, I think their attitudes toward resisters got more and more pro"; and (608): "Well, as the truth about the war in Vietnam became better known, people . . . would express sympathy." Resistance began to take on a more noble aura; (306): "Resistance was — well, [the] respectable sort of thing." Even one of the Canadian women in the commune quoted earlier said, "I am more sympathetic to draft dodgers than to any Americans who come up here and take a job away."

The second reason was time. To one, (407): "Well, I think just being here longer tends to sort of reduce the boogeyman effect." Things simply grew less tense over the years as Canadians became (612) "more accepting that we were here." This acceptance was often credited to assimilation; for example, (607): "There has been an increasing acceptance of resisters as part of the social fabric."

Third, many Canadians saw the resisters establish their permanent homes in Canada — it was not just a way-station. Williams (1971a: 50–51) agrees with these explanations and adds that Canadians saw these men as an antidote to outmigration.

> (613): Well, I think it's mellowed out a little and I think that was largely because the resisters and deserters sort of melted into society. They did not take a high profile at all. They took a very low profile so there was nothing for the Canadians to dislike. You know, it just ceased to be an issue.

> (415): People are — feel a bit more positive towards draft dodgers or deserters maybe because . . . of the war and also because of the fact that most of them have assimilated into Canadian life and have contributed.

The War Measures Act: Wake-up Call

> . . . The fear stemmed from discovering on the morning of October 16 that the country chosen as a refuge and whose government [everyone] praised for its tolerance had suddenly, without warning, decreed a police state.
>
> (Williams, 1971B:15)

The acceptance these resisters had begun to feel was threatened in 1970, by a series of events that changed forever an innocent view that most shared of Canada. In October of the year, Quebec Labor Minister Pierre LaPorte and British Trade Officer James Cross were kidnapped by the *Front de Liberation de Quebec (FLQ)*, with LaPorte eventually executed. In response, Prime Minister Pierre Trudeau instituted the War Measures Act, which suspended civil liberties for six months. Searches could be made without warrants and people could be detained without counsel for up to 90 days. (See Emerick, 1972: 280–283; Kasinsky, 198: 135–137; Williams, 1971b: 15–18).

The people of Quebec felt the brunt of this Act. Two thousand raids resulted in over 500 arrests in that province. Some feeling exists that provincial and local governments across Canada exploited the Act as an opportunity to crack down on dissidents, including resister organizations. One of the first actions under the Act involved a raid against the Montreal American Deserters' Committee Hostel (Colhoun 1977: 21–27; Emerick, 1972: 280–283; Kasinsky, 1978: 135–137). The response of the mayors of Vancouver and Toronto, Campbell and Dennison, exemplify how the act was, or could be, applied. Campbell said he would "pursue American draft dodgers, drug traffickers and other types of criminals." Campbell had commented earlier of resisters, "If they won't fight for their own country, what are they going to do for Canada?" (Kasinsky, 1978: 136–137). In both Toronto and Vancouver, resister organizations were raided and many resisters detained (Colhoun, 1977: 21–22).

The formal interviews by the Vietnam Era Research Project did not elicit much direct information on this Act. There were enough hints in these interviews, however, as well as suggestions in the literature, to encourage its pursuit on subsequent trips. When probed many responded as (607) did: the Act "disillusioned me a little bit . . . quite a bit, I should say. I reverted to cynicism." Another (419) told me, "Until Trudeau did this, I was pro-Canadian — I had Maple Leaves strung out of my ears and was a big hockey fan then. . . it scared me, it scares me still." The wife of a draft dodger agreed, saying, "For the first time, I sort of realized that there was another side of Canada and I didn't like it." Another (621) considered it "an indication that the government can take whatever measures it wants." A military deserter (405) reacted in this way:

> I had just come to Canada. I don't think I had any idea of what Canada was. I was in Montreal. I was terrified. I had just been in the American Army and it was disorganized — there was no longer any discipline in the army. You come to Canada and they're crack troops marching through the city. I was fearful that my name and address would show up and I would be arrested and deported.

One resister, fearful of being deported at that time, took action familiar to many draft avoiders in the United States in the mid-sixties:

(615): Whew! I was very nervous about it. They had a little provision where the government gets a sort of immediate control of immigration. I was having trouble getting landed. The woman I was going with is Canadian. I called her up and said, Let's get married right away. She has never ceased reminding me of this. How much of an opportunist I can be. [They are still married.]

. . . A lot of dodgers and deserters freaked. They felt this place was unrepressed and free and all of a sudden disillusionment . . . all of a sudden the bubble burst.

What disturbed many resisters about the War Measures Act was its ready acceptance by Canadians. Public opinion polls showed widespread support for the Act, subordinating individual liberties to law and order. The polls even reflected support for extreme measures such as firing teachers in Ontario and British Columbia for discussing these issues (Kasinsky, 1978: 135). A resister said:

(405): I was really appalled by the complacency about it by Canadians, instead of things in the States where they — all the groups would be up in arms. Here they were rallying around the flag — at the universities, yet.

Most discussed the War Measures Act as either a threat to them or as a factor which changed their attitude toward Canada. Others, a definite minority, felt unaffected. To one (412): "It did not actually affect me so I paid no attention"; another (317) "was vaguely aware of what was going on, but I was more concerned with bread and butter issues." A third (609) was surprised even to be asked about the Act: "That's a strange — that's a really strange question. Why do you ask that one?"

For the majority of the resisters, the War Measures Act placed Canada in a different light. For a time it introduced a threat to their permitted existence in Canada, and for a time it raised questions about whether they wanted to stay there. When the Act expired, it gradually ceased to be a major issue. By the time of this research, only probing could uncover it.

Canada's Role in Vietnam

A general misconception, in the United States and in Canada, is that Canada only watched Vietnam from the sidelines. Canada in fact participated heavily in supplying equipment directly used by the United States in Vietnam. This connection continued a long historic process.

On August 18, 1940, Canada's defense industry formally became linked to the United States, when a mutual assistance pact was signed leading to the establishment of the Canadian-American Permanent Joint Defense Board. By 1947 this pact expanded to establish shared expenditures such as the DEW line, NATO, and the stationing of American troops in Canada. British-made equipment began to be replaced by U.S. materials: the Canadian arms industry became geared to American specifications (Culhane, 1972: 119–121; Resnick, 1967: 17–21). This relationship intensified further in 1958 and 1959 with the implementation of the North American Air Defense (NORAD) and the Defense Production Sharing Agreement. Canada's defense was linked directly to that of the U.S. and integrated into the U.S. economy (Resnick, 1977: 99–110).

By the time of Vietnam, Canada functioned as an important supplier of hardware for the U.S. military. Under the Defense Production Sharing Agreement, Canada sold the United States over $500 million worth of ammunition and supplies for use in the war (Kasinsky, 1976: 58). "Soft money" research plums for Canada were plentiful: "every university in Canada received money from the U.S. defense complex" (Wiseman, 1972: 40).

At a speech at the University of Toronto, then Prime Minister Lester Pearson responded to suggestions that Canada stop helping the U.S. in Vietnam:

> It is clear that the imposition of an embargo on the export of military equipment to the United States, and concomitant termination of Production Sharing Agreements, would have far reaching consequences which no Canadian Government would contemplate with equanimity. It would be interpreted as a notice of withdrawal on our part from Continental Defense and even the Collective Defense of the Atlantic Alliance.
>
> (Cited in Resnick, 1970: 110)

Later, under the publicly "dovish" Prime Minister Pierre Elliot Trudeau, Canada still could not bring itself to face the "far reaching consequences" to which Pearson alluded. The reason was obvious. As one Canadian observer (Grant, 1969: 63–64) writes:

> Many Canadians who are forced to admit the sheer evil of what is being done in Vietnam say at the same time that we have no choice but to stand with Americans as the pillar of Western civilization. Beyond this kind of talk is, of course, the fact that this society is above all a

machine for greed, and our branch-plant industry is making a packet out of the demolition of Vietnam.

How big this "packet" had become can be seen in one startling statistic — by 1970 Canada rose to the position where, per capita, it earned more as an international arms exporter than any other nation in the world (Wiseman, 1972: 40).

Very few men in our sample expressed concern over or even knowledge of this aspect of Canada's role in Vietnam. Those who were aware considered this another example of Canada's general economic relationship to the United States. Canada, according to one military deserter (405), "is nothing but a colony." A draft dodger (401) expressed anger at Canada's "holier than thou" image during the war by saying, "Sure, they weren't doing the bombing, you know, or even making the bombs, but they were, you know, designing better crosshairs for bomb sights." The U.S. incursion into Canada's war industry represents, of course, only part of a general corporate involvement by this country in Canada. More of this is explored in the next chapter.

SUMMARY

"Complicated" may be the word that best describes the relationship between Canada and the resisters. Draft dodgers were basically welcome; this influx of generally middle- and upper-class men harmonized with Canada's selective immigration policy. On the other hand, military deserters received less hospitality. The government, and some of the citizenry, made many military deserters feel less than welcome. This selective hospitality reflects Canada's tendency toward discrimination as well as a commitment to a sense of duty, which these men ostensibly violated.

Skepticism about anything American was most obvious in criticism directed at the general class of resisters. Usually criticisms were legitimate. When Americans started arriving in large numbers, some Canadians were pushed out of their jobs, or lost opportunities for new ones. The United States, which had always been viewed as stealing the young through the brain drain, now exported employment rivals. The resisters' alleged lack of interest in Canada further irritated some Canadians. Resisters were seen as using Canada as a second class "mailing address" while waiting out the war.

Criticism was not a one-way street; the War Measures Act of 1970 shattered Canada's rather pristine image for many resisters (although some were unaware of its ramifications). Others were aware of Canada's selective and discriminatory immigration policies. A small minority recognized Canada's deep involvement with the U.S. war economy.

These issues were eventually minimized as draft, and even most military, resisters who remained, meshed with Canadian society. The fact that most Americans were seen as staying permanently in Canada, coupled with a generally positive record appeased many Canadians. However, as the 1977 *Times Magazine* flare-up illustrates, the skepticism and resentment never abated fully. Eventually, most resisters began looking toward Canada, rather than toward the United States, as "home"; however, they were looking through American lenses. The following chapter focuses on what they saw.

CHAPTER **6**

Resister Impressions: The Canada They Found

Q. What have you found most attractive about Canada?
A. (416) The peace and quiet.
Q. What have you found least attractive about Canada?
A. (416) Can I say the peace and quiet about that too?

(607): I suppose I liked, I've always liked Canada's being a second-rate power and therefore, not taking upon itself to be the policeman of the world, the defender of all that's right and true.

The treatment of new arrivals in Canada was central to the previous chapter. This chapter reverses the analysis, and focuses on what these men found and did not find in Canada. Most arrived with either the popular U.S. myth that Canada represents a bland copy of the United States, or without any ideas about Canada. Most of these men have since dramatically altered their views.

CANADIAN IDENTITY CRISES?

Many draft and military resisters, like many Canadians, have trouble deciding exactly what Canada represents to them. Some Canadians refer to the "Great Canadian Identity Crisis" — a crisis rooted in the very great influences of both Britain and the United States on Canada, (Fulford, 1968: 12; Porter, 1971: 5ff.). A Canadian woman living with a resister smiled in response to a question on this issue. She explained: "For years people in Canada laughed at 'What is Canada?' There is no such thing!" Two draft resisters agree, saying (612): "The country itself lacks an identity — it lacks a point of view," and (422) "I think it's mainly that the concept of Canada wasn't all that clear."

To many newcomers and Canadians, similarities between Canada and the U.S. are confusing:

> Canada was a kind of myth to them, back in the States, and when they
> came here to encounter the reality they find — a myth! Canada looks
> so much like America that they can't quite believe they've arrived
> someplace else; it's kind of fairyland. The Canadians, they aren't quite
> sure their country exists. . . . It's hard enough growing up with the
> Great Canadian Identity Crisis. Think how much harder it is to be
> forced to adopt it.
>
> (Fulford, 1969: 12).

Many Canadians and resisters who subscribe to the notion of an
identity crisis trace it to Canada's history. The Confederation of Canada was formed in 1867 with neither a revolution nor a true break
from the British crown. Freedom was not won, it was granted: first
as a part of the British Empire, and later, in 1931, with membership
in the British Commonwealth. The very gradual split promoted a
Canada, at least English-speaking Canada, reflecting many of the
characteristics and values of Great Britain (Lipset, 1971). Porter (1971:
2) observed that "there has never been in Canada, as in the United
States, a strong commitment to the creation of a new nation, a new
ethnicity."

It follows, adherents of this theory maintain, that because of the
lengthy and drawn-out separation from England, and then the economic dominance of the United States, Canada never developed an
identity of her own. Many characterize Canada's history as simply
slipping from English to American domination:

> A central aspect of the fate of being a Canadian is that our very existence
> has at all times been bound up with the interplay of various world
> empires. (Grant, 1969: 63–64).

Many resisters arrived subscribing to the "Great Canadian Identity
Crisis." Ultimately their views of this theory, and stereotypes of Canada, changed dramatically. Resisters' views of Canadian history,
economy, world role, social relations, and government, consistently
involve comparisons of the United States. In response to the questions
"What have you found most/least attractive about Canada?" these
men refer to their new home only in relation to the country where
they were raised and which they rejected. The comments include
both positive and negative impressions of Canada, the latter elicited
primarily by probes. The factors behind these impressions are the
focus for this chapter.

Economics and Psychology: Conflicts about Autonomy

> (305): The U.S. owns 75 to 80 percent of the economy here. They control
> a lot behind the scenes.

The last chapter detailed the relationship between the military industries of Canada and the U.S. While many were unaware of this relationship, the omnipresence of U.S. economic influence in Canada, which goes well beyond this sphere, absorbs the attention of most in this sample. One resister states, without smiling, (602): "It's sort of funny to see the extent of the American influence here." Two others agree: (304) "Most everything is American owned. I mean, the big stuff, you know, shit, Bell-Canada"; and (313) "Canada is owned by the U.S." (For more details, see especially Culhane, 1973; Laxer, 1973; Porter, 1965; and Resnick, 1970).

Others describe U.S. influence in terms of its psychological impact on Canadians. One comments (306): "Canada is really just plain subservient to the United States economically and therefore . . . there are tremendous mechanisms at work to keep people from really admitting that." One (607) sees a "kind of complacency. Canadians are basically complacent about the fact that the U.S. owns 70 percent of the manufacturing sector of the economy." And others go further; (610): "They have an inferiority complex. They're always looking over their shoulder nervously at the States."

Many, in and out of this sample, depict a cultural devouring of Canada by the United States:

> Anyone familiar with the reading habits of Canadians knows that the handful of magazines and periodicals published in Canada does not represent the ideological exposure of the general population. Publications from the United States circulate far more widely than do those of Canadian origin. The consumption of American periodicals in Canada is an ideological counterpart of the external control of the economic system.
>
> (Porter, 1965: 465)

Some resisters share this opinion; (405): "I think Canadians are primarily Americans. They've been immersed in American culture. They understand America and they are part of it." A notably pro-Canadian resister (614) agrees; "Canada's not as much of an independent country as it could be from the United States. We get things secondhand."

For a minority this influence came as a pleasant surprise: (418): "I was looking for similarities and I found them"; (609): "Well, in all honesty, a thing I find very attractive about Canada is it's very much like the States. In other words, it wasn't like cultural shock."

The majority, however, criticized "the bland carbon-copiness of the United States; the invasion of American culture" (410). What these resisters found "least attractive about Canada is the sort of tendency for the Canadians to follow in the footsteps and mimic the United States in various cultural and social trends" (317).

Undoubtedly, the United States has permeated the Canadian economy and culture since World War II. But many resisters see beyond the mimicry, the U.S. influences, and identify unique aspects: Canada's world role, social attitudes, and government structure.

Canada: Not a World Police Force

> (615): . ... The absence of this national vanity in imperialist adventure. You know, a saving grace in a smaller country, but — it isn't going to send 500,000 troops to save the world because it doesn't have them . . . this absence of imperialist mentality.

> (312): . . . It's more of a mellow type of country . . . I think Canadians tend to take things calmer and the rest of the world calmer. They don't get that upset over what happens in the Middle East. And if something happens in the Middle East, they don't expect to send the Canadian troops in there or anything like that or — the same thing with Vietnam.

Canada does not endeavor to "make the world safe." Many resisters discovered that Canada, unlike Britain, and later the U.S., was blessed with (615) "a lack of any kind of world ambitions." Often this was contrasted with the United States; (618): "Oh, Americans I think are — are probably out to conquer the world, be the biggest and the best and make a — the most impact." Canada avoids the obsessive sense of manifest destiny of the U.S. — (610): "The people here don't have a feeling of greatness or mission that Americans have."

The U.S. ambition for greatness and the illusion that it has been obtained were missing in Canada, and Canadian troops were missing from Vietnam. Canada's lack of a direct military role in world affairs impressed most resisters.

Canadians: Calmer at Home

> (305): I don't think that the Canadians have the big ego that I saw people in the States have.

> (416): Canadians do not imagine that they are the most important people in the world, that they are the best, that they're the most democratic, that they're the most anything . . . Americans have been loaded with suppositions that they're God's answer to everything.

Hand in hand with the absence of an aggressive international or national policy, resisters find a more relaxed lifestyle, a calmer people in Canada. The winner-take-all attitude, so characteristic of U.S. westward expansion, is not seen as a part of Canada's history. One dodger (616) put it: "There was never a Wild West in Canada . . . there is a frontier mentality in the States that doesn't exist in Canada." Another (411) said, "Canada, I guess, is the first orderly democracy, built on order rather than revolution or some sort of civil war. It's an involved democracy . . . [unlike] the U.S. having a Civil War under its belt, and very much a violent tradition," Lipset (1971: 34) agrees, writing, "The Queen's peace was maintained even in the mining camps, which were characteristically undisciplined in the United States."

To many resisters this refreshing lack of national aggression boils down to a lack of over-intensity in the people. A draft dodger (616) finds that his "relationship with people is a lot easier . . . the pace is just a little bit slower" and (414) notes that "they are less violent." Another (618) says, "The most attractive thing about Canada is [that] the people here seem to be a little less intense, a little more tolerant, and a little more rational."

Intense competition, domestic or international, is minimized. Thus (315): "Well, you can feel relaxed here . . . I always felt guarded in the States", and (314): "I think Canada isn't as intense and even in Toronto I feel much more relaxed than [in] say, Cleveland . . . it isn't as fast — bang, bang, bang, bang, you know."*

Problems, while recognized, shrink on a U.S. scale; e.g., (404): "I guess it [Canada] seems to me so trouble-free as compared to the U.S." A military resister (402) states, "In certain ways Canada is an easier place to live in because it's — it isn't faced with 14 or 15 simultaneous social crises — economic crises." Another resister (609) feels, "Canada has a lot of problems of the States but not in as great intensity . . . the problems aren't amplified as much as they are in the States because of the larger size."

Often these men compare the American personality to that of Canadians. As one puts it (318): "You can hear Americans when they come into restaurants." Another (304) comments, "Americans are more flamboyant. In everything they do."

Others harshly depict American "directness," which Canadians found obnoxious. As one draft dodger (410) notes, "When I first got here, I ran into a real problem with people thinking I was arrogant. And I didn't consider it arrogance, I considered it direct, and Canadians perhaps are a little bit more diplomatic." Another (611) says, "Americans tend to be more forthright, they tend to be more assertive, I think Americans generally feel they're more important — 'I'm

---

*As an aside, whether positively or negatively stated, almost the entire sample felt that the pace in Toronto was much slower than in the United States. However, the brothers who were raised in rural Virginia and West Virginia felt differently. One (404) states they were having trouble "keeping up with the way everyone is in such a hurry up here."

an American and I'm important because of it' — whereas a Canadian wouldn't feel that way."

You Can Take The Boy Out of The Country But —

> (315): I think mainly it's Canadians, I don't know, they have a — they have in many senses, they have a real, a real talent for mediocrity. Sort of inoffensive mediocrity, but it's still mediocrity.

The international and domestic characteristics respected by most, dismay a vocal minority. To them, one readily becomes (312) "rather bored [with] the city of Toronto". It is (419) the "slowness of life coming from New York City. [I got the] impression that the projector has been slowed down by another 15 percent." And (309): "The energy level tends to be a lot lower up here." Critical of this slower pace of life, these men give somewhat negative descriptions of Canadians. One (618) maintains, "Canadians are a little cautious, a little too reserved and they can at times seem cold," and another (610) observes that "the people themselves aren't as passionately committed [as Americans]. I think they're more apathetic about things." The Canadian wife of one dodger concurs: "I find Canadians on the whole a bit too careful. Not willing to take a chance."

Some identify Canadians as (408) "much much colder, less reactive people and they're not as — as friendly, they're not as alive as Americans. From what I can see [they're] far more reserved." Others agree, seeing people as (608), "not as warm and outgoing in Canada as in the States"; and (607): "Some Canadians . . . in the cities of English Canada, tend to be considerably more reserved and colder than American counterparts." Or (700): "There's a bit of a stiffness, a stuffiness [among Canadians]."

Pro or con, the vast majority of resisters observe a different lifestyle in Canada in both external and internal nuances. For the most part, they respect and admire these qualities. However, a vocal minority has difficulties respecting or adjusting to these differences.

Government: Plural and Popular

> (307): The thing I find most attractive about Canada is that there's much greater willingness to consider public kinds of approaches to public problems . . . The good aspect of it is that it means there's a real chance to work for better programs in medical care, housing, workers' rights.

The form and functioning of Canadian government generally impress these resisters. Many see the powers of the provincial governments as (309) "very strong and I like that." In contrast to the United States, which in 200 years has experienced increasing federal power over individual states, Canadian provinces maintain substantial autonomy and identity, illustrated perhaps most vividly in French-speaking Quebec (Porter, 1971: 1) The principle was reinforced most powerfully in 1980, when the provinces banded together to defeat an Ottowa attempt to change Canada's charter in the direction of more centralized power — and perhaps most concretely in 1981, when eight of the ten provinces continued to oppose Prime Minister Trudeau's attempts to centralize governmental power (Giniger, 1981: A11). This led to, typically, a compromise, with, also typically, only Quebec remaining in opposition. The relative lack of power of the Prime Minister, compared to the U.S. President, establishes a solid check on governmental abuse; (421): "In Canada you have a system — he's [the Prime Minister] the leader of the party but the opposition is still highly critical . . ."

Many remark on the degree to which Canadian government caters to people's needs, again in contrast to the United States. (610): "The government is more responsive [than the U.S.] to the people" and (412) "I have written to Cabinet, Federal Cabinet, ministers, and gotten answers from them, which I don't think I could do in the States."

The most frequently cited virtue of the Canadian Government is the comparatively "better social welfare schemes and programs than the U.S." (415). That is (407), ". . . In terms of social policies it's more liberal . . . well, health care is the biggest example. I think also in terms of welfare policies and some innovative training programs and innovative employment programs." Some resisters specify the (408) "good health insurance program." For instance (310): "I would have been in real poor shape last week for instance, without free hospitalization and doctors"; and (307): "I had an operation a couple of years ago. It cost me 25¢."

The Canadian government represents more opportunities and advantages for those in certain fields. There is (612), "funding for the arts, by comparison with the United States where you have a private market [and] you either make it or you don't." As judged by (310), Canada has "a reasonable system . . . some provinces up here they have like, socialized car insurance and you end up paying $25 a year."

Some men berate aspects of Canadian government; e.g., the War Measures Act and Canada's military relationship with the U.S. However, when they compare the parliamentary and provincial styles of Canada to the "Imperial Presidencies" of Johnson and Nixon, Canada comes out far ahead.

The Climate: Urban and Centrigrade

> (306): One of the most attractive things that I've found is that I can live in this city. For a city this size, it doesn't have the sort of uptight feeling that American cities have. There isn't the kind of social unrest and tension that there is in the U.S.

Among the remaining varied impressions these men harbor of Canada, two themes emerge: absence of urban problems and the weather.

Concerns about personal safety are repeatedly offered as the reasons men would not return to the U.S. Resisters enjoy the seemingly safe atmosphere in Canada, particularly Toronto; (403) speaks of "lack of — lack of crime, pleasant lack of crime." Toronto represents (605) "a safe city, particularly after living in New York where crime was, for me anyway, a constant consideration." For some, diminished crime rates reflect the general lack of intensity: (403) "Well, Canada has about one-tenth of — of everything except crime and I think it's probably less than one-tenth."

In contrast, a few resisters anticipate that Toronto will become increasingly like U.S. cities, in one most unpleasant aspect — racism. Minority resisters felt unwelcome in Toronto. Most re-assessed their exile, and opted to take their chances at home. This problem seems, to many, to be intensifying. One military deserter (304) remarks, "Recently there've been some incidents in Toronto. Young street gangs beating up on black Pakistanis and Indians. That's the new quote National Nigger." Others agree adding that Canada is sadly catching up in this area with the U.S. As (621) says, "The racism is just starting to be very apparent here," and (314) agrees: "There's a certain amount of racial tension cropping up here — which seems to be an omen."

As the urban "climate" in Canada received mixed reviews, so too did the physical environment. Some enjoy (609), "the scenery, the wide open spaces," and (410), "the beauty of the country." Some describe taking advantage of the great outdoors:

> (405): Well, I like the vastness of the country. . . . I've wanted to go into the bush at least once a summer — canoe trips that are well out of the way. I've done probably all the major trips of the explorers that were in the fur trade and so that part [of being in Canada] is fantastic.

For still others, the environment poses drawbacks. Quite often men volunteered, "Weather," in response to the question, "What have you found least attractive about Canada?" The responses were brief and to the point, as with (605): "I don't know, the weather, maybe. The damn weather. Ya. It's cold man," and "I'm still not wild about the climate." Those damning the cold winters far outnumber those praising the great outdoors. In fact, the weather constitutes a major reason why a number of resisters consider eventually returning to the United States.

SUMMARY

Those resisters willing to look discovered that Canada exists as a distinct country, with a unique population. Resisters who stress either cultural or economic subjugation to the United States base their impressions on limited information. To see only these aspects of Canada obscures the reality; those who found only these parts of Canada missed a great deal. Those men who go beyond the surface are apt to offer useful insights about Canada, its institutions, and people. That these insights are based almost exclusively on comparisons with the United States is not surprising — after all, these resisters came of age in the U.S.

Many resisters praise Canada's role in the world. Canada, they note, is not driven by God or a national mission to make the world "safe". Canada remains as likely to avoid potential trouble spots as the United States is to become engaged. This same quality characterizes the Canadian people. Resisters depict them, in contrast to people in the U.S., as more mellow, less involved in a national "rat race." People in the U.S., on the other hand, are often described as louder, pushier, with a need and desire to get more done than Canadians. While most men in our sample uniformly portray Canada and Canadians as less aggressive than Americans, their evaluations of the difference vary. The majority find it very refreshing; a minority are bored and put off by the same qualities the others praise.

A related difference between the two nations which respondents identify concerns national government. Again most see Canadian government as far more responsive to people's needs, particularly in the area of services and funding. Regionalism is widely recognized and generally admired.

Despite the ever increasing economic and cultural influences of the U.S. on Canada, the "Great Canadian Identity Crisis" pales when resisters identify the numerous qualities which distinguish Canada and Canadians. Lack of world aggression is confused, by some, as a lack of purpose. Lack of cultural competitiveness is mistaken for lack of directions. Decentralized government is mislabeled weak government. It is often forgotten that Canada is a confederation, rather than a nation, by constitutional choice. What is totally incorrect is to assume that Canada is merely our little brother in the North.

On the whole, these men like what they found. What they respect most contrasts with their recollections of life in the United States. The nature of this study necessarily precluded gathering further details in this general area, since the emphasis was on questions more directly related to the U.S. and the Vietnam War. This chapter has investigated some of what these resisters were willing and able to discover about Canada. The next two chapters explore their desires for and abilities to become a part of that nation.

PART FOUR

ASSIMILATION: AN UNEASY PROCESS

Previously we discussed a rapid period of resocialization witnessing the transformation of all-American boys into war resisters. This section focuses on the resocialization which occurred once the border was crossed: comparing and constrasting the process for these Political Refugees to that of other immigrant groups.

Chapter Seven, "Individuals and Resisters: Identity Crises," concentrates on the time beginning immediately after their arrival in Canada. Individuals generally developed, for a short time, a sense of resister consciousness. Like most immigrants they were bonded by mutual dependencies. Never creating a united front, this resister consciousness was soon marked by schisms within the resister community: dodgers versus deserters, and those wishing to assimilate versus those wishing to retain an American identity.

Chapter Eight, "Assimilate or Return?" continues to examine the pathways of these men, up to the present. As the resister community gradually diminished in importance in most of their lives, the complexities of assimilation grew. Reasons for remaining in Canada, for many, were as compelling as reasons for returning to the United States. This chapter concludes with an analysis of the "clemency" and "amnesty" programs of Presidents Ford and Carter, respectively. Amnesty provided a litmus test for distinguishing those who wished to stay in Canada, in the abstract, from those who wished to stay in Canada, period.

Central to this section is the understanding that this is a sample of men I have called "survivors." These men have remained in Canada and retain at least limited contact with each other. In measuring assimilation, we are not measuring those least and most assimilated war resisters. Our sample excludes those who have returned to the U.S. and those who have disappeared into the Canadian woods (and woodwork).

CHAPTER **7**

Individuals and Resisters: Identity Crises

(617): A sense of loss at the United States that I had left behind. And at that point I thought, you know, that I would never be able to go back to the United States, that I would lose contact with everyone that I knew.

Earlier chapters established that the men who chose Canada shared a certain degree of homogeneity based in their generally privileged social class backgrounds. Nevertheless, they arrived as distinct individuals whose family experiences and routes to exile were quite diverse. Once the border had been crossed, these men were bonded together as *political refugees.*[1] This bond, at least temporarily, fostered a sense of community and interdependence among previously unconnected individuals. These individuals were resocialized as resisters.

FREEDOM AND DEPRESSION

(318): As soon as I crossed the border, I got out of my car and kissed the ground.

(701): . . . This big void . . . what the hell have I done?

General studies on immigrants, as well as specific writings on resisters, identify two reactions common to those who arrive in a new country. Depression or disorganization often follows an initial feeling of elation or jubilation. Richardson (1967: 6–12) identifies the elation as a response to the novelty of the new nation, a social freedom from obligations, and self-justification for leaving home. The subsequent depression, he writes, can be traced to culture shock, nostalgia, and initial non-acceptance by the host society.

Dr. Saul Levine, a psychiatrist who worked with war resisters in Canada, found that they too passed through these stages. He observed (1972: 434) an "immediate sense of relief," often "based more on fantasy and wish fulfillment than reality." When it passed, the feeling was replaced by a "sense of isolation, loneliness, and psychic pain."

Not surprisingly, men in this sample followed this pattern. For them, the "immediate sense of relief" often involved a lifting of anxiety — anxiety of course caused by threat of induction or being a member of the military. According to one draft dodger (406), "There was a great deal of paranoia building up, you know, and all of a sudden that was lifted and I felt safe." For another (408), "The draft was behind me and I didn't have to hassle about it anymore." This feeling may be best captured by one dodger who describes his arrival in Canada as (417) "having a monkey off my back."

Relief allowed the freedom to put one's life back in order; (304) — "I felt I could start getting myself together." There was freedom to move. "I could walk around. I could use my real name, you know. I could laugh and boast and tell stories" (633).

But freedom, for some, left a tremendous sense of trauma. The joy of arrival often gave way to a stronger feeling of depression. The natural question, "What do I do now?", was compounded by the knowledge that there was no turning back, and natural feelings like those of (418) "I was lonely," or (404) "I found it real hard to make friends when I got here."

For deserters in particular, this reaction stemmed from the real or magnified dangers of deportation. One (304) felt constantly "scared . . . I didn't know if you could be sent back," and for some the fear led to "anxiety attacks, almost physical anxiety attacks" (414). Even among the legally landed, depression, fear, and feelings of isolation emerged as common reactions.

It should be noted here that while most resisters arrived in Canada alone, a minority — in the case of this sample, 25 men (42 percent) — at least traveled across the border with one or more other persons. But for the most part, these men traveled with people with whom they were not particularly close: (304) — "Don't even remember what he looks like", and (607), who went with people he had just met, "They wanted to visit the organization in Vancouver and I was going anyway, so they gave me a ride." Some came with friends or relatives who would stay for only a few days: (313) "It was a weekend trip. My brother and I — we'll go a long ways"; and (609), "Well, he [a close friend] thought it would be quite a shock to be going by myself, so he decided to make the trip with me and stay with me a few days." In a few days, these men were left as alone as if they crossed the border by themselves.

However, an even smaller minority in this sample, approximately 15 percent, were accompanied by a wife or a girl friend. Some resisters were influenced by these women — "It was her suggestion" (605) — others arrived at a mutual decision, e.g., (612) "Well, we were in on it all the way — I don't know — we made the decision to come to Canada together and she was behind me all the way. She stuck with that commitment."

In addition, and this is often overlooked, a small but significant group of expatriate American women arrived independent of any man. These women often left the U.S. for political reasons similar to those of the male resisters. Although Levine (1972: 432) estimates the male-to-female expatriate rate to be about five to one, these women, also resisters, whether they arrived independently or with a male, played important roles in many resister organizations (Colhoun, 1972:53).

Unique Immigrants

Despite the feelings of elation/depression which many of these men shared with other immigrants, many distinctions characterize the resister experience. While none of these differences is absolutely unique to war resisters, their combination sets these men apart.

First, most resisters arrived, or were soon left, alone, without close friends or family and with little expectation that friends or family would follow. Of course other immigrants often arrive alone; however, they do so with the comforting knowledge that their isolation is temporary — their loved ones will eventually follow. The resisters had to face the fact that those closest to them were likely to remain in the United States. This knowledge only magnified the feelings of isolation normally associated with immigration.

Second, the resisters lacked the option to return to their home country without negative repercussions if things did not work out. Immigrants, particularly young single males, often arrive in the host society fully planning to return "home" after a season or even a number of years. Resisters could not entertain this possibility.

Third, the war resisters arrived without a shared sense of common identity as resisters. After arrival, they were grouped neither by occupation nor by neighborhood — although many did share houses or communes. Other immigrants arrive knowing that others share their history; they often live in the same ethnic neighborhoods and hold similar jobs, sometimes for generations. This lack of an enclave, past or present, again distinguishes the resisters from most immigrant groups.

In some respects the resisters had advantages which set them apart from other immigrants. They arrived from a nation which shared the same language as Canada. They also carried with them basically interchangeable education and occupational training as well as similar cultural trappings. The draft dodgers in particular faced few of the traditional barriers imposed on, and by, other immigrants. In this sense they were truly elite immigrants.

Finally, the resisters arrived as *political refugees*. They did not come to Canada looking for improved living conditions. The draft and military resisters left the U.S. because of the Vietnam War. They were not seeking new lives; they were rejecting old ones.

SOCIAL COHESION

Despite these distinguishing factors, resisters repeated a traditional immigration pattern. Most developed a certain sense of community despite their lack of a common past before arrival and of shared neighborhoods or jobs after arrival. In fact, the resisters are not unique in developing social cohesion without historic, occupational, or geographic ties. Fermi's study (1968) of intellectuals who migrated to the United States from different locations in Europe shows parallels with the experience of the Toronto exiles. Resisters and intellectuals chose Toronto and New York, respectively, as the hubs of their exile activity in the belief that they were the most vibrant cities in the new nations. In their respective cities, the immigrants sought out their own people for primary associations, quickly establishing a common identity where none had before existed.

Gordon (1964) demonstrates that cohesive groups can be formed even by previously unconnected non-immigrants. He too uses the example of intellectuals to illustrate that strong common associations, selected sources of information, and voluntary by-passing of the common culture can facilitate a solid sense of identity. At least initially, the majority of resisters chose to exclude themselves from mainstream Canada in a similar manner.

Sider, in his discussion of excluded peoples (1976), contends that a strong sense of group identity need not depend on traditional commonalities. The crucial factor is not history but rather a current "sense of rootedness outside the state" (p. 163). Indeed, this very bond unified the resisters upon arrival in Canada — their place of exile.

Role of Resister Organizations

If individuals enjoy no traditional links with which to build a sense of community, they must share a purpose for unity. For the draft dodgers and military deserters, this purpose was often transmitted through the various resister organizations, with 56 of the 60 men in this sample initially having contact with one or more groups. Gordon (1964) identifies three basic support group functions: *psychological security; refraction of the dominant society from the individual to the group; and the establishment of network patterns among previously unconnected individuals.* To varying degrees, the resister organizations served all of these functions for most resisters.

Psychological Security

During the early period of depression, confusion, or isolation, immigrants tend to rely on each other. Henry (1958: 827) describes a universal need for group support, with "every socialized human being" needing others "on which he can rely for approval and support." This functional aspect of a support group is defined by Gordon (1964: 25–26) as a "sense of peoplehood" — an answer to the fundamental question, "Who am I?" Richardson (1967: 13) stresses the fundamental need to be able to think in terms of "we" and "our".

Most resisters arrived alone, but through the resister organizations individuals discovered that they were part of something. As one (420) puts it: "I finally knew I wasn't alone." Another (307) found in his organization "a sense of being in this with a group of other people — that I wasn't alone up here." A third (414) learned to his surprise that "thousands have come over."

The groups' ability to alleviate loneliness diminshed the fear and insecurity many felt. Being in a group (414) "calmed me down. I was just panic-stricken." The groups did this in a variety of ways but in essence (312), "they encouraged me" and helped resisters become (409) "more confident".

Refraction of the Dominant Society

Support groups also screen members from outside pressures. A major role of resister organizations involved guiding men through the complexities of the new nation: a nation where some feared legal rejection; others were unwelcome, and all were scrutinized. The resister groups created a context in which no one had to face these pressures alone. Individuals were not the isolated targets of examination; Canadian attention focused on general categories of people — "dodgers" and "deserters". Or, conversely (Levine, 1972: 439) "When one dodger is arrested, the whole group is (metaphorically) indicted."

Such refraction provided a shield. The groups informed newcomers of the facts of life — Canadian life. As one states (622), "They sat me down and told me everything I needed to do to get immigrated." They provided (413) a "background on what life was like there, what to expect." The groups "gave me some pointers on, you know, how to survive" (406) and provided a set of rules on "how to play the game properly" (620).

The resister organizations were particularly useful in helping some exiles obtain legal status. For those illegally landed, the organizations provided expertise on how to leave and re-enter as a legal immigrant. Sometimes aid included lending "flash" money for the border; adjusting personal histories; and providing letters from sympathetic employers assuring the resister of a job. Much of this assistance was geared toward achieving the 50 points necessary for legal entry.

Some groups helped locate employment opportunities; they lent money and hired some men for part-time employment, or more accurately, full-time employment with part-time pay — "movement wages".

(313): AMEX [a resister organization] has a referment system where they had asked for people to volunteer rooms. Um, for rather small change — I stayed for three months.

Perhaps the most significant form of help in this area provided by the resister organizations was housing. While there were no resister enclaves, in the way Italian or Greek immigrant neighborhoods emerged, there were a large number of "houses" or "communes," to which newly arrived resisters were often sent by exile organizations on a "temporary basis." As (307) says, "I went there for the night — that's where I stayed for the next five or six months." The groups buffered; they served a resocialization role, and they channeled men into legal status, jobs, and housing.

Establishment of Networks

We have discussed how immigrants, and resisters in particular, generally arrive alone. Immigrant organizations traditionally serve as the first base for what Leeds (1964: 329) refers to as a "social genealogy." Barnes (1954: 43) demonstrates the significance of social networks which link individuals who know each other directly, and put each member "in touch with a number of other people, some of whom are directly in touch with each other and some who are not." For the resisters, Levine (1972: 435) describes these connections as a "network of support mechanisms."

The development of friendship patterns, often coupled with shared housing, could temporarily fill the void left by abandoned friends and family. With 56 of these 60 men turning to at least one of the resister organizations, it was virtually a matter of course that the organizations would cultivate their first social contacts in Canada. One remembers (605): "There was a little community of friends around." Many simply (315), "hung around with dodgers and deserters" or, at least, (313) "talked with those folks . . . well, about twice a week."

The resister organizations usually supplied the three important supports needed by these new arrivals. They calmed newcomers and provided a sense of community, undermining the loneliness and isolation. They protected them from hostile elements in society, and provided the basis for first friendships in the new nation. They gave these men what they needed — critical support. For a time, previously unconnected individuals were connected by their mutual dependencies as immigrants. They were indeed resocialized from isolated individuals into a community of resisters.

Limited Tenure

(313); [I was] very unimpressed . . . people were sitting around on the floor with bare feet and stringy dirty hair and so on. That wasn't my thing.

(404): I was in contact for about a year or so, but other people I knew left and went, either back to the States or various parts of Canada. So I left . . .

For most, the resister organizations constituted legitimate support groups. However, a minority of men remained in contact for only one or two meetings. Those who quickly severed their ties had come to seek help with a specific problem, usually gaining legal landed status — and then saw no further use for the groups. To them, the groups were nothing more than service organizations, whose (620) "main role was to facilitate the arrivals of immigrants, people like me." After such assistance, this minority saw (621) "no reason" to remain, because (606) they had "no other use for them." These men (413) "didn't think that they had too much in common other than the war," with those in the groups.

Personalities also alienated a few from these groups relatively quickly. Some simply did not like the resisters who were involved in these organizations. This is put bluntly by (420): ". . . Most of the people running them are assholes . . . [who] left a bad taste in my mouth." These men almost immediately cut their contact with the resister organizations. Most were involved longer. Few sustained high levels of activity beyond their first years in Canada. As we shall see in the next chapter, the need for such peer support rapidly dwindled. Except for a minority, continued immersion in, or even direct contact with, the exile community proved an impediment to a new goal: Canadianization. Paradoxically, the resister groups so important in resocializing these men for survival at first, were later roadblocks to change. That is, they "made the process of adaptation considerably easier for many, but on the other hand they ensured a kind of isolation or even elitism" (Levine, 1972: 435).

NO UNITED FRONT

To this point the resister organizations have been depicted as almost monolithic entities. This, of course, is not the full reality. Many groups existed with distinct political and strategic directions. The directions, at times quite divergent, created factional bitterness which often outlived the groups themselves.[2]

From one or two in the early sixties, the number of organizations in Canada aiding resisters rose to between 26 and 32 by the late sixties and early seventies, falling back to one by the time of our research. In the early sixties, U.S. refugees from the McCarthy period often led the groups. By the end of the decade, these people had all but disappeared, replaced mainly by resisters of the Vietnam Era.

During their numerical zenith, the resister organizations reflected much of the political range of the antiwar movement, from the barely liberal to the anarchist. The titles of their publications reflect the political tone of the various groups: the American Deserter Committee (ADC) in Montreal — *The Rebel;* Ottawa's ADC — *Ambush;* Toronto's Red, White and Black — *Alternative;* from France — *Act;* and from Sweden — *Paper Grenade.* Not all resister groups had such militant-sounding titles, as illustrated by Vancouver's *American Refugee News* and *Yankee Refugee.*

The Student Union for Peace Action (SUPA), established in 1966, was the first major organization in Canada to center its activities totally on incoming war resisters. Once loosely affiliated with Students for a Democratic Society (SDS) in the United States, the two split in 1967 over the issue of whether men should go to Canada or fight it out at home. SUPA represented the former perspective; SDS felt that Canada represented less than the strongest political stance.

SUPA, like many of the anti-war groups in the States, was comprised largely of members of the middle and upper classes — in this case, draft dodgers. Like many of these groups in the U.S., SUPA was not only nonrepresentative of the lower classes, but failed to understand their specific problems. As a result, SUPA erroneously "made the assumption that deserters could not legally remain in Canada" (Kasinsky, 1976: 109). (This sort of error was typical of much of the draft dodger insensitivity to, and lack of knowledge of, military deserter issues.)

In late 1967 SUPA experienced a series of upheavals which led to its demise. Specifically, SUPA's own integrity suffered when it was discovered that both Canadian opposition parties provided it with financial assistance.

The largest group to emerge from SUPA, the Toronto Anti-Draft Programme (TADP), was founded in late 1967. As the spelling of "programme" suggests, the TADP favored resister assimilation into mainstream Canada. Its energies focused on obtaining legally-landed immigration status, employment, and housing. It published the widely circulated *Manual for Draft Age Immigrants to Canada*, the Bible of immigration literature used by draft and military counselors as well as potential resisters in the United States. According to Williams (1971a: 67), the 1968 edition of the *Manual* was the first entirely Canadian best-seller on U.S. book charts.

The TADP was somewhat more attuned to military deserters than SUPA; military deserters even served as counselors from time to time. However, particularly in its early years, TADP repeated SUPA's largely class-based insensitivity toward deserters. The TADP represented a predominantly higher class draft dodger constituency whose publicly-stated goal was assimilation. In order to retain its rather favorable image with the Canadian public and government, the TADP initially did not deal directly with deserters, but referred them to counselors away from their offices. The often illegally landed, relatively undertrained deserters did not fit into the mold of easy and quiet assimilation.

The militant Union of American Exiles (UAE) also emerged out of SUPA. The UAE quickly differentiated itself from the TADP. It publicly dealt with deserters and openly protested policies of the U.S. The TADP argued that these stances would "rock the boat" and be counterproductive to the goal of quick assimilation. The UAE maintained that these issues could not be swept under the rug.

Perhaps because of its militancy, the UAE offered a relatively

short-lived alternative to the TADP. However, from the UAE arose
the only Toronto organization which would survive the Vietnam Era,
remaining viable even beyond Carter's amnesty. This group was
AMEX. While retaining the UAE's deserters and more militant dodgers as a constituency, AMEX offered an alternative to the TADP's
assimilation and the UAE's exile activism. This was underscored in
the subtlety of the change in meaning of the AMEX acronym; in 1969,
AMEX ceased to mean The American Exile in Canada, and became
The American Expatriate in Canada. While still urging activism directed toward the United States, AMEX also recognized the potential
for working within Canadian society. AMEX thus established a much
broader base than UAE.

The UAE and AMEX both recognized that counseling military
deserters was a much more long-term proposition than the TADP's
efforts with draft dodgers. Because of their often illegal methods of
entry and their more limited ability to pay for housing or obtain
employment, the deserters usually required much more aid than
dodgers.

AMEX and the TADP both descended from SUPA. Distance
nevertheless characterized their relationship. Much of the conflict
centered on the dodger/deserter issue. In addition, TADP received
establishment funds; AMEX did not. Some AMEX members in this
sample, as well as in other studies, charge that the TADP failed to
share resources. Others claim the TADP's fear of rocking the boat
made it more cautious than effective. One AMEX activist charges that
TADP went so far as to urge AMEX to stop mailing its magazine to
the United States, for fear that drawing too much attention to exiles
in Canada would change the generally receptive climate.

The root of the schism was TADP's determination to ease assimilation and AMEX's commitment to keeping the exile community
alive. One draft dodger (615) sums up the critical view on the TADP
as follows:

> TADP wanted straight counseling. They said keep a low profile —
> you're nice young guys — on personal beliefs, moral issues. . . .

> The rest of us thought we had a political problem here in terms of it's
> not a bunch of unrelated individuals. We needed, in fact, an anti-
> imperialist anti-war movement. We should in fact be in an anti-war
> movement for Christ sakes, we shouldn't drop out of it . . . a lot of us
> were young and militant and somewhat experienced anti-war fighters
> and the TADP said we don't want this public — you're not a bunch
> of exiles plotting like governments in exile. Don't get the TADP in-
> volved in sectarian politics which alienated the public.

Altogether resisters in this sample were involved at one time in over 20 groups, with many involved in more than one. However, among the many resister groups, none influenced this sample to the extent that TADP and AMEX did. Other important groups, particularly the various American Deserter Committees and the Black Refugee Organization, simply were not central to the men in this survivor sample. The remainder of this discussion, therefore, centers on the positions represented by the TADP and AMEX. The divergent stances of these two organizations on dodger/deserter and exile/expatriate issues illustrate the major schisms which emerged within the broader resister community.

Dodging the Deserters?

> (606): Personally I suppose I sort of resent [that] it took them [deserters] so long to wake up.

> (422): They [deserters] were obviously people who thought they were doing the right thing, but then they saw the light, and I'm all for that.

Dodgers and deserters often came from very different backgrounds. These differences were exacerbated in Canada by economics, social rejection, and the politics of some resister groups. Serious charges in the literature, and from some men in this sample, accuse the TADP of being unwilling and/or unable to deal effectively with many deserters. One deserter (304), trying to be objective, politely notes that some groups were "more cautious with deserters." Others, more analytical, include one dodger (406), who maintains that dodgers controlled the TADP and "dodgers as a group really don't understand the mechanics of the military and so in their realm of experience the whole thing of being a deserter, while sympathetic to that, [they] were not terribly aware of what it means."

Dodgers could easily obtain legal status in Canada and gain employment; deserters encountered more problems. The same dodger quoted above continues about the TADP's reluctance: deserters "were the hardest group to deal with, to get anything done for . . . [there was] a fear of the unknown." A deserter (405), understandably less patient, says, "I've seen a lot of organizations that did not know how to deal with the problems of deserters . . . and they would have trouble getting them landed. They [deserters] were not college kids . . ."

AMEX worked with deserters and anyone else unable or unwilling to assimilate in Canada. TADP aimed, predominantly, to accelerate assimilation. Deserters, lower-class dodgers who also had trouble adjusting, and men wishing to return to the U.S., could not be accommodated by the TADP position. AMEX, with a broader mission, absorbed these "more difficult cases" as well as those men wishing to remain active in the exile community. For this reason, AMEX remained somewhat unpopular among those resisters who wished only to assimilate. Also for this reason, AMEX outlasted other organizations.

Dodgers who express negative feelings toward deserters, almost to a man begin their statements with "I sympathize with them, but. . . ." These "buts" generally overlook the fact that many working-class deserters had to make military decisions at age 18, while the relatively elite dodgers could delay their moves until after college. Typically, a dodger states that he was "a little regretful that they didn't decide before going in" (607). These statements were too frequently echoed: (613) — "I am glad that they finally wised up"; and (618) — "I feel that it's unfortunate that they didn't reach the decision earlier, you know."

Some dodgers critical of deserters go beyond denigrating them as slow learners. In a group discussion one dodger declared, "People who came up as deserters, many of them, most of them, were sociopathic personalities as opposed to being political." Another in this group dismissed the possibility that deserters could learn or grow within the military, saying, "Deserters I know just couldn't take the army . . . how can you have a political revelation in the army?"

Dodgers sympathetic to the deserters were likely to feel that deserters had entered the military unaware, largely, of other options. To these men the dodger and deserter acts of resistance were the same; the only difference was time. One (306) said, "I feel that they did what they did for the same reason that I did what I did"; (406): "Well, they came up here for the same reasons I did. . . . the only difference that I see about deserters is, [the ones] who got drafted in the army were lower class, if not just outrightly poor folks, you know, who, as a result of that, didn't have a chance to get exposed to the sort of conditions that would allow them to articulate their situations . . . not really seeing any out."

Many other dodgers have modified their previously negative views of deserters. One (418) now says, "Just recently I've actually realized the racism involved and understand that and that has I think helped my positive association with the situation for deserters"; another (617), "I used to wonder why they didn't make the decision beforehand. I can't wonder that any more, because when a person is drafted right out of high school or something like that, they really don't know enough to make a decision."

Still other dodgers express direct admiration for the deserters, with many feeling that they themselves had got off easily compared to what the deserters had had to face, before and even after coming to Canada. Here is a sample of opinion from this dodger group:

> (414): I respect them because they had more at stake than I did . . . there but for the grace of God go I. . . . In general I'd say I'm — I have even more respect for them than for the average dodger.

> (415): . . . A remarkable thing, that — a very courageous act and remarkable in the sense that it shows a great resilience of spirit.

> (313): They've got a really hard row to hoe . . . generally getting a raw deal, much more, much worse than the draft dodgers.

Dodgers who did not share this respect often looked down on the deserters, who in some cases felt a certain bitterness in return. It would seem that, where negative feelings existed on either side, social class was a major factor. There were many other dodgers, and some deserters, for whom this ceased to be an issue as they moved rapidly down the road towards assimilation. As assimilation opportunities grew more and more available, the dodger/deserter split evolved into a new political division: those interested in staying or going back to the U.S. After the war, the rift was subsumed for the most part under this more salient schism between those wishing and/or able to assimilate (the TADP position) and those remaining oriented toward the United States (the AMEX position).

Assimilation or Cop-Out?

> (612): There was a whole American community forming of people who were waiting for amnesty and I wanted to get going with my own life. I didn't want to become part of a ghetto mentality up here.

> (405): Some people are unpolitical and simply don't understand or like politicals.

As the dodger/deserter rift permeated the resister organizations, so too did the split between those who wished to stay in Canada (*assimilationists*) and those who intended to return to the United States (*exiles*). Deserters and lower class dodgers were often forced into the latter category. For these men, assimilation opportunities were limited. For some others, assimilation simply was not preferred, with exile activity the more desirable alternative. With the ending of the war, the rift divided the sole surviving Toronto group — AMEX — from most who were trying to assimilate.

Once the large influx of resisters into Canada ended, organizations directed at rapid assimilation lost their function and faded into history. AMEX remained, serving as an organization for those who were not easily assimilated into Canada; a platform for those wishing to keep resister issues alive; and a force in the drive for amnesty. By surviving, AMEX became the center of controversy. Many of those fully or partially assimilated resented its existence; those still involved felt that others had abandoned their politics.

This rift grew most noticeable when the TADP and other assimilation groups were still in existence. Charges of sellout were raised by the UAE, AMEX, and various American Deserter Committees which existed throughout Canada. The exiles charged that assimilationists, after arriving in Canada, betrayed the political commitments they held when they resisted. Some argued that eventual return to the United States was needed to realize full political change. The exiles, the assimilationists countered, lived in the past, in a dream world, and should get on with their lives. To be truly political, the assimilations said, required involvement in Canadian politics because "that's where we live now."[3]

Among those resisters oriented toward assimilation, many criticized AMEX's very existence; (310) — "I didn't see myself as an exile in that sense of some little groups of Americans here. I saw myself as coming to Canada"; or (417) "I did not see myself as an American exile. Once I came to Canada I saw myself as — as a new Canadian." Another (611) aptly described (although failing to understand) AMEX and its members, when he said, "They weren't trying to make permanent adjustment to Canada . . . they would return to the United States when the opportunity presented itself."

The majority of this sample, while not so critical of AMEX, nevertheless separated themselves from AMEX's philosophy without open bitterness. A minority bore harsher feelings. One (318) refers to AMEX as "an American exile club. I'd had enough of that garbage." Another dodger (401) accuses the head of AMEX of being "like a general up here, leading an army that is not behind him." One draft dodger (417) argues that those who remained active, although a minority, got more than their share of publicity:

> There is the other group — those who have — have avoided becoming absorbed into Canadian culture and have maintained a more radical posture, who tend to live somewhat on the sidelines in Canada, [in] less of a — of an acceptable social position, this sort of thing. These tend to be the more vocal among the — among the draft dodgers, and

it's easy to assume that that is what a Canadian draft dodger is, and under these circumstances to feel either disgust or pity [for] these people, or, if you're of that persuasion, to hold them as being the — the true patriots, as they view themselves.

Those who remain politically active consider these charges off the mark. One deserter, not in our original sample, says that many just came to Canada "to cover their asses and when we get publicity, we remind them of this and they feel guilty." A dodger, also not in the original survey and no longer active in AMEX (but still quite sympathetic) concurs: "Whenever AMEX is in the news, it reminds the guys who are trying to out-Canadianize Canada that they are not Canadians — it makes them feel a bit like jerks."

Men who chose assimilation and are no longer active in the resister community contend that AMEX members used Canada only as a mailing address. By not getting involved in Canadian politics or culture, the exiles, they contend, simply exploited Canadian hospitality. One dodger (401) states:

> . . . They [AMEX members] lived in this little dream world, a gunboat parked on the coast off the United States. They weren't part of the political, the everyday politics of what was going on here . . . if you did a social network you would not find much linkage with other groups . . . AMEX didn't even circulate to other leftist groups.

Again, these charges were denied. In fact, many AMEX members became quite involved in Canadian politics, particularly with the working classes and French activists. Svirchev (1972: 34), an exile writing in *AMEX-Canada* magazine even charged that those who were assimilating were strictly men who "looked down their noses at the Quebec and Canadian working classes." Another (421) said "Sure, those guys [who assimilated] are active but they're only active in safe Canadian politics — they don't care about change."

Even language was a matter where the assimilationists and exiles found an opportunity for confrontation. A number of resisters readily admit to a conscious attempt to "fit in" linguistically. One dodger (617) describes how he and his American friends would purposely try to mimic Canadian speech patterns such as "ending my sentences with 'eh', and using the negative differently like 'was that not her?' " Another (401) reports a phase during which he used certain word patterns to sound more Canadian — "You've eaten, haven't you?" Needless to say, this brought a certain amount of ridicule from those opposed to assimilation. An exile activist (406) speaks of the hypocrisy of those who "tend to become super-Canadian, learn the words, all the words, to *Oh, Canada,* all the traffic laws, all the premiers . . . how to say certain things in Canadian dialect which probably a lot of Canadians don't even bother with."

One group of dodgers who consider themselves very Canadianized were asked about their frequent use of "we" and "back home" in reference to the United States. Asked to explain this seeming contradiction, one (617) responds, "If I make a slip of the tongue, it's because two-thirds of my life was in the States and it doesn't mean I am looking back," and another (419) says, "I used to be an American, by mistake." Assimilation to them does not negate their past; it corrects it.

AMEX itself facilitates this linguistic drift. In one of the early issues of *AMEX-Canada* (Kane, 1968: 2) as part of a three-part series on survival, definitions such as "chips" meaning french fries, "biscuits" for cookies, etc., were provided. What some call survival, others consider assimilation.

Some of the charges leveled by both factions seem valid, but many are stated as polemic. If many resisters were not committed to any major political action in their lives other than resisting — so what? As one deserter (405) states, "Well, their act of resistance was probably the main political thing that any of them ever did, but that is a lot more than most people." He is right.

At the same time, charges that the exile faction live in the past are as inaccurate. Those making this allegation may be denying their own past, rationalizing their decision or easier ability to assimilate. Active resisters persist as a disquieting reminder for those who wish to assimilate clean and easy. Feelings of guilt for not being active themselves undoubtedly compound the problem. Lewin's analysis (1948: 67) of Jews trying to pass as non-Jews may be applied to these resisters: "He dislikes or even hates his own group because it is nothing but a burden to him."

Nor does it appear that the AMEX members were living in an isolated dream world. Because of the very concrete goals of amnesty and strategies for returning to the U.S., they remained uninterested in establishing deep roots in Canada. However, this did not mandate isolation. AMEX established very solid links with progressive Canadian organizations. As one dodger (406) says, "Charges of setting up an enclave were unfair because they [the AMEX group] were serving as a forum for the U.S. community."

Criticisms that those wishing to assimilate were only involved in "safe" Canadian political parties also seem to be unfounded. Most joined the New Democratic Party (NDP) which offered a sharp departure from the Tories and the Liberals. While it is an established minority party, it is not the establishment.

SUMMARY

In this chapter it has been shown that for brief periods (of varied duration), previously unconnected individuals shared a communal resister identity centered around resister groups. The organizations served their members in many of the traditional roles of immigrant groups. The needs of the resisters were both similar and different from those other immigrants. However, their problems were magnified by their status as political exiles, their frequent isolation at arrival, and their minimal chance for return. For a time, most were resocialized as resisters.

The resister organizations had a rolling membership, consisting of both a core of committed activists and a constant flow of newcomers. Most resisters left the organizations after less than a year in Canada. With the cessation of hostilities in Vietnam, the number of Toronto groups decreased to one, and its membership sharply declined. Indeed by the time of this research, only nine in this sample were active in AMEX; only 11 claimed any contact. (Both these figures are somewhat deflated as 29 out of the 60 attended AMEX's last conference.)

The resister community in Canada incorporated a spectrum of political perspectives fraught by deep divisions. Bitterness still exists over the partly class-related issues surrounding the dodger/deserter rift; the question of whether or not to assimilate continues to create animosity.

NOTES

1. Although they were never granted political refugee status by the Canadian government, these men certainly qualify for this descriptive label. A discussion with Dr. Robert Laufer added much to my understanding on this issue.

2. Background on this material comes from the author's own work experience as a draft and military counselor; the men in this sample; and several printed sources (particularly, Campbell, 1970; Colhoun, 1977; Cooney and Spitzer, 1969; Kasinsky, 1976; Williams, 1971a.) Of particular assistance was a series of personal communications with Jack Colhoun of AMEX in the spring of 1981.

3. This debate is borne out not only in these data, but in many back issues of *AMEX-Canada*; Colhoun, 1977; Emerick, 1972; Kasinsky, 1976; Williams, 1971a; and again a series of personal communications with Jack Colhoun in the spring of 1981.)

CHAPTER **8**

Assimilate or Return?

Assimilation is a process of interpenetration and fusion in which persons and groups
acquire memories, sentiments, and attitudes of other persons or groups, and by sharing
their experience and history are incorporated with them in a common cultural life.
(Park and Burgess, Introduction to the Science of Sociology, *1924: 735.)*

What has happened to these men in the years since the end of the
Vietnam War? This question provides the framework for this chapter:
an analysis of the process of assimilation experienced by the men in
this sample. In this context, it is again important to remember that
those resisters most and least adapted to Canada would not appear
in this survivor sample. Those who have assimilated beyond resister
networks as well as those who have returned to the United States
were not interviewed.

The previous chapter examined the resisters' experiences immediately after arrival. Most underwent a short-lived period of "resister" consciousness and interdependency. Only for a minority, did
this consciousness extend beyond the first years of exile. The patterns
of assimilation pursued by and available to the resisters differ, in
many ways, from those of most other immigrants. They are political
refugees who faced fewer roadblocks in the way of acceptance in,
and adaptation to, Canada. The white draft dodgers, in particular,
were not stigmatized "immigrants" like the Haitians, Pakistanis,
black Americans, and many deserters. For most survivors, the discriminatory barriers which immigrants traditionally face were largely
absent. These men, who spoke the language, looked like "natives,"
and brought educational and occupational skills, were, in fact, welcomed into Canada.

Even the once illegally landed resisters, largely deserters, received an opportunity to build lives in Canada with the 1973 implementation of the 60-day *Immigration Adjustment of Status Program*. This
program granted to immigrants who were illegally landed in Canada,

legal landed status (independent of the required 50 points). Approximately 50,000 people took advantage of the program including nearly 2500 U.S. war resisters (Kasinsky, 1976: 200–205).

At the time this research began, 62 percent of these men said they definitely wished to stay in Canada. Legal status, the passing years, and the natural desire to become rooted combined to pull the war resisters toward assimilation, into Canada and away from an identification with both the U.S. and resister organizations. An additional force pulling these men toward Canada involved the distinct circumstances under which they arrived. Except for a significant minority, they came alone, without spouses, mates or family, and without expectations that they would be joined by these people. Since the resister community was predominantly, although not exclusively male, most of these men sought intimate relationships outside the important resister networks discussed in the last chapter. Seeking and obtaining these relationships added a strong pull towards mainstream Canadian society.

Concurrently, strong pulls toward the U.S. persisted. Some men remained "marginal" in Canada; others felt nostalgia for the U.S.; some retained a political commitment to the U.S. and others longed for career opportunities they envisioned to be available in the U.S. Once President Carter granted his limited amnesty, in 1977 (after the 62% figure mentioned above was derived), many reported second thoughts about "wishing to stay." Prior to 1977, Canada was, for most, the only realistic game in town; after 1977, remaining was a matter of choice.

Assimilation, as a process, takes time. For this elite group of survivors, the time required was relatively short. In the remainder of this chapter we explore this process for these war resisters, in terms of the complicated pulls toward and away from Canada, and the effects of Carter's amnesty on this process.

THE PROCESS OF ASSIMILATION

Assimilation is often divided into two major phases. The first, here called *Formal Assimilation*, reflects the extent to which an individual is connected to the institutions and structures of the new society. What is labeled here as *Social Assimilation* concerns the degree to which an individual is connected to the people in the host society.

In order to study the process of assimilation, social scientists have developed elaborate measures to assess the extent and nature of connections to the host society.[1] These measures, which trace assimilation processes and barriers more complex than those faced by this sample, are replaced in this study by additive indices loosely based on the same theoretical models. To assess the process of entering the host society, indices of formal and social group membership were created; a third index, exile activity, tests the winds that were blowing in the opposite direction — the men's activities directed toward returning to the U.S.[2] To supplement these indices, a number of individual items are used to determine extent of formal and social assimilation, as well as exile activity.

It may be argued that for those who desire it, who are socially invited and permitted, assimilation involves a linear process in which formal attachments precede social connections. Formal assimilation is easier for both immigrants and the host society. While it involves contacts in limited spheres, such as a labor union, the person still identifies himself and is identified as an immigrant. By establishing these formal connections, neither the identity of the immigrant group nor the fabric of the host society is substantially changed.

Unlike formal assimilation, social assimilation involves penetrating the host society, and leaving the immigrant group. This process, however, can be delayed for years, even generations. Even with extensive formal connections to the host society, an immigrant may remain socially sheltered in the immigrant group, through constricted loyalty, religion, friendship patterns, recreational activities and marriage. Only when barriers to social assimilation are lifted can the identity of the immigrant switch toward the host society.

The fact that formal assimilation precedes social assimilation is of course quite logical. First, most immigrants must become connected to some institutions if they are to survive. Second, despite those connections, one is able to retain, at first, comfortable, informal primary relationships and identity with the immigrant community. Third, the host society poses fewer barriers to formal assimilation than to social entry — workers are accepted; equals are not.

The history of war resisters in Canada, as political refugees, only approximates this time model of formal preceding social assimilation. As we will see, these men arrived with educational and occupational tools which expedited formal assimilation. Particularly for draft dodgers, restrictions on social assimilation were largely due to their own temporary reluctance to commit permanently to Canada.

The formal-social sequence which characterizes most immigrant patterns, therefore, does not as clearly hold up for the resisters. While time in the host society does facilitate formal assimilation, social connections develop less clearly along a time-line. An analysis of formal assimilation, social assimilation and continued exile identity follows.

Formal Assimilation

(421): I have a career in Canada . . . I have a few months to go before I'm a journey carpenter.

(612): I've got a career started and I can do everything here.

Three indicators of formal assimilation assess the extent of formal connections established with Canadian institutions. *Current occupation* and *educational levels* comprise the first indicator of formal assimilation; a *Formal Group Membership Index* comprises the second component; and *Canadian citizenship* or *plans to become a citizen,* constitutes the third measure of formal assimilation.

(611): I've got a good job now with a large Canadian company, I can begin to see some career potential for the first time in my life.

(310): I mean, I wouldn't fit into a lot of that stuff [music scene in U.S.] . . . I know how the Ontario Municipal Act works and the Metropolitan Toronto Act and so on. I don't know the first thing about covering New York City. Where would you start?

High levels of occupation and education achievement can represent either pulls toward remaining in Canada, or, as we will see below, toward seeking greener pastures in the U.S. Many with specifically educationally tied careers, i.e., in this sample lawyers, simply could not pick up and practice their craft in the U.S.

This survivor sample came to Canada well educated, and then pursued their education further once in Canada. At the initiation of this research, 34 men had at least a college degree. Similarly, these men as a group arrived quite profession-oriented and were welcomed with opportunities for professional advancement. Thirty-two men held professional or managerial positions at the time this research began. Once so established, it was very difficult for some to return to the United States.

Despite these rather impressive findings, the marginality of deserters resurfaces. Although this sample reflects only a slight deserter disadvantage in terms of formal assimilation, Kasinsky (1976: 194), with her much larger deserter sample, documents that deserters suffered three times the unemployment rate of dodgers.

In a follow-up on this issue, not only were a number of unemployed deserters located, but information was obtained about many more who had returned to the United States to try their luck there. Many of those who returned did so prior to Carter's amnesty program, preferring potential arrest to the economic marginality in Canada.

(421): There are a lot of names that come up of civil servants, people who are involved in politics that turn out to be dodgers, and they are accepted. They are not Canadian citizens. But there are no deserters that pop up in the news as having made it.

The Formal Membership Index provides another means to explore how these men connect to Canadian institutions:

–Labor unions
–Business or civic groups
–Professional organizations
–Political organizations
–Issue action-oriented groups.

This index measures structural connections to work, political, business, or civic groups. Labor unions are by far the most popular of these groups, with 22 men joining them. They are followed by membership in political parties, usually the New Democratic Party, with 13 men. Nine have joined issue action-oriented groups; eight belong to a professional organization, and only one participates in a business group. Of the sample of 60, 26 participate in no groups; 23 belong to only one group and 11 have joined more than one. These three categories are rated as low, medium, and high on the Formal Membership Index.

Obviously not all war resisters joined these formal groups. As might be predicted, draft dodgers evidence higher levels of formal membership than military deserters; resisters who arrived early tend to rate higher on the formal assimilation index than those who arrived later.

Fifty-five percent of deserters in this sample versus 41 percent of the dodgers fall in the low Formal Membership category. Deserters' marginality in occupational status is reinforced in their lack of formal connections. This again is substantiated by other works (Kasinsky, 1976; Levine, 1972; Williams, 1971a).

Even more strikingly than military status, time of arrival influenced the question of who could reach high levels of formal group membership. Thirty percent of the early arrivals (27 men arrived in 1968 or earlier) versus nine percent of the late arrivals (33 men arrived post-1968) score in the high category of Formal Membership. As predicted, formal assimilation, assumed to be the easier mode of assimilation, is facilitated by time.

Two factors shed further light on these findings. First, the early arrivals are significantly older and therefore more likely to be established into Canadian formal structures. Second, as a whole, the early group derived from a higher social class than the later group (when deserters and lower-class dodgers began to arrive in large numbers) and thus had a leg up in terms of Formal Group Membership. Both of these features contribute to the accelerated formal assimilation for the early arrivals.

(406): Right now there is no main advantage of becoming a Canadian citizen.

The final component of formal assimilation which will be examined in this work involves Canadian citizenship. In the case of resisters, this is by far the most complicated indicator of assimilation. At the time this research began, twenty-eight men had already become Canadian citizens; another nine were seriously considering it. Since then, another dozen have either become citizens, or started the process toward attaining citizenship.

With Canadian citizenship, one's U.S. citizenship is automatically revoked. Even after amnesty was granted, a person who had become a Canadian citizen could technically be refused entry into the U.S. as an undesirable alien. Many men, although they intended to remain in Canada indefinitely, therefore did not become citizens of that country. One draft dodger (700) describes his reluctance as a matter of "leaving one's options open . . . mainly I prefer long-term visits to the States." Another (607) states he would gladly become a citizen, "but not so long as they can keep me out of the U.S." A politically active deserter (405), who briefly returned to the U.S. with other deserters under Carter's discharge plan, was amused at the consternation of a rather innocent fellow deserter, who had become a lawyer in Canada. The lawyer was a Canadian citizen, unaware that there would be travel restrictions, and he "threw a fit when he found out."

One small group of men who definitely wanted to return to the U.S., or were seriously considering it, nonetheless became citizens of Canada. The reason, particularly among deserters, was a fear of arrest. One (421) described his motivation: "If you get into any kind of trouble, you get deported [if not a citizen] and I thought at the time that if I was deported, I would go to jail in the States."

Despite these complicated motivations, a clear relationship between citizenship and formal assimilation exists. Those men who ultimately became or planned to become citizens at the time of the initial research, tended to score high on the Formal Membership Index (25 percent) relative to the noncitizens (8 percent). In addition, those men who became or planned to become citizens reported a much greater commitment to Canada, prior to amnesty. Seventy-five percent of these men "wish to stay" in Canada, while only 42 percent of the others "wish to stay". This contrast is even greater today, as more men have elected Canadian citizenship. Indeed, citizenship marks a major commitment to the host country.

Formal assimilation has been described as the first step toward assimilation into a host society. The high educational and occupational levels imported to Canada by these survivors accelerated this process; as our time-of-arrival information indicates, the process still continues. These data, substantiated by that of other researchers, document that social class, age, and time of arrival pace formal assimilation; once again, the military deserters are more marginal than draft dodgers.

Social Assimilation

(616): I grew up in Toronto — I really did. This is my home town now.

(312): I feel attached towards Canada now.

The chief difference between social and formal assimilation is that the former deals with interpersonal relations while the latter reflects institutional integration. Newcomers who become formally connected can choose, or be forced, to remain socially isolated within their group. Social assimilation erodes this isolation. The ability to assimilate depends on the willingness of the newcomer to leave the past behind and the ability to remove the barriers imposed by the host society.

Four indicators are used to measure social assimilation: an analysis of *Social Group Membership Index* which measures involvement in social/community groups; *friendship patterns* which assess degree of American versus Canadian dominance in personal networks; *marriage* to a Canadian; and most important, *thematic descriptions* offered by the resisters for choosing to remain in Canada.

In exploring social assimilation, the factors which distinguish resisters from other immigrants are most prominent. War resisters in Canada lacked the security and isolation of an enclave. They did not live in the same neighborhoods as other war resisters; they did not work at the same jobs. Therefore, if they were to expand their networks beyond their initial friendship associations, their new friends had to be Canadians. In the even more significant realm of marriage or establishing new permanent relationships with women, most of these men had no choice but to go beyond their resister circles. Other immigrant groups consist primarily of young, unattached males. However, these men either expect to be joined by, or return to, their own people; this discourages social access to the host society. Resisters who did not come with partners had few such hopes.

Assimilation theory predicts that length of time in the host society influences levels of social assimilation. This is true for many immigrant populations, but not for this survivor sample of resisters. Unlike formal assimilation, those who arrived early were as likely to be socially assimilated as those who arrived later.

There are several explanations for this. First, age does not logically facilitate membership in social groups as it does membership in formal groups. Some social groups draw a young constituency (e.g., a sporting group); others attract an older population (e.g., a parent-teacher association). Second, resisters experienced a heightened need for social assimilation, compared to other immigrants; to make new social connections, they had to travel beyond their resisters' networks. Third, and perhaps most important, Canadian public opinion polls and government policy eventually shifted in favor of accepting resisters into their country. Aided by the trail blazers who preceded them, the men who arrived later faced fewer obstacles to social assimilation. For these three reasons those who arrived early have not out-assimilated the later arrivals, at least socially.

The *Social Group Membership Index* computes involvement in social and community groups:

-church
-church committee
-fraternal lodge
-parent-teacher association
-youth group
-community center
-neighborhood association
-social or card-playing group
-sporting club
-country club
-charity club.

This sample of men includes few "joiners" of social groups. With no more than six men belonging to any one kind of group, community centers and neighborhood associations are the most popular. Overall, 37 men belong to no group; 14 have joined only one, and 9 participate in more than one group.

Most interesting, among this sample of resisters, a greater proportion joined at least one formal group than joined at least one social group (57 percent versus 38 percent respectively). Despite the need for social contacts, formal assimilation seems to be more central to survival, explaining the different levels of joining behavior.

Beyond group membership, at the heart of social assimilation are the resisters' primary relationships: friends and spouses. Friendship patterns perhaps best indicate the degree to which these men left their resister enclaves and moved toward Canadianization. Despite the fact that this sample was obtained by snowballing from resisters, and therefore these men were at least somewhat connected, 68 percent of these resisters report that over half their "best friends" are Canadian. This trend holds true for dodgers and deserters; for men who arrived early and men who arrived later.

Shifting friendship patterns away from one's immigrant support group to members of the host society fosters social assimilation and precipitates a shift in self-identification. Whether by choice or by the lifting of social barriers, "they" become "we". As one says:

> (422): A lot of my attitudes . . . are not American attitudes anymore. They are Canadian.

Marriage to a Canadian obviously represents an even more intimate form of social assimilation. Eighteen resisters were married to Canadians at the beginning of this research; more are now. For these men, and at least the 15 more who were living intimately with Canadian men or women, the line toward "amalgamation" had been crossed. The several men who have Canadian children, in particular, are firmly enmeshed in the social fabric of their new nation. One (622) associates his new identification as a Canadian with "personal commitments and affairs of the heart in Canada."

> (305): If I would go back to Virginia, I probably would have been shot after. I'd have to go back armed if I went.

Earlier we described the job-related reasons why men chose to remain in Canada. Social reasons were even more frequently cited. Many wish to stay primarily because they have found personal happiness. One resister (618) simply says, "I like it here," and another (417) feels that "there is considerably less tension in Canada . . . well, greater awareness of what it means to live in the world, and I think personally a greater respect for . . . human beings."

Some present very positive reasons for remaining in Canada: (422) "I'm a Canadian now." More reflect on the societal differences between Canada and the U.S., presented in Chapters Three and Four. For instance, (314) states: "There are very few places in Toronto that you can walk that you have to be afraid for your life. You know . . . there are places in Cleveland, you drive through with a tank and you're still worried about seeing the end of the street." Another (412), agrees: "My wife and I can walk around any place in the city [Toronto] any time, day or night, relatively freely without any hassles. And you can't say that for many places in the States."

Others express fear that they would not be welcomed back. U.S. attitudes would impose social or economic marginality at home. For instance, a dodger (325) feels, "With my record as a draft resister . . . many, many Americans still strongly disagree." A dodger (416) puts it that "Americans are no longer aware of their responsibilities in a democracy. And they're no longer willing to have individuals in their midst. They want, what the nation as a whole wants, really wants, the majority of the nation, is conformity."

Others are sharply critical of Americans. In the words of (422), "God knows I would never go back to my home state, it's an awful place. . . . There's no challenge to a jerkwater factory town." Along these lines, another (311) finds, "I just didn't want to be surrounded by Midwesterners at any rate, who think God is white. I find Midwesterners so provincial."

Finally, a dodger (613) seems to capture many of these subthemes associated with social assimilation:

> I just don't like by and large the pace of life there. I think people are too caught up — if you can make such broad generalizations about 200 million people — with some of the wrong things. I don't like the direction society is taking . . . an excessive concern for commercialism. Money is too important. Business is too important. The military is too important. Politically the American government certainly needs a big overhaul . . . it's, well a police state is much too strong a term to use, but you know what I mean. When you have situations where the FBI is busy infiltrating everybody that they can, I find it distasteful.

Formal and social assimilation cannot be assumed to be natural and ongoing. One's age, social class, and the host society's public opinions affect the pace and breadth of assimilation, and the potential for it. Yet another factor affects the assimilation process for war resisters: exile orientation. Immigration does not automatically promote a one-way road to assimilation. In the next section we examine the factors which tempt men to return to the United States.

EXILE ORIENTATION

> (623): I cherish the United States. I like the people, I love the country too. You know, I'm not big on flags and shit, but I love the country and I want to be there. It means something to me spiritually.

> (609): I would go back because of the weather.

The fact that these men are political refugees distinguishes them from other immigrants. They chose Canada in rejection of the Vietnam War. They did not seek Canada as a "promised land" but rather as an escape from broken promises. As time wore on, many retained the hope of returning to the U.S.; most came to view Canada as a preferable residence for the reasons already discussed. Even for the men most committed to Canada, totally severing their relations with the U.S. proved most difficult.

For our purposes, exile orientation involves those actions taken by resisters to retain their connection to the U.S. Such a perspective on immigrant groups is too often overlooked, on the assumption that all immigrants want only to assimilate and that once immigration has occurred, there is no turning back. This view ignores those people who are unwilling, unable, or unsure about assimilating into the host society.

Exile orientation is explored here by examining four aspects of exile life: *current friendship patterns; original and current membership in exile organizations; levels of exile activity,* and *expressed desire to return to the U.S.* Using these varied measures of exile orientation, one finds only minimal evidence of exile-oriented behavior for only a small core of resisters.

Earlier it was stated that 68 percent of these men report friendship patterns dominated by Canadians (*over* 50 percent of friends are Canadian). Conversely, one third of the sample retains friendship patterns of which *at least* 50 percent are American. This latter group substantiates the presence of an exile core. Over twice as many men have American-based friendships (32 percent) as are active in AMEX, the exile organization (15 percent). Letting go of organizations appears to be easier than letting go of people. This is the natural inverse of our discussion of assimilation in which linking to organizations precedes linking to new social groups.

To further explore exile orientation, an Exile Activity Index was constructed, consisting of the following items:

> –exile organization membership
> –exile organization contact and
> –did you vote in the U.S. in the last presidential election?

By examining the pattern of responses to these items, as a composite, the varied levels of exile activity can be deduced. In Chapter Seven, political stances of the resister organizations toward assimilation were discussed; "exile" and "assimilation" oriented groups were identified. Of the 47 men initially involved with assimilation groups, only six (13 percent) retain membership and only 9 maintain any form of contact (19 percent) with AMEX, the sole surviving group. Of the 17 who were initially involved with exile groups, seven (41 percent) retain membership and eight (47 percent) maintain some contact. Although the exile groups attracted fewer people in this sample from the start, their drop-off rate was considerably less than that of the assimilation groups, as illustrated in Table 8-1.

As stated in the previous chapter, AMEX survived largely because organizations oriented toward assimilation served a gradually reduced purpose. Assimilation groups attracted those men who could most easily merge into Canadian society. AMEX attracted both those individuals who wished to return to the U.S. and those who were not as easily accepted into Canadian society. AMEX has survived beyond all other groups because the needs that originally attracted men to exile groups persist. In fact, almost half of the men who initially joined an exile-oriented group retained contact at the time of this research. Certainly an exile core has survived.

It must be pointed out that others, many who claim no contact with AMEX, nevertheless turn to it on occasions of need — specifically over immigration problems, information about amnesty, and family matters. For instance, one resister (607) got in touch because his "mother was sick and I wanted to find out how I might be able to visit her." In all, 29 of this sample of 60 showed up at the last AMEX Conference. The need for a support group may have dwindled, but it has not disappeared.

Voting in the U.S. indicates further retention of a U.S. political orientation — some exiled resisters could legally vote by absentee ballot in the U.S. elections. Only four exercised this option in the last pre-amnesty Presidential election. Many were no longer interested; others were skeptical of all candidates. The four who did vote reflect one "exile" stance of trying to affect political change in the U.S.

The Exile Activity Index, consisting of the items identified above, was constructed to distinguish those involved in exile-oriented activity. Not surprisingly, 70 percent of these resisters are involved in *no* exile-related activity. As expected, time in the host society and dodger

Table 8-1 Original Organizations by Current Contact and Current Membership in Exile Group (AMEX)

	Exile	Assimilationist
Contact (N = 11)	47%	19%
Membership (N = 9)	41	13
	(N = 17)	(N = 47)

status negatively predict exile activity. Comparing early arrivals to late arrivals, 22 percent of the former versus 37 percent of the latter participate in at least one aspect of exile activity. Time proves to be somewhat of a broker for assimilation, and a brake on exile identity.

Military status also affects one's exile activity. From the beginning, deserters were more exile-oriented than dodgers: 46 percent of the deserters initially joined exile groups, versus 24 percent of the dodgers. These initial proclivities have endured. Deserters report much greater exile activism than dodgers. Forty-six percent of the deserters, compared to 27 percent of the dodgers, participate in at least one exile activity. (This finding would be even more dramatic with a larger pool of deserters.)

The existence of an exile core may reflect marginality: self-imposed or created by a lack of Canadian opportunities. Returning to the U.S. remains a hope for many who find themselves on the periphery of Canadian society. A large group of resisters remains marginal to Canadian society, but not by choice. While they are underrepresented in this sample of survivors, these men were never permitted the opportunity to assimilate fully, because of their racial, social class, and/or military status backgrounds. Many of these men returned to the U.S. prior to amnesty, accepting the potential consequences of bad paper discharge or imprisonment, rather than remaining in Canada.

Some resisters elect to be marginal. Those who always intended to return to the U.S. chose not to establish deep roots in Canada. In this sample, evidence of a tight exile community is demonstrated by those who retain American friends, are still members of AMEX, and those who report contact with AMEX. Their exile activity involved their continued struggle for amnesty. Once amnesty was granted, many of these men intended to return to the U.S., and most of them have in fact returned.

> (602): . . . I have very deep roots and emotional ties in the part of the country I came from, Deep South. I miss it . . .

> (622): I do miss that — that spirit of the States — that enthusiasm . . . I mean, there's a thing about home, I don't feel here.

Other resisters remain marginal to Canadian society, again by choice, because of their strong social roots in the U.S. They miss their families, their traditions, and the American lifestyle, and long to return.

A dodger (316) was going to return because of "family ties . . . I miss my family", and another (611) expressed the possibility of going back in those terms: "I have a lot of friends in the States." One (408) is concerned with losing the continuity of generations, saying, "My children, I would like them to see their grandparents and other relatives more often."

A different form of cultural longing was described by the only black deserter (409) in the sample. (He too has since returned.) He felt excluded from the largely white resister community and the black West Indians in Toronto. He wanted to go back because "I like American black people . . . I like American blacks in general, I like American black women."

Those who wished to return to the U.S. because of these forms of marginality must be distinguished from those who wished to return to the U.S. because of economic opportunities. These men, as stated in earlier chapters, are perhaps the most Canadian of all. Like many Canadians, they see more opportunities to the south, and wish to emigrate to the U.S. to advance their professional lives.

During the structured interviews, a few men discuss returning to the States for employment opportunities; for example, (309): "If I got a job in the States, I'd take the job in the States," or (413): "If I was offered a really . . . be offered a job which I'm really interested in down there." For the more ambivalent, return hinged on specific occupations. They would go only as a last resort. For instance, (615): "If I finished my Ph.D. and the only teaching job in my field opened up in the States, then I'd really consider it," or (304), who would go back "only if my career took me there. Say, if I found my art would be accepted a lot quicker than here."

However, slightly over a year later, with amnesty, more men considered returning to the U.S. for occupational reasons. If the jobs were there, these men would go, without the hesitation expressed a year earlier; (412): "I'd grab an academic appointment," and (401): "I would gladly return to the United States for employment opportunities in the educational field."

Before Carter's amnesty, 23 men (38 percent) were interested in, or considering returning to the U.S. Nine (15 percent) of the men stated definitely that they wanted to go back to the United States; another 14 (23 percent) were still deciding. Not surprisingly, draft dodgers and military deserters differed in their desire to return to the U.S. Only 35 percent of these dodgers (as opposed to 55 percent of the deserters) either definitely wished to return to the U.S. or were unsure about their plans. The greater obstacles encountered by deserters clearly contributed to their lower level of commitment to Canada.

The reasons for returning to the U.S. notwithstanding, most of these men (like most resisters) had decided, or were leaning toward a decision, to remain in Canada. This commitment to Canada became clearer and less questionable once Carter's amnesty failed to open the flood gates for returning resisters.

PUSHES AND PULLS

To this point we have independently considered pulls toward and away from Canada. What has been neglected is the fact that many concurrently experience both pushes toward the U.S. and pulls toward Canada. Indicative of this are the 14 men (23 percent) who, even prior to Carter's amnesty, remained unsure about whether they "wished to stay" in Canada.

Most of these men leaned toward permanent residence in Canada with assimilation into Canadian society. However, this did not in their minds, preclude exile-oriented activities. Some men who rated high in terms of formal and social group membership also reported exile-oriented activities. Thirty-four percent of the men scoring high on formal membership versus 15 percent of the men low on this index are exile-oriented. Likewise, 45 percent of the men high in social group membership versus 27 percent low on this index are exile-oriented. To be exile-oriented does not require a rejection of Canadian society. In fact, a significant proportion of those most connected to Canadian society participate in exile-oriented functions. These findings suggest that these active resisters pursue two seemingly conflicting directions at the same time. Many remain conflicted about other aspects of formal assimilation, such as whether to establish Canadian citizenship or pursue Canadian career opportunities. Others struggle with the often impossible task of planting new social roots while maintaining old ones.

Before amnesty was granted, most of these conflicts could not be resolved in ways other than remaining in Canada or returning to the U.S. to face punitive consequences. Once amnesty was granted, and more varied choices were available, many men began to reassess their positions. The final section of this chapter explores the impact of amnesty on these men, Canada, and the U.S.

Amnesty: Same Stacked Deck

(405): There was nothing magnanimous about Carter's amnesty program. It was very conservative. It was the least that he could do. Deserters are discriminated against on the basis of class and race. Deserters are still given bad paper discharges. Deserters are lower-class and still are being made to pay for it.

(The Canadian Wife of a Resister): The fact that they chose to be discriminatory in something that was supposed to be the last final act to start the healing process . . . showed that amnesty was just another American snow job.

Before the option of amnesty, most draft dodgers and military deserters could not realistically consider returning to the United States.[3] Not until 1977 was a *true* amnesty granted. And this amnesty was *true* to 300 years of discrimination, rather than to justice.

Dr. Saul Levine, a psychiatrist who spent a great deal of time working with war resisters, writes (1972) that the uncertainty of amnesty increased the psychological stresses experienced by these men. In this work, and in a follow-up interview (Colhoun and Jones, 1974), Levine details the pressures which amnesty could introduce. For instance, he describes the professional who completed his Canadian education, began a career in Canada, and married a Canadian. With amnesty, this resister suddenly faced pressures from his family to return "home," as well as new options for career advancement in the United States. A once unattainable option would suddenly force a harsh decision.

On the other hand, almost all resisters expected, eventually, some form of amnesty. This expectation, too, provoked stress. Until the time of actual amnesty, Levine notes (Ibid: 44) that the resisters "are subject to a continuing and potentially detrimental ambivalence, as long as the question of returning home is not resolved." The prospects of amnesty involved both hope and stress. Indeed the question "Do you wish to remain in Canada?" could not be answered realistically until the choice was available.

American Civil Liberties Union: . . . We consider this "clemency" program . . . offensive in its moral and political assumptions and outrageous in its implementation. The Ford "Clemency" program is worse than no amnesty at all. It is punitive and demeaning . . .
(Cited in Kasinsky, 1976: 257)

In 1974, President Ford complemented his full and absolute pardon of Richard Nixon with a shallow "clemency" program for five categories of persons from the Vietnam Era:

- –convicted draft violators
- –convicted deserters
- –convicted AWOLs
- –unconvicted selective service violators
- –unconvicted veterans with less-than-honorable discharges.

Nixon was allowed to get off free; the resisters had major strings attached to "clemency," including a required maximum 24 months' alternative service for both returning dodgers and deserters. Military deserters were initially granted an "undesirable discharge". After a cumbersome case-by-case review, these discharges could be up-graded to a "clemency discharge" under "other than honorable" conditions, precluding the reception of veterans' benefits (Baskir and Strauss, 1978; Kasinsky, 1976).

After two extensions, even the government admitted that its "clemency" program failed. Approximately 20 percent of the 350,000 eligibles took "advantage" of it before it stumbled to a halt in Sep-tember 1975. These were mostly men in the United States, not exiles (Baskir and Strauss, 1978; Colhoun, 1977: 46–47).

The reasons for the program's failure were simple. The majority of those eligible considered the 24-month alternate service and the still punitive discharge for deserters, to be not clemency, but pun-ishment. An international conference of exiles held in Toronto in September 1974 urged boycotting of the program. The boycott was very successful (Efaw, 1975; Kasinsky, 1976).

President Ford's clemency had little effect on the war resisters in Canada. It failed to offer an acceptable option for those men wish-ing to return to the U.S. The 24 months alternative service was viewed as punishment for an action which those in exile felt deserved praise.

A central thesis of this work is that historically, socio-economic class has influenced men's opportunities into and out of the military. This influence, of course, continued beyond the Vietnam Era, and was reinforced dramatically in President Jimmy Carter's "uncondi-tional" amnesty. President Carter proclaimed what amounted to a first and second class amnesty in 1977 (for greater details see *AMEX-Canada*, Vol. 6, No. 2: 7; Halloran, 1977: 11; Laufer, Sloan, Joyce and Surrey, 1981). In January he granted draft dodgers an unconditional amnesty, providing they had no other charges pending against them. This act covered almost all the dodgers in our sample, as well as the vast majority of those residing both in Canada and elsewhere.

Later that year, Carter implemented a limited two-stage pardon for deserters — again if no other charges were pending against them. The first stage provided a less-than-honorable discharge, followed by a possible second stage discharge upgrade. The second stage was contingent on a case-by-case review. Under this program, the less-than-honorable discharge both *prevented* deserters from cleaning the slate and specifically *barred* them from obtaining the Veterans Admin-istration benefits which other men (not deserters) with less-than-hon-orable discharges received.

The comparatively higher class dodgers *automatically* received what amounted to a blanket amnesty, with no blemish on their rec-ords. Deserters, generally representative of lower classes, *had to apply* for a limited pardon which institutionalized punitive actions. Because of the "no-other-charges-pending" provision, only 4,200 deserters proved eligible for Carter's program. Of these, less than one-quarter were actually processed with less-than-honorable discharges. Carter's "amnesty" also included a possible case-by-case upgrade for 430,000 bad-paper non-deserters — again those from comparatively lower class backgrounds. Only 16,227 benefited from this complicated procedure (*AMEX-Canada*, Vol. 6, No. 2: 7; Halloran, 1977: 11; Personal Communication John Landow, Staff Attorney, *Central Committee for Conscientious Objectors*).

The distinction between the automatic amnesty for dodgers and the "need to apply" catch for deserters has remained. In May of 1981, four years after Carter's program, John Gonzales, an Air Force deserter, was arrested while visiting Alaska from Canada. He was eventually permitted to submit his resignation from the military, and allowed to go, after spending several weeks in jail. Had he been a draft dodger, he would not have been detained (Toth, 1981: A4.).

Amnesty, like so many of the issues discussed in this work, was reduced to a matter of class — this time by the President of the United States. Those generally from the lower classes bore the characteristic brunt of discrimination. Those who had the greatest socio-economic disadvantages initially were leveled one more disadvantage. Those with more initial advantages, had one more.

Despite these shortcomings, Carter's program was acceptable to many more exiles than Ford's clemency. This was primarily due to its automatically being granted to dodgers and its absence of required 24-months alternate service for all. At a conference in January 1977, resisters from the United States, Canada, and those living in Europe voted not to boycott Carter's plan, but rather to take advantage of this opportunity to work for true amnesty for all resisters, not just higher class dodgers.

The potential effects of Carter's amnesty were enormous. These men, so long without a choice, now had to choose; the borders were open. Not surprisingly, the U.S. media appeared in full force at the 1977 conference, fully expecting to follow resisters home to joyful reunions with their families. What they got instead, generally, were brief visits to Buffalo before the men returned to Canada to resume their lives. On the other hand, the pressures on the resisters to return did heighten. The author, in Canada at the time of Carter's amnesty, noted that the "potentially detrimental ambivalence" Levine referred to in 1974, had arrived. The discomfort of this ambivalence, in follow-up interviews, was quickly resolved by difficult decisions.

On a return visit, resisters were asked what their American and

Canadian friends expected them to do now that they had the opportunity to return to the States. The large majority stated that their American friends expected them to go back. A smaller majority said that most of their Canadian friends also expected them to return.

In most cases both sets of friends were wrong. As one puts it (419): "There is nothing better to Americans, even expatriate Americans, than the good old United States of America. They just couldn't believe that I wouldn't go back when I had the chance." Another (404) said, "Most Americans have this misconception that we had been waiting all these years at the border, and would just go when the gate was lifted. They don't know Canada." A third (401) felt that much of this misconception was perpetuated by the "American newspaper reporters who all had this idea that we were just aching to be back to our roots . . . that we were really suffering up here . . . they didn't believe it when I told them I didn't want to go back."

Canadian friends concurred. As one American (407) said, this reflected the "sort of Canadianism that [makes] even Canadians sometimes have inferiority complexes about living in Canada . . . [they think] if anybody ever had the opportunity to live in the States they would." Another (405) agreed, saying that his Canadian friends "expected me to split, out of that self-effacing thing that Canadians have. They always expect that they are not good enough." And a third (621) said that his Canadian friends expected him to go back because "things are economically better down there."

That U.S. friends would expect resisters to return is not surprising, given the ignorance about Canada which typifies many Americans, for whom anything beyond our border is simply considered a wasteland. That many Canadians endorsed this perspective illustrates just how much U.S. chauvinism has infiltrated that nation.

Amnesty for (607) "allowed me to return . . . *to visit*, otherwise, not much" (Italics mine). This was the actual effect of amnesty for the majority of war resisters. It provided them with an opportunity to visit what they no longer called home. What is ironic, but not surprising, is that military deserters were more likely to return to live in the U.S. than draft dodgers, despite the fact that they were not fully covered by Carter's amnesty. Dodgers, who could return to the United States with a clean slate, usually elected to remain in Canada.

Along with the generally more marginal deserters, the racial minorities who lasted in Canada were also more likely to return. A few men, for reasons discussed in the last section, also came back to the U.S. to seek jobs; slightly more returned for social reasons. Most predictable, of the small core who remained involved in exile-oriented activities, in and out of the sample, almost all returned.

Despite the diversity of reasons for returning, the actual numbers are relatively small. Those who "made it" in Canada, until 1977, were survivors; the majority of the most marginal had long since returned. The survivors liked Canada and thrived there. These men had generally good jobs, new families, new friends, and new roots — some extending back to the early 1960s. Perhaps most important, these men left the United States for reasons of which Vietnam was merely a symptom. The war had ended; the United States, to them, had not changed substantially.

SUMMARY

In the last two chapters, we examined assimilation as a dynamic process, influenced by U.S. policies toward resisters, Canadian attitudes toward the immigrant group, the opportunity structures available for incoming resisters, the interpersonal relationships within the exile community, and the individual motives of the resisters. Occurring within a context, assimilation is not always the choice of the immigrant. Establishing ties with new structures and people, assimilation often involves letting go of old structures and people.

Assimilation was largely a matter of choice of most of the resisters both inside and outside of this sample, because of their relatively privileged class backgrounds and the similarities of the two nations. Assimilation even for these men followed traditional patterns, with formal preceding social. The process occurred at a greatly accelerated rate, however. For minorities and deserters, assimilation has been much more difficult, underscoring the influences of class demonstrated throughout this work: throughout the history of military procurement and assignment. That complete amnesty has yet to be granted extends this history of class discrimination into the 1980's.

NOTES

1. The most influential theorists for the following section are Bar-Yosef, 1968; Chadwick and Strauss, 1976; Gordon, 1964; Porter, 1965; Richardson, 1967; Roy, 1962; Thompson, 1974.
2. The concept of the indices was originally suggested by Dr. Charles Kadushin, who was also instrumental in determining which items to include. Final responsibility for what was included and for interpretation lies with the author. The indices were developed by extracting face valid items and re-coding them in the consistent directions; the

items were weighted equally and added together. The first two indices, Formal and Social, were trichotomized into low, medium, and high categories. Exile activity was dichotomized.

3. A number of draft resisters had already been "pardoned." The Justice Department simply dropped their cases, for a variety of reasons, over the years. Baskir and Strauss (1978: 221) put this figure at over 13,000 men.

PART FIVE

WHATEVER HAPPENED
TO VIETNAM?

Williams. But if the cause be not good, the king himself hath a heavy reckoning to make, when all those legs and arms and heads, chopped off in a battle, shall join together at the latter day and cry all, "We died at such a place," some swearing, some crying for a surgeon, some upon their wives left poor behind them, some upon the debts they owe, some upon their children rawly left. I am afeard there are few die well that die in a battle; for how can they charitably dispose of anything when blood is their argument?

(A common soldier in Shakespeare's *Henry V,* IV.i.134–143)

As I was going up the stair
I met a man who wasn't there.
He wasn't there again to-day.
I wish, I wish, he'd stay away.

(Hughes Mearns, *The Psychoed [Antigonish]*)

CHAPTER **9**

Reflections: Past, Present and Future

(411): One of the best things that's ever happened to me . . . we got out of Kentucky.

(618: I would resist and stay in the United States . . . because I would be more effective there . . . as a catalyst.

This final chapter begins with hindsight: How do the war resisters *now* view their decision to resist through exile? What effects of exile, that is, changes in lifestyle, opportunities, and outlooks, do these men identify? This discussion provides the foundation for a final examination of the Vietnam Era's enduring impact on the United States. It is time to sort out what has lasted and what was merely a sign of the times.

We have seen that prior to their exile (Chapter Four), a number of war resisters questioned Canada as the "best" moral or political response to the Vietnam War. Many considered other alternatives, especially seeking conscientious objector status or going to prison. However, when these 60 men were asked, during the structured interviews, "If you could relive those years, would you choose to resist again?", only eight regretted not taking strong actions within the U.S. Of the remaining 52, retrospective views of the best tactics for resistance — avoidance versus exile — varied.

The eight men who would now consider more militant U.S.-based action question whether coming to Canada was indeed a proper political alternative to Vietnam. To them perhaps the best course would have been to (615) ". . . go into the army and organize against the war." Another (314) suggests that if he had to do it over again, he "probably would have gone to prison . . . gone to jail for the draft . . . outwardly just said no, I will not go." For these men, the fundamental issue is whether these actions would have accomplished more toward ending the war.

Others question, not the decision to seek exile, but the timing of their resistance. Military deserters, more than dodgers, say they would have resisted earlier. For example, (304): "If I had the information that I have now, I would have avoided it before I even had to go in"; or (307): "I would not have gone into the service in the first place."

Some draft dodgers maintain that if they could do it over again, they would avoid exile altogether. For instance, (404): "I think what I would have done if I knew what I know now is try and get out by other methods . . . go into the induction center stoned out of my head." Another (612) learned, after exile, about the broadened basis for determining CO status (Chapter Two). Had he known earlier that he was qualified, he "would have filed for a CO."

In retrospect, these dodgers would have avoided exile, while the deserters would have exiled themselves prior to the service. This discrepancy, even in hindsight, reveals the importance of their class-related starting points. The class-gap has still not closed: draft dodgers fantasize "avoidance" and military deserters visualize premilitary exile.

Although some of the men say they might have taken different courses of action, most question neither their decision to go to Canada nor their timing. They would go again; (315) — "Absolutely . . . for the same reasons . . . because there was no other way out." To these men there is not, (613), ". . . any alternative. Nothing has changed." The move is justified, (313), ". . . 'cause it was the right thing to do," and (609) says, "The whole process, everything I did was right." These men express no regrets ". . . except for those goddamn winters" (403).

DISILLUSIONMENT

The disillusionment with the United States which so typified the decision to go to Canada (Chapter Four) was usually strengthened during exile. These men had been socialized to believe in the U.S. system of government. Such ideals were shattered during the Vietnam Era. With exposure to, and increasing acceptance by Canadian society, these men have grown even more cynical about the U.S. That this disillusionment has not receded over the years, is evidenced by the limited numbers who returned after Carter's amnesty. This disillusionment, however, goes well beyond these resisters. The northeast Vietnam Era Research data indicate that an entire generation of Vietnam Era age-eligible men remain substantially disillusioned with the U.S. government, and its major institutions. (See Table 9-1).

More than two-thirds of any specific group in this generation

Table 9-1 Current Attitudes by Northeast Vietnam Era Research Project Sample

Question	Response	Vietnam Veterans	Vietnam Era Veterans	College Nonveterans	Non-college Nonveterans	Draft Dodgers	Military Deserters
How much of the time do you think you trust the United States government to do what's right?	Some of the time/never*	67%	78%	76%	71%	80%	100%
	Always/most of the time	29	20	21	25	16	0
Would you say the government is run pretty much for a few big interests or would you say it is run for the benefit of the people?	Big Interests	76%	73%	75%	65%	84%	100%
	All the People	18	15	16	38	6	0
	Dk/NR	6	12	9	5	10	0
Would you agree or disagree that public officials don't care what people like me think?	Agree	72%	71%	58%	59%	59%	91%
	Disagree	22	24	38	35	31	9
	Dk/NR	6	5	4	6	10	0
		(N = 82)	(N = 101)	(N = 102)	(N = 95)	(N = 49)	(N = 11)

*Originally respondents could select one of four answers: Always; most of the time; some of the time; never. For our purposes these categories have been collapsed into two.

feel that the United States government cannot be trusted to do what is right; an equal percentage are cynical about who benefits from the government. Over half the men in each group agree that public officials do not care what they think. There is little faith in the government to do what is right, work for the people, or care about public opinions.

While the responses in Table 9-1 reflect disillusionment across groups, it runs deepest for the war resisters. Table 9-2 reports responses to the question "How much confidence do you have in the people running [the following U.S. institutions]?" These responses of the war resisters and the other men in the generation are even more distinct. While all are disillusioned, the resisters are the most consistent and extreme.

On the first five items in Table 9-2, war resisters express the least faith in the leaders of power broker institutions in this country. To them, the government, military, major companies, banks and financial institutions all shared responsibility for the Vietnam conflict. Television, except at the very end, did not provide a forum for questioning any aspect of U.S. involvement in Vietnam.

In contrast, the resisters do not express, relatively, a lack of confidence in the press, the Supreme Court (except for deserters), or the U.S. Congress. During the late 1960's and nearly 1970's, these institutions were often sympathetic to the cause of resistance. Eventually more segments of the written press than television rallied against the war. The Warren Court often advanced the cause of these men, and in Congress a number of strong dissenters emerged against the war. Accordingly, resisters are least cynical about these three institutions.[1]

Overall, faith in the U.S. and in its leaders was virtually shattered by the Vietnam experience. Most particularly this affected those men who opted for exile. To them the cliché of "my country right or wrong . . ." could no longer be seriously voiced. Years after the war has ended, the general assumption remains — "My country is wrong." These attitudes appear to characterize not only the exiles, but an entire generation of men — those who went to Vietnam, stayed home, or opted for Canada. The generation became and has remained disillusioned.

EXILES' REWARDS: LIFESTYLE AND AWARENESS

(318): I guess it made it totally different . . . I died as a being . . . living in America. And I had to be reborn as one in Canada.

(305): If an H-bomb would hit me in the head it couldn't have had a bigger change in me (than coming to Canada).

The most frequent responses to the question, "How did exile affect your life?" describe lifestyle changes and new levels of political awareness. A less frantic, calmer approach to life has been gained by those men no longer caught up in what they consider the American ethos of ". . . materialistic involvement and dealing in the material world" (313). As another put it, (419): "Personally, I've really slowed down a lot . . . [I'm] happy and comfortable." Many see themselves as having adopted the cultural style of Canadians. (Chapters Five and Six).

Another effect of exile involves a deepened political awareness; a broader understanding of, and interest in, the dynamics behind world events. These men often developed a critical perspective of the U.S. government, big business, and to a lesser extent, the American people. Awareness prior to exile (Chapter Four) generally focused on the Vietnam War; immediately after arrival (Chapter Seven), it centered on the resister movement. Now it embodies more global issues. As one military deserter puts it (421): "When we came here we had no choice but to see things politically. Once you're forced to do it, you never let go."

No Longer Activists

These resisters remain politically aware, enormously disillusioned with the United States, but essentially non-activist. Once relatively militant as a group, they have long ceased trying to reshape society. The active commitment they felt toward change in the United States has long disappeared; the commitment most feel toward Canada, while genuine, is relatively passive.

The return to prewar minimal levels of activism may be attributed to a variety of factors. Disillusionment led many to view change as impossible. The tragedies of the Vietnam Era, which began in the turbulent sixties, including the political assassinations (the two Kennedys and Martin Luther King), the shootings of black (Jackson State) and white (Kent State) students, and finally Watergate, dashed hopes of making the United States more liveable.

Another contributing element is the fact that it is virtually impossible to sustain high levels of political activism for a number of years. "Burnout," or simply moving on to new spheres, naturally occurs. As one draft dodger (411) puts it, he would "hate to spend the rest of my life as a professional exile." The majority opinion of these war resisters holds that it would be quixotic to devote one's life to political struggle.

Third, these men are now doing, on the whole, quite well within

Table 9-2 Confidence in People Running Institutions by the N.E. Vietnam Era Project Sample

Institution	Response (Confidence)	Vietnam Veterans	Vietnam Era Veterans	College Nonveterans	Non-college Nonveterans	Draft Dodgers	Military Deserters
Government	Hardly any	15%	19%	20%	22%	49%	55%
	Some	61	54	66	44	43	36
	Great Deal	17	22	12	26	2	9
	Dk/NR*	7	5	2	8	5	—
Military	Hardly any	23	34	41	31	61	64
	Some	55	50	41	43	27	27
	Great deal	16	12	16	16	6	9
	Dk/NR	6	4	2	10	6	—
Major Companies	Hardly any	37	25	36	40	63	73
	Some	43	41	36	32	31	18
	Great deal	14	27	23	20	4	—
	Dk/NR	6	7	5	8	2	9
Banks and Financial Institutions	Hardly any	38	26	41	38	63	63
	Some	37	54	37	37	23	27
	Great deal	18	16	19	21	14	—
	Dk/NR	7	4	3	4	—	—

Table 9-2 (Continued)

Institution	Response (Confidence)	Vietnam Veterans	Vietnam Era Veterans	College Nonveterans	Non-college Nonveterans	Draft Dodgers	Military Deserters
Television	Hardly any	40	38	39	32	61	55
	Some	34	45	47	40	33	45
	Great deal	16	13	10	24	6	—
	Dk/NR	10	4	4	4	—	—
Press	Hardly any	27	21	21	20	16	18
	Some	42	54	60	51	59	82
	Great deal	23	23	18	23	23	—
	Dk/NR	8	2	1	6	2	—
Supreme Court	Hardly any	35	21	18	32	16	73
	Some	38	53	62	38	53	27
	Great deal	18	22	18	24	27	—
	Dk/NR	9	4	2	6	4	—
Congress	Hardly any	32	24	38	28	29	18
	Some	55	35	54	47	67	82
	Great deal	6	8	7	16	4	—
	Dk/NR	7	4	1	9	—	—
		(N = 82)	(N = 101)	(N = 102)	(N = 95)	(N = 49)	(N = 11)

*Dk = Don't know. NR = No response.

the once taboo "establishment". Promoting radical change while reaping success is difficult. Nevertheless, it is less difficult for these men in Canada, in which the "establishment" is viewed as morally superior to that of the U.S.

EXILE'S COSTS

> (409): I was snatched away from an environment I was kind of used to . . . If I'd stayed . . . I would have, you know, been getting the GI Bill and all that other stuff and could have gone back to school. And probably and a — you know — pretty good job. . . .

Almost to a man, the enormous effects of exile are recognized by these war resisters. Most consider these changes to be very positive. (See Chapters Six and Eight.) A minority judge exile to be a hindrance to their goals. The military deserter quoted above presents such a view. Unable to mesh with Canadian society, he has since returned to the U.S., accepting the consequences of a bad paper discharge over the isolation and lack of opportunities away from home.

Those who feel exile had negative effects are often among the more economically or socially marginal (Chapter Eight). Had they stayed in the U.S., some maintain, they would have been more successful, would not have lost their G.I. benefits or disrupted their careers. One (612) put it, "I could always get by in California on freelance work, as an illustrator. But in Canada most of the advertising is done in the States . . . [exile] ruined certain career objectives that I've had." Others, socially unattached, are simply unable or unwilling to plant cultural roots in Canada. Many feel politically uprooted: that their work in the States has been delayed. Those who feel exile has been a negative experience are underrepresented in this sample of survivors. Had we interviewed more military deserters or reached those who had already returned to the U.S., this viewpoint would have been more pervasive.

VIETNAM UNDER THE RUG: HISTORY DENIED

> (405): No one wanted to talk about where I had been [when he returned to the U.S. for a visit]. A cousin of mine had been to Canada on a fishing trip and they asked him questions about Canada and they didn't ask me. This was at a party for me.

During the structured interviews, it became obvious that the questions pursued about the Vietnam Era experience represented issues no longer salient to most of these resisters. These men, as a group, had progressed personally, socially, and professionally beyond the stage when resistance organized their existence. Typical of comments at the end of the interviews are (419): "I haven't thought about this stuff lately," or (403): "That was a long, long time ago."

During follow-up interviews it became clear that visits to the United States, made possible by Carter's amnesty, renewed an awareness by these men of their resister status (Chapter Eight). The visits were generally quite pleasant. The following statement is fairly typical:

> (411): It was fine. My friends and relatives were great. I was treated like visiting royalty . . . we had a great time, renewed old friendships and had a real whoop-to-do Kentucky vacation.

However, one major area of disappointment was consistently mentioned. While the war exiles through amnesty gained a renewed sense of their historic roles, most of the people "back home" were unwilling to talk about either the resistance or the war. A dodger (621) who returned for his sister's wedding said, "Nobody said anything I could remember about me being a resister — like it had never happened. It was not even mentioned." Another (407) notes that the issue of his resistance was "usually avoided in some way or another." A dodger (414) talks of his anticipation as he and his wife approached the Canadian/U.S. border. He was a Canadian citizen, and he expected a hassle[2] — there was none. He recalls this as a letdown —"after eight years, is that all there is?"

For these resisters the Vietnam Era had generally ceased to be a central issue — at least until Carter's amnesty. Their families and friends — even after amnesty — were reluctant to discuss it. Such evidence of denial harmonized well with the general attitudes of the U.S. public. Since the cessation of our military involvement, Vietnam has become virtually a taboo topic. It is rarely taught in high schools, or even colleges. It is neither acclaimed nor criticized; it is ignored.

Those who weave our national myths have been unable to incorporate Vietnam. The traditional stories of American victories and heroism remain unheralded for the Vietnam war. Incidents of heroism, of course, existed, but they cannot be "packaged" in the context of this conflict. There are no Pershings, Eisenhowers, Pattons, MacArthurs. From Vietnam the names most likely to be remembered are Calley and Garwood.

For almost a decade, Vietnam did not make it on commercial television as either comedy or drama. Unlike World War II (*Combat* or *Hogan's Heroes*) or Korea (*M.A.S.H.*) there have been no successful television series about Vietnam. The closest thing to a lasting television series on Vietnam was the horror transmitted by the six o'clock news. In the movies there are no modern day Audie Murphys going *To Hell and Back*. Indeed, even our biggest movie folk hero, John Wayne, could not pull off a celebration of this war with his *Green Berets* — a war movie so at variance with public attitudes that one is hard pressed to find it on late night television.

On the other hand, at the outset of the 1980's, we find nationwide denial reluctantly and selectively giving way to only the terror of war. Movies have been belatedly produced about Vietnam — largely as caricatures. Some dwell on the absolute horrors *(Deerhunter* and *Apocalypse Now!)*, while others create unrealistic saints of their chief characters *(Coming Home)*. These negative images of Vietnam have been transplanted to television where, if the Vietnam veteran is portrayed at all, he is usually a tragic "psycho" unable to cope.[3]

Newspapers sensationalize Vietnam veterans involved in crimes, while they might not cover a nonveteran in a parallel situation. The media, after months of speculating to the contrary, were crushed to learn that New York's "Son of Sam" killer had only served in peacetime Korea. The single exception to the one-sided coverage of Vietnam is a number of excellent and undercirculated books.

The reason for the distorted coverage of this military conflict is obvious. We lost; it was not a clean war; and most *believe now* we shouldn't have been there. There is simply no way that history can be rewoven to fit this war into our national self-image of invincible "good guys". After years of denial, when Vietnam is dealt with, only its most grotesque and extreme aspects are considered.

LEGACIES

Despite the fact that Vietnam has largely been relegated to the closet, its legacies remain. The broad disillusionment of the war resisters and an entire generation, already discussed, has been inherited from the Vietnam Era. Vietnam's impact, however, goes beyond this. The marginality of military deserters and, as we will see, Vietnam veterans, reflects another legacy of Vietnam. The questionable quality of the post-Vietnam military can also be construed as a legacy. And, finally, the no longer passive political responses, by a significant portion of the U.S. public, may be the one legacy most likely to help us avoid Vietnams in the future.

Most Americans, including the majority of draft dodgers who participated in this study, have been able to leave Vietnam behind them. True to history, those who have suffered the most do not have this luxury. While the draft dodgers can generally select their future paths, the relatively lower class deserters are often restricted to a choice of marginality in Canada or in the U.S. The class-biased amnesty further stigmatizes deserters, reinforcing a peripheral existence for many.

The Vietnam veterans, as well as all veterans holding bad paper discharges, too, continue to bear heavy burdens. Negatively stereotyped by the media and segments of the public for years, they remain largely ignored by government agencies. Only after denial and consequent embarrassment, for instance, has the government belatedly and barely begun to attend to the problems created by the Agent Orange chemical catastrophe.

The most comprehensive study of the Vietnam Era, the Congressionally mandated *Legacies of Vietnam: Comparative Adjustment of Veterans and Their Peers* (Vietnam Era Research Project, Center for Policy Research) summarizes the legacy of the Vietnam Veteran.

> The majority of Vietnam Veterans we interviewed have not made substantial headway in working through their war experiences.
>
> (Volume 1, xxvii)

While the implications of this conclusion are major, it must be recognized that not all Vietnam veterans suffer these or other problems. Efforts designed to identify Vietnam's impact, run the risk of being misconstrued to reinforce negative stereotypes of Vietnam veterans. Nonetheless, the findings in *Legacies of Vietnam* (Egendorf et al., 1981) reveal major negative effects. Among the most startling are the following:

–Vietnam veterans have not achieved the educational levels of their age peers.

–Vietnam veterans hold lower level jobs than Vietnam Era veterans, as well as nonveterans.

–Black Vietnam veterans are three times more likely to experience career unemployment than others.

–Those exposed to "heavy combat" are more likely to suffer drug, alcohol, and/or (after 1968) stress-related problems than other men.

–One-third of those engaged in "heavy combat" are "stressed," as opposed to less than 20 percent of their age peers.

–A total of 24 percent of the Vietnam veterans in "heavy combat" have later been arrested. (This figure is deflated because the otherwise representative sampling technique systematically excluded incarcerated veterans.)

Any analysis of these findings requires one to remember the class-related military channeling procedures (Chapter Two). Social class of origin influenced greatly who went to Vietnam and who was involved in combat. Due to our class structure, even without Vietnam, these men, like the deserters, would undoubtedly face more problems today than those from higher social classes. Their Vietnam experiences, and their treatment afterwards have clearly exacerbated their initial class disadvantages.

In 1981, the dramatic return of the hostages from Iran ironically drew attention to the Vietnam veterans — by disappointing contrast. The hostages were greeted as heroes in our most traditional sense; they were presented symbols such as the yellow ribbon and American flags. Most marched in parades. They were provided free hotel rooms, cars, shopping sprees and lifetime baseball passes. The government shepherded them through formal and informal "decompression" sessions. Most important, they could tell their fellow citizens who they were without facing scorn. They were encouraged and supported to feel proud of their status.

The Vietnam veterans, in contrast to both the hostages and veterans of previous wars, were not treated as heroes. They were given few symbols and fewer parades and as soon as possible were forced into the background. Often they returned to antiwar protesters as their only greeters. Neither the government nor the public has made much effort to make them feel good about themselves, thus magnifying and even creating many of their problems.

Deserters, bad paper veterans and Vietnam veterans represent, perhaps, the most devastating legacy of Vietnam. But other effects defy our national attempts at denial. The widespread disillusionment, described earlier, captures another facet of the legacy of Vietnam. A significant portion of an entire generation stopped believing in this country and its leaders during the war. The high hopes of the 1960's represented by the New Camelot of the Kennedy Administration ended with the fall of Saigon and a very divided nation. Hopes were shattered and faith has yet to be rekindled.

Another, more concrete legacy of the Vietnam Era is represented by the military's current all-volunteer force (AVF). Both the selective service and the military itself were in a shambles by the end of the war (Chapter Two). The alternative post-Vietnam AVF, established in 1973, continues the tradition of 300 years of channeling the less advantaged into the military. Indeed, regardless of where one stands on the political spectrum, opinion is virtually unanimous that the AVF is a throwback to the notion of the poorest classes serving, in far greater proportions than during the Vietnam conflict.[4]

Lovell (1981: 33), using education as a rough indicator of social class, documents the "regressive effects" of enlistments. He notes, in early 1981, that of male recruits over the past six months to a year, only five percent have at least a semester of college versus 40 percent of all 18- or 19-year-old males. Race, again, is reflected in patterns of channeling. In 1981, 33 percent of the AVF are black (Middleton, 1981: B20) versus 11.7 percent of the national population (Herbes, 1981: E5).

The AVF's composition is consistent with history. It offers low pay compared to civilian work, few benefits, and an image which still has not recovered from Vietnam. Generally, only those with the fewest alternatives would consider joining.

It is not surprising, therefore, that those seeking more qualified military personnel have long been agitating for the reinstitution of the draft. Jimmy Carter's last-ditch attempt to hold onto the White House included a traditional rally-round-the-flag draft registration during the Iranian crisis to provide the military with these more qualified personnel. Ronald Reagan, immediately upon taking office, began "studying" resumption of the draft. He has begun selective Justice Department investigations of men who refuse to register, to set examples for possible resisters in the 1980's (Halloran 1981: Al).

This time its proponents promise the draft will be fair. On the basis of trial balloons, the claim is made that deferments will not be discriminatory. However, 300 years of history assure us that discrimination will surely re-emerge. After the draft riots of the Civil War, overt discrimination was replaced by covert class-biased deferments, which evolved into increasingly sophisticated "channeling" by the time of the Vietnam Era. Should "deferments" be dropped, new bureaucratic euphemisms will be used to replace them.

The incipient resistance to draft registration and President Reagan's evocation of memories of our early involvement in Vietnam, with the placement of advisors in El Salvador, indicate another legacy from the Vietnam Era. By mid-1981, non-registration had reached the point where the government took action. A poll by the National Center for Education Statistics concludes that almost 30 percent of the 1980 high school seniors would try to avoid any form, military or civilian, of mandatory service (*New York Times*, April 16, 1981: A21). The first national anti-draft rally in years was held in Washington, D.C., on March 22, 1980, with at least 30,000 attending — an impressive number considering there were neither troops deployed nor a draft call (Ibid., March 23: A24). On May 3, 1981, upwards of 100,000 rallied in Washington to protest the draft and the presence of U.S. military advisors in El Salvador (deOnis, 1981: 31; Trinkl, 1981: 1).

A major reason for the collapse of our efforts in Vietnam was the extensive breakdown of procedures for establishing and maintaining an effective military force. Enough Americans refused to be a part of this process to damage it seriously. The more recent re-emergence of an anti-draft, anti-intervention movement may indicate a final legacy of Vietnam: significant numbers of Americans may no longer blindly follow our leaders into war. With the dialectic between the generally conceded failure of the all-volunteer force and military advisors again being sent abroad, the strength of this last legacy may be tested sooner than we hope.

The experiences before, during, and after Vietnam of the war resisters who went to Canada represent in microcosm the turmoil and changes which this nation underwent as a result of that conflict. These men left the United States because of what they viewed as an immoral war. Few have returned. Those who remain in exile, and those who are forced to remain marginal, symbolize the loss of a large portion of the Vietnam War generation. The legacies of the Vietnam Era belong to the entire nation. Unless Vietnam is honestly examined, the mistakes which led us into this conflict and the wounds which we have not attempted to heal, will continue to haunt our nation.

NOTES

1. Once again, Dr. Robert Laufer was instrumental in helping to sort out and interpret the material above.
2. Technically, the men who became Canadian citizens would be denied re-entry as "undesirable aliens." This rarely happened.
3. The stars of a few current television series (1981) are "good-guy" Vietnam vets; however this is almost mandated by their generation. When Vietnam is referred to in these shows, it is inevitably in hushed tones, or through gruesome flashbacks.
4. For example, see "The Rise and Fall of the Volunteer Army," *Society* (March/April, 1981), 28–60, for a representative analysis of this issue.

BIBLIOGRAPHY

Adams, Michael J. 1970. "American refugee study." University of Toronto:
  Unpublished master's thesis.
AMEX-Canada. 1977. "SDRP statistics." 6(2): 7.
Badillo, Gilbert and David G. Curry. 1976. "The social incidence of Vietnam
  casualties: social class or race?" *Armed Forces and Society*, 2(3): 397-406.
Barnes, J.A. 1954. "Class and committees in a Norwegian island parish."
  Human Relations, 7(1): 39-58.
Bar-Yosef, Rivka Weiss. 1968. "Desocialization and resocialization: the ad-
  justment process of immigrants." *The International Migration Review*,
  2(3): 27-45.
Baskir, Lawrence M. and William A. Strauss. 1978. *Chance and circumstance;
  the draft, the war and the Vietnam generation*. New York: Random House
  (Vintage).
Beals, Ralph. 1953. "Acculturation." In *Anthropology Today*, Alfred Kroeber,
  ed. Chicago: University of Chicago Press.
Bell, Bruce D. and Thomas J. Houston. 1976. "The Vietnam era deserter:
  characteristics of unconvicted army deserters participating in the pres-
  idential clemency program." Arlington: U.S. Army Research Institute
  for the Behavioral and Social Sciences.
Bond, Thomas C., M.D. 1976. "The why of fragging." *American Journal of
  Psychiatry*. 133(11): 1328-1331.
Bowles, Samuel and Herbert Gintis. 1976. *Schooling in capitalist America: ed-
  ucational reform and the contradictions of economic life*. New York: Basic
  Books, Inc.
Braverman, Harry. 1974. *Labor and monopoly capital: the degradation of work in
  the twentieth century*. New York: Monthly Review Press.
Brown, Wallace. 1969. *The good Americans: the loyalists in the American Revo-
  lution*. New York: Morrow Press.
Campbell, Charles. 1970. "How I dodged the draft and found God." *AMEX-
  Canada*, 2(2): 20.
Canadian Pocket Encyclopedia. 1977. Toronto: Quick Canadian Facts. 33rd ed.
Chadwick, Bruce A. and Joseph H. Strauss. 1975. "The assimilation of Amer-
  ican Indians into urban society: the Seattle case." *Human Organization*,
  34(4): 359-369.
Chatfield, Charles. 1971. *For peace and justice: pacification in America, 1914-1941*.
  Knoxville: The University of Tennessee Press.
Chatterjee, Pranab and Barbara F. 1970. "Some structural dilemmas of se-
  lective service boards." *Human Organization*, 29(4): 288-293.

Clifford, John G. 1973. "Grenville Clark and the origins of selective service." *Review of Politics*, 35(1): 17-40.

Cocking, Clive. 1970. "How did the Canadian Mounties develop their unfortunate habit of deporting people they don't happen to like?" *Saturday Night*, 85(6): 28-30.

Colhoun, Jack. 1972. "On exile." *AMEX-Canada*, 3(5): 53-56.

_____. 1976. "The antiwar movement they don't talk about." *AMEX-Canada*, 5(6): 31-36.

_____. 1977. "War resisters in exile: the memoirs of AMEX-Canada." *AMEX-Canada*, 6(2): 11-78.

_____. 1981a. "The draft protests and the Vietnam war." *The Guardian*, 6 May: 10.

_____. 1981b. "Antidraft movement: from protest to resistance." *The Guardian*, 13 May: 9.

_____. 1981c. "Draft: one step nearer with classification." *The Guardian*, 20 May: 4.

_____. 1981d. "Antiwar movement: vets, exiles played a role." *The Guardian*, 20 May: 9, 18.

Colhoun, Jack and Joe Jones. 1974. " 'Future stress': the psychology of exile." *AMEX-Canada*, 4(6): 42-44.

Cook, Adrian. 1974. *The armies of the streets: the New York City draft riots of 1863.* Lexington: The University Press of Kentucky.

Cook, Blanche. 1973. "Democracy in wartime: antimilitarism in England and the United States, 1914-1918." Charles Chatfield, ed., *Peace Movements in America*, pp. 39-56. New York: Schocken Books.

Cooney, John and Dana Spitzer. 1969. "American deserters in Sweden and Canada." *Transaction*, 6(10): 53-62.

Cortright, David. 1975. *Soldiers in revolt: the American military today.* Garden City: Anchor Press/Doubleday.

Culhane, Claire. 1972. *Why is Canada in Vietnam?* Toronto: New Canada Publications.

_____. 1973. "Canada and Vietnam." *Our Generation*, 9(2): 63-64.

Damico, Alfonso, J. 1974. "In defense of amnesty." *Dissent*, 21(Winter): 90-94.

Davis, James and Kenneth Dolbeare. 1968. *Little groups of neighbors: the selective service system.* Chicago: Markham Publishing.

_____. 1969. "A social profile of local draft board members: the case of Wisconsin." Roger W. Little, ed., *Selective Service and American Society*, 53-58. New York: Russell Sage Foundation.

deOnis, Juan. 1981. "Capital rally assails arms to Salvador." *New York Times*, 4 May: A3.

Dullea, Georgia. 1981. "Women speaking out on effects of duty in Vietnam." *New York Times*, 23 March: A1; B12.

Economist. 1970. "Doves or dodgers?" 29 June: 48-49.

Efaw, Fritz. 1975. "Why Ford's amnesty failed," *New Statesman*, 28 February: 265-266.

Egendorf, Arthur, Charles Kadushin, Robert Laufer, George Rothbart, and

Lee Sloan. 1981. "Legacies of Vietnam: comparative adjustment of veterans and their peers." Volumes I-V, Final Report to the Veterans Administration and the U.S. Congress. New York: Center for Policy Research.

Emerick, Kenneth Fred. 1972. *War Resisters in Canada.* Knox, Pennsylvania: Pennsylvania Free Press.

Epp, Frank H. 1970. ". . . My own history allows me no escape." Frank H. Epp, ed., *I would like to dodge the draft-dodgers but . . . (including deserters)*, 8-19. Winnipeg: Conrad Press.

Etzioni, Amitai. 1959. "The ghetto—a re-evaluation." *Social Forces*, 37(3): 255-262.

Ferber, Michael and Staughton Lynd. 1971. *The resistance.* Boston: Beacon Press.

Fermi, Laura. 1968. *Illustrious immigrants: The intellectual migration from Europe, 1930-41.* Chicago: University of Chicago Press.

Fite, Emerson David. 1930. *Social and industrial conditions in the north during the Civil War.* New York: Frederick Ungar Publishers Company. (New York: P. Smith.)

Flacks, Richard, Florence Howe, and Paul Lauter. 1967. "On the draft." *The New York Review of Books*, 6 April: 3-5.

Fleuret, Anne K. 1974. "Incorporation into networks among Sikhs in Los Angeles." *Urban Anthropology*, 3(1): 27-33.

Fligstein, Neil. 1981. "Militarism, not service." *Society*, 18(3): 43-44.

Franks, Lucinda. 1974. *Waiting out a war: the exile of Private John Picciano.* New York: Coward, McCann and Geoghegan Inc.

Fulford, Robert. 1968. "On draft dodgers." *Saturday Night*, 83 (Nov.): 11-12.

Gallup, George. 1972. *The Gallup poll, public opinion, 1935-1971* (Vol. 3, 1959-1971). New York: Random House.

————. 1978. *The Gallup poll, public opinion, 1972-1977* (Vol. 1, 1972-1975). Wilmington, Delaware: Scholarly Resources, Publishers.

Gates, Thomas (Chairman). 1970. *The report of president's commission on an all-volunteer armed forces.* New York: The Macmillan Company.

Giniger, Henry. 1981. "High court ruling encourages Ottawa and its foes." *New York Times*, 29 September: A11.

Glass, Andrew. 1970. "Defense report/draftees shoulder the burden of fighting and dying in Vietnam." *National Journal*, 15 August: 1747-1755.

Gordon, Milton M. 1964. *Assimilation in American life: the role of race, religion, and national origins.* New York: Oxford University Press.

Gory, Adrian E. and David C. McClelland. 1947. "Characteristics of conscientious objectors in World War II." *Journal of Consulting Psychology*, 11(5): 245-257.

Gosselin, Van Allen. 1969. "Are we exiles or expatriots?" *The American Exile*, I (15): 12-13.

Graham, John. 1974. "The American amnesty debate." *New Statesman*, 15 March: 348-349.

Grant, George. 1969. *Technology and empire: perspective on North America.* Toronto: House of Anansi.

Grant, Zalin. 1969. "Revolt in the Pentagon?" *New Republic,* 4 October: 17-20.

Grossman, Steve. 1977. "I want to go home, but. . . . " *New York Times Magazine,* 2 January: 8, 9, 40, 47, 50.

Halloran, Richard. 1977. "The dispute over amnesty for deserters: a legacy of the Vietnam War." *New York Times,* 11 March: A11.

————. 1981. "U.S. to prosecute youths to compel sign-up for draft." *The New York Times,* 21 July: A1 and B20.

Hansard. 1967. Debate: Canadian House of Commons, 27th Parliament, 1st Session, Vol. XII.

————. 1967. Debate: Canadian House of Commons, 27th Parliament, 2nd Session, Vol. IV.

————. 1968. Debate: Canadian House of Commons, 27th Parliament, 2nd Session, Vol. VII.

————. 1969. Debate: Canadian House of Commons, 28th Parliament, 1st Session, Vol. VI.

————. 1969. Debate: Canadian House of Commons, 28th Parliament, 2nd Session, Vol. II.

————. 1969. Debate: Canadian House of Commons, 28th Parliament, 2nd Session, Vol. VI.

————. 1970. Debate: Canadian House of Commons, 28th Parliament, 2nd Session, Vol. III.

————. 1970. Debate: Canadian House of Commons, 28th Parliament, 2nd Session, Vol. IV.

————. 1970. Debate: Canadian House of Commons, 28th Parliament, 2nd Session, Vol. VI.

Hawkins, Freda. 1972. *Canada and immigration: public policy and public concern.* Montreal: McGill-Queen's University Press.

Hayes, James R. 1975. "The dialectics of resistance: an analysis of the G.I. movement." *Journal of Social Issues,* 31(4): 125-139.

Headley, Joel Tyler. 1970 (1873). *The great riots of New York: 1712-1873.* New York: The Bobbs-Merrill Company, Inc. (New York: E. B. Treat.)

Helmer, John. 1974. *Bringing the war home: the American soldier before Vietnam and after.* New York: The Free Press.

Henry, Jules. 1958. "The personal community and its invariant properties." *American Anthropologist,* 60(5): 827-831.

Herbes, John. 1981. "Census totals show nation is as diverse as before." *New York Times,* 6 September: E5.

Higginbotham, Don. 1971. *The war of American independence: military attitudes, policies, and practice, 1763-1789.* New York: The Macmillan Company.

Janowitz, Morris and Charles C. Moskos Jr. 1979. "Five years of the all-volunteer force: 1973-1978." *Armed Forces and Society,* 5(2): 171-218.

Jones, Frank E. and Wallace E. Lambert. 1968. "Attitudes toward immigrants in a Canadian community." Bernard R. Blishen, Frank E. Jones, Kaspar

B. Naegele and John Porter, eds., *Canadian society: sociological perspective*, Third Ed., 95-103. Toronto: Macmillan Press of Canada.

Kage, Joseph. 1967. "The recent changes in Canadian immigration legislation." *The International Migration Review*, 2(1): 47-50.

Kane, Tom. 1968. "Surviving in Toronto." *American Exile*, 5(1): 22.

Karpinos, Bernard D. 1967. "Mental test failures." Sol Tax, ed., *The draft*. Chicago: The University of Chicago Press. pp. 35-53.

Kasinsky, Renee. 1976. *Refugees from militarism: draft-age Americans in Canada*. New Brunswick, N.J.: Transaction Books.

Kilmer, Richard, Robert Lecky, and Deborah S. Wiley. 1971. *They can't go home again*. Philadelphia: United Church Press.

Kirshner, Lewis A. 1973. "Countertransference issues in the treatment of the military dissenter." *American Journal of Orthopsychiatry*, 43(4): 654-659.

Kline, Carl, Katherine Rider, Karen Berry, and J. McRee Elrod. "The young American expatriots in Canada: alienated or self-defined." *American Journal Of Orthopsychiatry*, 41(1): 74-84.

Klineberg, Otto. 1935. *Negro intelligence and selective migration*. New York: Columbia University Press.

Kome, Penny. 1977. "Letters to editor." *The Toronto Globe and Mail*, 13 January: A6.

Lang, Kurt. 1981. "Service inequality." *Society*, 18(3): 40-43.

Laufer, Robert, Lee Sloan, Kathy Joyce, and David Surrey. 1981. "Attitudes toward amnesty within the Vietnam generation." *Journal of American Culture*, 4(2): 166-194.

Lauter, Paul and Florence Howe. 1970. *The conspiracy of the young*. New York: The World Publishing Company.

Laxer, Robert M. (ed.) 1973. *Canada Ltd.: the political economy of dependency*. Toronto: McClelland and Stewart, Limited.

Leeds, Anthony. 1964. "Brazilian careers and social structure: an evolutionary model and case history." *American Anthropologist*, 66 (6:1): 1321-1347.

Levine, Saul V., M.D. 1972. "Draft dodgers: coping with stress, adapting to exile." *American Journal of Orthopsychiatry*, 42(3): 431-440.

Lewin, Kurt. 1948. *Resolving social conflicts: selected papers on group dynamics*. Gertrude Weiss Lewin, ed. New York: Harper and Row Publishers.

Lifton, Robert J. 1973. *Home from the war: Vietnam Veterans; neither victims nor executioners*. New York: Simon and Schuster.

Linden, Eugene. 1972. "The demoralization of an army: fragging and other withdrawal symptoms." *Saturday Review*, 8 January: 12–17, 55.

Lingeman, Richard R. 1970. *Don't you know there's a war on?: the American home front 1941–1945*. New York: G. P. Putnams' Sons.

Lipset, Seymour M. 1971. "Revolution and counter-revolution: the United States and Canada." W.E. Mann, ed., *Canada: A Sociological Profile*: 24–36. Toronto: Copp Clark Publishing Company.

Little, Roger. 1981. "For choice, not chance." *Society*, 18(3): 49–51.

Lonn, Ella. 1928. *Desertion during the Civil War*. Gloucester, Mass.: Peter Smith.

Lovell, John P. 1981. "Fears, slogans, and choices." *Society*, 18(3): 33–35.

McCague, James. 1968. *The second rebellion: the story of the New York city draft riots of 1863*. New York: The Dial Press, Inc.

McFadden, Robert D. 1981. "U.S. study of veterans ties combat strain to several impairments." *New York Times*, 23 March: A6 and B12.

Man, Albon P. Jr. 1951. "Labor competition and the New York draft riots of 1863." *The Journal of Negro History*, 36(4): 375–405.

Mantell, David Mark. 1974. *True Americanism Green Berets and War Resisters: A study of commitment*. New York: Teachers College Press.

Marmion, Harry A. 1967. "A critique of selective service with emphasis on student deferments." Sol Tax, ed., *The Draft*, 54–61. Chicago: The University of Chicago Press.

———. 1969. "Historical background of the selective service in the United States." Roger W. Little, ed. *Selective service and American society*, 35–52. New York: Russell Sage.

Mathews, Robin. 1970. "On draft dodging and U.S. imperialism in Canada." *Canadian Dimension*, 6(7): 10–11.

Mayer, Albert J. and Thomas Ford Hoult. 1955. "Social stratification and combat survival." *Social Forces*, 34(2): 155–159.

Melnyk, George. 1973. "Confession to an American friend." *Our Generation*, 9(1): 23.

Middleton, Drew. 1981. "Manpower: most urgent problem for the military." *New York Times*, 21 July: B20.

Milton, George Fort. 1942. *Abraham Lincoln and the fifth column*. New York: Vanguard Press.

Mitchell, Broadus. 1974. *The price of independence*. New York: Oxford University Press.

Mitchell, James Clyde. 1969. "The concept and use of social networks." J. Clyde Mitchell, ed., *Social networks, urban situations: analyses of personal relationships in central African towns*, 1–50. New York: Humanities Press Incorporated.

Moskos, Charles C. Jr. 1978. "The enlisted ranks in the all-volunteer army." John B. Keeley, ed., *The all-volunteer force and American society*, 39–80. Charlottesville, Virginia: University Press of Virginia.

Murdock, Eugene Converse. 1967. *Patriotism limited: 1862–1865. The Civil War draft and the bounty system*. Kent, Ohio: Kent State University Press.

———. 1971. *One million men: the Civil War draft in the North*. Worcester, Mass.: Heffernan Press Incorporated.

Murray, Paul T. 1971. "Local draft board composition and institutional racism." *Social Problems*, 19(1): 129–136.

Musil, Robert K. 1973. "The truth about deserters." *The Nation*, 16 April: 495–499.

New York Times. 1863. "The mob in New York." 14 July: 1.

———. 1979. "Record-keeping ended for Vietnam deserters." 5 March: B5.

_____. 1980. "Foes of proposal on draft signup rally in capital." 23 March: A24.

_____. 1981. "30% of pupils say they would try to avoid a draft." 16 April: A21.

_____. 1981. "Call of the draft." 10 May A37.

O'Sullivan, John and Alan Meckler. 1974. *The draft and its enemies: a documentary history.* Urbana: University of Illinois Press.

Otto, Luther, B. 1975. "Class and status in family research." *Journal of Marriage and the Family,* 37: 315–32.

Park, Robert E. and Ernest W. Burgess. 1924. *Introduction to the science of sociology.* Chicago: University of Chicago Press.

Porter, John. 1965. *The vertical mosaic: an analysis of social class and power in Canada.* Toronto: University of Toronto Press.

_____. 1971. "Canadian character in the twentieth century." W. E. Mann, ed., *Canada: A sociological profile,* 1–8. Toronto: Copp Clark Publishing Company.

Reeves, Thomas and Karl Hess. 1970. *The end of the draft.* New York: Random House.

Resnick, Philip. 1970. "Canadian defense policy and the American empire." Ian Lumsden, ed., *Close the 49th Parallel, etc.: the Americanization of Canada,* 93–115. Toronto: University of Toronto Press.

_____. 1967. "Canadian war industries and Vietnam." *Our Generation,* 5(3): 16–27.

Richardson, Allen. 1967. "A theory and a method for the psychological study of assimilation." *The International Migration Review,* 2(1): 3–29.

Richmond, Anthony. 1969. "Immigration and pluralism in Canada." *The International Migration Review,* 4(1): 5–24.

Rinaldi, Matthew. 1974. "Olive-drab rebels: military organizing during the Vietnam war." *Radical America,* 8(3): 17–52.

Ross, D.A. 1918. "Protest against Mennonites." *Winnipeg Free Press,* 4 September: 1.

Roy, Prodipto. 1962. "The measurements of assimilation: the Spokane Indians." *American Journal of Sociology,* 67(5): 541–551.

Sarkesian, Sam C. 1981. "Who serves?" *Society,* 18(3): 57–60.

Savage, Paul L. and Richard A. Gabriel. 1976. "Cohesion and disintegration in the American army: an alternative perspective." *Armed Forces and Society,* 2(2): 340–376.

Schlissel, Lillian (ed.). 1968. *Conscience in America: a documentary history of conscientious objection in America, 1757–1967.* New York: E.P. Dutton and Company Incorporated.

Seeley, Robert A. 1981. *Handbook for conscientious objectors.* 13th ed. Philadelphia: Central Committee for Conscientious Objectors.

Segal, David R. 1981. "How equal is equity?" *Society,* 18(3): 31–33.

Segall, Marshall H. 1976. *Human behavior and public policy: a political psychology.* New York: Pergamon Press, Inc.

Sherman, Edward F. 1968. "Dissenters and deserters." *The New Republic,* 6 January: 23–36.

Sherrill, Robert. 1970. *Military justice is to justice as military music is to music.* New York: Harper and Row Publishers.

Shikes, Ralph E. (ed.). 1976. *Amnesty: an unresolved national question.* New York: Fund for New Priorities in America.

Sibley, Mulford Q. and Philip E. Jacob. 1952. *Conscription of conscience: The American state and the conscientious objector, 1940–1947.* Ithaca: Cornell University Press.

Sider, Gerald M. 1976. "Lumbee Indian cultural nationalism and ethnogenesis." *Dialectical Anthropology,* 1(2): 161–172.

Siebert, Wilbur H. 1966. "The dispersion of the American Tories." Esmond Wright, ed., *Causes and consequences of the American Revolution,* 249–258. Chicago: Quadrangle Books.

Smith, Robert B. 1971. "Disaffection, delegitimation and consequences: aggregate trends for World War II, Korea and Vietnam." Charles C. Moskos, Jr., ed., *Public opinion and the military establishment,* 221–254. Beverly Hills: Sage Publishers.

Society. 1981. "The rise and fall of the volunteer army." 18(3): 28–60.

Stapp, Andy. 1970. *Up against the brass.* New York: Simon and Schuster.

Starr, Paul. 1973. *The discarded army: veterans after Vietnam.* New York: Charterhouse.

Svirchev, Lawrence M. 1972. "Exiles and expatriots: two world outlooks, two classes." *AMEX-Canada,* 3(6): 32–35.

Szymanski, Alfred. 1972. "Trends in the American class structure." *Socialist Revolution,* 2(4): 101–122.

Teske, Raymond H.C. and Bardin H. Nelson. 1974. "Acculturation and assimilation: a clarification." *American Ethnologist,* 1(2): 351–367.

Thompson, Edward Palmer. 1964. *The making of the English working class.* New York: Pantheon Books.

Thompson, Stephen. 1974. "Survival of ethnicity in the Japanese community of Lima, Peru." *Urban Anthropology,* 3(2): 243–261.

Toronto Daily Star. 1970. "U.S. deserters: the ardent exiles." 17 December: A11.

Toronto Globe and Mail. 1969. "American exiles, strangers in Canada." 7 January: A6.

Toth, Robert C. 1981. "Air Force allows deserter to resign." *Washington Post,* 2 August: A4.

Trinkl, John. 1981. "100,000 unite against war and Reagan." *Guardian,* May 13: 1, 5–8.

U.S. Bureau of the Census.

————. 1953. *Statistical abstract of the United States* (74th annual edition). Washington, D.C., Government Printing Office.

————. 1955. *Statistical abstract of the United States* (76th annual edition), Washington, D.C., Government Printing Office.

————. 1965. *Statistical abstract of the United States* (86th annual edition), Washington, D.C., Government Printing Office.

————. 1975. *Statistical abstract of the United States* (96th annual edition), Washington, D.C., Government Printing Office.

_____. 1976. *Historical statistics of the United States, Colonial times to 1970: Bicentennial edition, Part 1*. Washington, D.C., Government Printing Office.

_____. 1976. *Statistical abstract of the United States* (97th annual edition), Washington, D.C., Government Printing Office.

_____. 1979. *Statistical abstract of the United States* (100th annual edition), Washington, D.C., Government Printing Office.

U.S. National Advisory Commission on Selective Service. 1967. "In pursuit of equity: who serves when not all serve?" Washington, D.C.: Government Printing Office.

U.S. News and World Report. 1953. "Why Korea is called 'poor man's war'." 20 February: 18–20.

Useem, Michael. 1973. *Conscription, protest and social conflict: the life and death of a draft resistance movement*. New York: John Wiley and Sons, Incorporated.

_____. 1981. "Conscription and class." *Society*, 18(3): 28–30.

Walz, Jay. 1969. "Canada to admit any U.S. deserter." *New York Times*, 23 April: A5.

Waterhouse, Larry G. and Marianne G. Wizard. 1971. *Turning the guns around*. New York: Praeger.

Weigley, Russell Frank. 1967. *History of the United States army*. New York: Macmillan Publishing Company.

Weinstein, James. 1959. "Antiwar sentiment and the socialist party, 1917–1918." *Political Science Quarterly*, 74(2): 215–239.

Werstein, Irving. 1971. *The draft riots: July 1863*. New York: Julian Messner.

Wilcox, Jim. 1970. ". . . They are up against the Canadian border." Frank H. Epp., ed., *I would like to dodge the draft dodgers but . . . (including deserters)*, 43–59. Winnipeg: Conrad Press.

Williams, Roger Neville. 1971a. *The new exiles: American war resisters in Canada*. New York: Liveright Publishers.

_____. 1971b. "Strong-arm rule in Canada." *New Republic*, 30 January: 15–18.

Winsborough, Halliman H. 1975. "Statistical histories of the life cycle of birth cohorts: the transition from school boy to adult male." A paper presented at the Conference on Social Demography, July 1975, University of Wisconsin. Center for Demography and Ecology, University of Wisconsin.

Wiseman, Ian. 1972. *Canada's role in war research*. Ottawa: Canadian University Press Service.

Wittner, Lawrence. 1969. *Rebels against war: the American peace movement, 1941–1960*. New York: Columbia University Press.

Young, Patricia. 1969. "On draft dodgers." *Straight Talk*, 1 August: 7.

Zietlin, Maurice, Kenneth Lutterman, and James Russell. 1973. "Death in Vietnam: class, poverty, and risks of war." *Politics and Society*, 3(Spring): 313–328.

Index

Absentee ballots, 163

Absent Without Official Leave (AWOL) and Vietnam, 58–61, 100, 167

Act, 142

Adams, Michael J., 68, 69, 70, 72, 77, 78

Age: and assimilation of resisters in Canada, 158; and immigration in Canada, *110*; as social indicator, 6

Agent Orange, 185

Agnew, Spiro T., 101

Agronsky, Martin, 58

Alabama, Selective Service in, 35, 36

Ali, Muhammed, 52

All-volunteer force (AVF), 186, 188 (*see also* Volunteerism)

Alternative, 142

Ambush, 142

American Civil Liberties Union, 167

American Deserter Committee (ADC), 142, 145, 148

American Exile in Canada, 144

American Expatriate in Canada, 144

American Refugee News, 142

American Revolution: desertion in, 10–11; military conscription for, 9–11, 32 [commutation, 10; substitution, 10]

American Servicemen's Union (ASU), 54

AMEX, 114–15, 140, 144–51, 162, 163, *163*, 164; *AMEX-Canada*, 149, 150, 151, 168, 169

Amnesty in U.S. for resisters in Canada, 148, 153, 164, 166–71; and military discharge, 168–69, 183; and socio-economic class, 168–69

Apocalypse Now!, 184

Arkansas, Selective Service in, 35

Armed Forces Qualification Test (AFQT), 40, 41

Assassination, political, 179

Assimilation of resisters in Canada, 133–72; and age, 158; ambivalence on (pushes/pulls), 166–71; and education, 155, 158; and group-organizational differences, 142–50; and marriage, 158; and occupation, 155, 158; phases of, 153–61 [formal, 153–58; social, 153, 158–61]; and retention of U.S. connections (exile orientation), 161–66, *163*; and social cohesion, 138–42 [resister organizations, 139–41; limited tenure, 141–42]; and socio-economic status, 158; summary on, 151, 171 (*see also* Immigration)

Axton, Hoyt, 87

Badillo, Gilbert, 48

Baez, Joan, 99

Banks-financial institutions, confidence in, *180*

Baptists, 77

Barnes, J.A., 140

Bar-Yosef, Rivka Weiss, 171

Baskir, Lawrence M., 20, 21, 24, 35–44, 46, 48, 50, 51, 53, 56, 57, 59–63, 99, 100, 111, 168, 172

Battle of Gettysburg, Civil War, 16

Bell, Bruce D., 59, 60, 68, 99

Berrigan brothers, 50

Black Refugee Organization, 145

Blacks, 104; and exile in Canada, 76; and Selective Service system, 36; unemployment of, 185; in World War II, 27 (*see also* Race)

Block, N.J., 63

Bond, Julian, 52

Bond, Thomas C., 56

Bounties, federal/state, in Civil War, 12–13, 18–19, *18*, *19*

Bowles, Samuel, 63

Braverman, Harry, 6

Bribery and selective conscription, 7, 10

Page numbers in italics indicate material in tables.

199

Culhane, Claire, 120, 125
Curry, David G., 48
Czechoslovakians, immigration of, 110

Damico, Alfonso J., 6
Davis, James, 35, 36, 37
Deerhunter, 184
Defense Production Sharing Agreement, 120
Defoliation, 92
Delaware: commutation payments in, Civil War, *18*; draft riots in, Civil War, 15
deOnis, Juan, 187
Dependents and exclusion from military, 14
Depression/elation of resisters in Canada, 135–38
Deserters, military, 2, 4, 65, *78*, 186; assimilation of in Canada, 145–47, 164; and expectations of military service, 88; and immigration, Canada, 110, 111–13; and income, 68, 72, *73*, *74*, *75*; and Korea, 29–31, *59*; and socio-economic class, 104, 185; two-stage pardon for, 168; in Vietnam, 27, 55, 58–59, *59*, *60*, 61; in World War II, 27, *59* (*see also* Amnesty; Family background of deserters/dodgers in military)
DEW line, 120
Dickens, Charles, 16
Discharge, military: and amnesty, 168; types of, and Vietnam, 57–58
Dolbeare, Kenneth, 35, 36, 37
Draft: and American Revolution, 9–11, 32; and Civil War, 12–20, 31, 32, 61 [failure of, 18–20, *18*, *19*; resistance to, 15–17; suspension of, 17–18]; and destruction of records, 32; and Korea, 27–31, *29*, *30*, *59* [exemptions, 28]; and War of 1812, 11–12; and World War I, 20–23, 31, 32 [avoidance, 21; evasion, 21–22; success, 22–23]; and World War II, 23–27, *24*, *25*, *26* (*see also* Canada, deserters/dodgers in; Draft dodgers; Selective Service)
Draft dodger as term, 2, 3, 4 (*see also* Family background of deserters/dodgers in Canada; Canada, deserters/dodgers in)
Draft Insurance Societies, 14

Draft resister as term, 4
Dullea, 1
Dworkin, Gerald, 63

Education, 68, 69, *70*, *71*; and assimilation of resisters in Canada, 155, 158; and casualties, Vietnam, 48–49, *49*; and enlistment, Vietnam, 46, *47*; and immigration, Canada, *109*; as social indicator, 3, 6; of Vietnam veterans, 185
Efaw, Fritz, 168
Elation/depression of resisters in Canada, 135–38
El Salvador, U.S. advisers in, 187
Emancipation Proclamation, 16
Emerick, Kenneth Fred, 68, 76, 77, 118, 151
Engendof, Arthur, ix, 185
Enrollment Act of 1863, 19
Episcopalians, 77, *77*
Epp, Frank H., 22
Exile Activity Index, 162, 163
Exile orientation (*see* Assimilation of resisters in Canada, and retention of U.S. connections)

Family background of deserters/dodgers in Canada, 67–87; quality of, 77–85 [and politics, 83–86; and religion, 82–83, *84*; and resister status, 84–85, *85*]; and socio-economic status, 68–77, 82–86 [education, 68, 69, *70*, *71*; and family composition, 77, *78*; income, 68, 72, *73*, *74*, *75*; occupation, parental, 68, 69, 72; and race, 76; and religion, 76–77, *77*, 82–86]
Family hardship deferment, 63*n.*
Federal Enrollment Act of 1863, 13–15
Ferber, Michael, 50, 53
Fermi, Laura, 138
First World War (*see* World War I)
Fite, Emerson, David, 16
Flacks, Richard, 36, 52
Ford, Gerald, 3, 61, 133, 167, 168, 169
Formal Group Membership Index, 155
Formal Membership Index, 156, 157
Fragging in Vietnam, 56, 60
France and Canadian identity, 129
Franklin, Benjamin, 9
Franks, Lucinda, 6, 111
Fulford, Robert, 107, 108, 109, 116, 123, 124

Typography and Binding design by Jeanne Ray Juster
Edited by Betty Chandler Hunt
Set in Palatino by Trade Composition Inc., Chicopee, Massachusetts
Printed and Bound by Edwards Brothers, Inc., Ann Arbor, Michigan